A VISION OF THE ORIENT:
TEXTS, INTERTEXTS, AND CONTEXTS OF
MADAME BUTTERFLY

A Vision of the Orient

Texts, Intertexts, and Contexts of Madame Butterfly

Edited by Jonathan Wisenthal, Sherrill Grace, Melinda Boyd, Brian McIlroy, and Vera Micznik

UNIVERSITY OF TORONTO PRESS
Toronto Buffalo London

© University of Toronto Press Incorporated 2006
Toronto Buffalo London
Printed in Canada

ISBN-13: 978-0-8020-8801-7 (cloth)
ISBN-10: 0-8020-8801-5 (cloth)
ISBN-13: 978-1-4426-1328-7 (paper)

Printed on acid-free paper

Library and Archives Canada Cataloguing in Publication

A vision of the Orient : texts, intertexts, and contexts of Madame Butterfly / edited by Jonathan Wisenthal ... [et al.].

Includes bibliographical references and index.
ISBN 0-8020-8801-5

1. Puccini, Giacomo, 1858–1924 – Adaptations. 2. Puccini, Giacomo, 1858–1924. Madama Butterfly. 3. Long, John Luther, 1861–1927 – Adaptations. 4. Long, John Luther, 1861–1927. Madame Butterfly.

NX652.M23V58 2006   809′.93351   C2006-901120-6

'Your Cio-Cio San' by Martin Manalansan is reproduced by permission of the author.

University of Toronto Press acknowledges the financial assistance to its publishing program of the Canada Council for the Arts and the Ontario Arts Council.

University of Toronto Press acknowledges the financial support for its publishing activities of the Government of Canada through the Book Publishing Industry Development Program (BPIDP).

GALLIMARD: There is a vision of the Orient that I have. Of slender women in chong sams and kimonos who die for the love of unworthy foreign devils. Who are born and raised to be the perfect women. Who take whatever punishment we give them, and bounce back, strengthened by love, unconditionally. It is a vision that has become my life.

(Hwang, *M. Butterfly* act 3, scene 3)

Contents

Madame Butterfly: A Selective Chronology   ix

Preface   xi

PART ONE: PRE-TEXTS

Inventing the Orient   3
JONATHAN WISENTHAL

PART TWO: TEXTS

Mounting Butterflies   21
SUSAN McCLARY

Cio-Cio-San the Geisha   36
VERA MICZNIK

'Re-Orienting' the Vision: Ethnicity and Authenticity from Suzuki to Comrade Chin   59
MELINDA BOYD

That Old Familiar Song: The Theatre of Culture in David Henry Hwang's *M. Butterfly*   72
KATE McINTURFF

PART THREE: INTERTEXTS

Late Mutations of Cinema's Butterfly   91
BART TESTA

White Nagasaki / White Japan and a Post-Atomic Butterfly:
Joshua Logan's *Sayonara* (1957)   123
BRIAN McILROY

Playing Butterfly with David Henry Hwang and Robert Lepage   136
SHERRILL GRACE

PART FOUR: CONTEXTS

Madama Butterfly and the Absence of Empire   155
RICHARD CAVELL

The Taming of the Oriental Shrew: The Two Asias in
Puccini's *Madama Butterfly* and *Turandot*   170
MARIA NG

Iron Butterfly: Cio-Cio-San and Japanese Imperialism   181
JOSHUA S. MOSTOW

Madame Butterfly: Behind Every Great Woman ...   196
JOY JAMES

M. Butterfly: Staging Choices and Their Meanings   227
RACHEL DITOR AND JAN SELMAN

Bibliography   239
Contributors   255
Index   257

Madame Butterfly: A Selective Chronology

1853 8 July: Commodore Matthew Perry enters Uraga harbour
1885 Summer: 'Marriage' of Lieutenant Julien Viaud (Pierre Loti) and Okane-San, Nagasaki
Gilbert and Sullivan's *The Mikado*
1887 Pierre Loti, *Madame Chrysanthème*
1898 John Luther Long, *Madame Butterfly*
1899 United States takes control of the Philippines
Rudyard Kipling, 'The White Man's Burden'
1900 David Belasco, *Madame Butterfly*
1901 Rudyard Kipling, *Kim*
1904 8 February: Beginning of Russo-Japanese War
17 February: Giacomo Puccini's *Madama Butterfly* opens at La Scala, Milan
Joseph Conrad, *Nostromo*
1915 Sidney Olcott's film *Madame Butterfly*, starring Mary Pickford
1922 Chester Franklin's film *The Toll of the Sea*, starring Anna May Wong
1941 7 December: Japan attacks Pearl Harbor
1945 6 and 9 August: United States drops atomic bombs on Hiroshima and Nagasaki
1949 Rodgers and Hammerstein's *South Pacific*
1954 French are defeated at Dien Bien Phu
James Michener, *Sayonara*
1957 Joshua Logan's film *Sayonara*, starring Marlon Brando
1975 April: American withdrawal from Vietnam
1986 Bernard Bouriscot sentenced to prison for spying for China

1988   10 February: David Henry Hwang's *M. Butterfly* opens in Washington, DC
1989   Boublil and Schönberg's *Miss Saigon*
1993   David Cronenberg's film *M. Butterfly*
1996   Robert Lepage's play *The Seven Streams of the River Ota*
1998   A.R. Gurney's play *Far East*

Preface

The five editors of *A Vision of the Orient: Texts, Intertexts, and Contexts of Madame Butterfly* have been working together as an interdisciplinary team since the spring of 1996, and we wish at the outset of this volume to express our gratitude towards the Hampton Fund of the University of British Columbia, which has generously provided the funding for our research. We have tried to make our inquiry as collaborative as possible, and have deliberately avoided just dividing the subject up into our respective disciplinary areas of literature, music, and film. Instead, we have made a point of meeting regularly to focus on particular texts and issues from the shared, multiple perspectives of different disciplines. In the fall of 1997 we organized an interdisciplinary graduate seminar on the Madame Butterfly theme, and for thirteen weeks our research team met with a group of twelve graduate students from a wide range of disciplinary backgrounds. We also organized a two-day symposium in April 1997, which provided the origin of several of the following essays, and at other times we brought a number of visiting speakers to the University of British Columbia, including Anne McClintock and Linda and Michael Hutcheon, to give talks on issues connected with our research.

One of our principles in this research project has been to resist any pressure for consensus, and to allow contradictory positions to stand and issues to remain unresolved. In this volume, therefore, there is no attempt to impose a monolithic view of the subject; what we want is a book that is full of opinions in conflict with each other, on the Blakean assumption that without Contraries is no progression and that Opposition is true Friendship. Thus, the reader will find, for example, very different evaluations of Puccini's opera, from **Vera Micznik**'s[1] defence of its thematic coherence to her fellow musicologist **Susan McClary**'s spirited demolition of it as a pernicious anachronism. And our volume contains radically different responses to David Henry Hwang's Madame Butterfly play and David Cronenberg's film version of it, from **Kate McInturff**'s examination of the play's subtle ironies to **Sherrill Grace**'s and **Rachel Ditor and Jan Selman**'s reservations about aspects of it and **Bart Testa**'s preference for the film over the play.

Underlying such disagreements, though, is a unifying sense among contributors about why the Madame Butterfly[2] narrative is worth sustained attention in the early twenty-first century. Broadly speaking, our volume presents a cultural and political reading of Puccini's opera and the texts that surround it. If our contributors believed (with Gallimard's wife in *M. Butterfly*) that one should just hear Puccini's *Madama Butterfly* as a piece of beautiful music, then *A Vision of the Orient* would never have been written. We do have a keen sense of the power of Puccini's music, but we are interested in this very power as culturally and politically significant in the context of Western culture. That is why Hwang's fascinating, ingenious play, along with Cronenberg's film version of it, figures so prominently in our study, for *M. Butterfly* is definitely a cultural and political response to Puccini's opera.

Another issue on which we have deliberately avoided unanimity is a fundamental one to do with the very nature of the project itself: How central to our inquiry is Puccini's opera? Is it *the* privileged Butterfly text, or is it just one among a number of cultural artefacts that we are examining? We leave this as an open question, but we certainly do assume that a crucial way to enrich one's understanding of Puccini's *Madama Butterfly* is to see it in a very wide context that includes the main predecessor and successor texts that we discuss in the introductory section that follows (Loti, Long, Belasco, Hwang, Cronenberg) – as well as films like the early *Madame Butterfly* with Mary Pickford and Joshua Logan's *Sayonara* from the 1950s; and the richly intertextual 1990s play by the Canadian Robert Lepage, *The Seven Streams of the River Ota*; and Gauguin's 1892 Tahiti painting *Manao Tupapau*; and Puccini's later Oriental opera *Turandot*; and ways of staging Hwang's play; and a great variety of other texts and issues that are taken up by contributors to this volume. *Madama Butterfly* is among the two or three most popular operas of all time, and 'Madame Butterfly' is also a compelling and highly influential modern myth that has achieved expressions in many forms over more than a century, from Loti's 1887 novel *Madame Chrysanthème* to the 1999 play by A.R. Gurney, *Far East*, in which an American marine stationed in Japan in the 1950s plans to marry a Japanese girl (whom one character calls his 'Madame Butterfly'). It is a narrative that is well worth examining closely in its original texts, and in its widest contexts. That is what we are doing in this volume.

We want to thank everyone who contributed to our inquiry, directly and indirectly. This includes each of the contributors to this volume, each of the members of our graduate seminar, each of the visiting speakers who came to the University of British Columbia to share their insights with us, each of the participants in our symposium, and other UBC colleagues and students who involved themselves in our project. And our gratitude also extends to the anonymous readers who have evaluated the manuscript for University of Toronto Press and the Humanities and Social Sciences Federation of Canada respectively; their careful, detailed, thoughtful reports have been immensely valuable to us in our revisions. As an editorial team, we have learned much from all these people – and from each other. We also thank our editors at University of Toronto Press, and in particular our eagle-eyed copy-editor, John St James.

With the exception of figure 12.3, all illustrations in chapter 12 are believed to be in the collection of the Loti Museum at Rochefort. Figure 12.3 is in the private collection of Christiane Pierre-Loti-Viaud. Figures 12.1–12.5 and 12.7–12.8 are reproduced in Christian Genet and Daniel Hervé, *Pierre Loti L'enchanteur* (Gémozac: La Caillerie, 1988). Figure 12.6 is reproduced in Bruno Vercier, *Pierre Loti Portraits: Les fantaisies changeantes* (Paris: Flammarion, 2002).

Notes

1 Throughout this volume, names in bold-face type refer to contributors' chapters.
2 Throughout this book we will use 'Madame Butterfly' to refer to the character who appears in a variety of texts and to refer to her generic story and 'Madama Butterfly' (or Cio-Cio-San) to refer to Puccini's heroine, and 'Puccini' as convenient shorthand for 'Puccini and Giacosa and Illica.'

PART ONE

Pre-Texts

Inventing the Orient

JONATHAN WISENTHAL

GALLIMARD: They hate it because the white man gets the girl. Sour grapes if you ask me.
HELGA: Politics again? Why can't they just hear it as a piece of beautiful music?
Hwang, M. Butterfly act 1, scene 7

VIVIAN: No great artist ever sees things as they really are. If he did, he would cease to be an artist. Take an example from our own day. I know you are fond of Japanese things. Now, do you really imagine that the Japanese people, as they are presented to us in art, have any existence? If you do, you have never understood Japanese art at all. The Japanese people are the deliberate self-conscious creation of certain individual artists. If you set a picture by Hokusai, or Hokkei, or any of the great native painters, beside a real Japanese gentleman or lady, you will see that there is not the slightest resemblance between them. The actual people who live in Japan are not unlike the general run of English people; that is to say, they are extremely commonplace, and have nothing curious or extraordinary about them. In fact the whole of Japan is a pure invention. There is no such country, there are no such people.
Wilde, The Decay of Lying 315

The texts that constitute the subject of this book take a wide variety of forms – opera, drama, film, prose narrative, musical comedy, painting – and they come from several countries. But all of these countries are in the Western Hemisphere, and it is a striking fact that this narrative of 'the Orient'[1] is entirely a cultural construct of white, Western nations that were vigorously engaged in the attempted conquest of other parts of the world during the period in which the Butterfly myth has flourished, the past hundred years or so. The three principal nations that have produced these Butterfly narratives are France, Italy, and the United States. France was exerting power in the South Pacific in the late nineteenth century at the time when the sailor Julien Viaud (Pierre Loti) was making sexual conquests 'dovunque al mondo' that he configured as semi-autobiographical narratives like *Madame Chrysanthème* (1887). Italy was pursuing imperialist ambitions in Ethiopia in the late nineteenth and early twentieth century[2] at the time when the composer Giacomo Puccini and his librettists Giuseppe Giacosa and Luigi Illica were creating *Madama Butterfly* (1904). The United States was engaged in adventures of conquest in places like the Philippines and Cuba at the time when the Philadelphia lawyer John Luther Long produced his novella *Madame Butterfly* (1898) and the San Francisco playwright David Belasco wrote his one-act play of the same name (1900); and the United States was attempting to control parts of Southeast Asia at the time that the American-born playwright David Henry Hwang was growing up in San Gabriel, California, and studying at Stanford University before he wrote the decidedly post-Vietnam work *M. Butterfly* (1988). The film of Hwang's play (1993), directed by a Canadian, David Cronenberg,[3] has an American actor playing the Chinese singer-spy Song Liling, while the only actual Asian figures on the screen are extras, and it stars a British actor playing a French diplomat. Moreover, most of the numerous other film treatments of the Butterfly story are American, as are musicals like Rodgers and Hammerstein's *South Pacific* (1949), Sondheim's *Pacific Overtures* (1976), and Boublil and Schönberg's *Miss Saigon* (1989).

Miss Saigon, though an American production on an American subject, was written by a French composer and librettist, which executes a nice return to the starting point of the Butterfly myth. For it was a hundred years earlier, in 1887, that Pierre Loti published his remarkable travel narrative from which all these other works ultimately flow. Or one can trace the point of origin back two years earlier than that, when Lieutenant Julien Viaud, like Lieutenant Benjamin Franklin Pinkerton, was a naval officer stationed for a few months in the treaty port of Nagasaki (his ship was called the 'Triomphante,' precursor of Pinkerton's 'Abramo Lincoln' in the Puccini opera). 'Last week,' Loti wrote to a friend back in France, 'I was married ... to a young girl of seventeen. She is called Okane-San. We celebrated with a lantern procession and a tea party. The validity of the marriage is entirely at the whim of the two parties.'[4] Viaud's purchased 'wife' for the summer of 1885, Okane-San, became the semi-fictional Madame Chrysanthemum, the first precursor of Madame Butterfly. Such temporary marriages were not uncommon in a port that was much visited by sailors from Western countries,[5] and Long knew of another case through his sister, who was married to an American missionary in Nagasaki.[6]

Madame Butterfly narratives, though they differ in many respects, have in common a Western man who has journeyed to Asia, where he pursues his vision of the Orient by 'marrying' a woman there – or, in the case of Hwang and Cronenberg, 'marrying' a 'woman.' And the point about Hwang's Gallimard (and Cronenberg's very different Gallimard too) is that he is a Westerner who is totally innocent of the political, social, and human realities of Asia. Gallimard's Orient is altogether a construction from the outside, and in this respect he is like Loti, Long, Belasco, Puccini, Giacosa, Illica, Cronenberg, and even Hwang, all of whom wrote works about – and at the same time paradoxically *were* – Westerners who tried to appropriate and impose an identity on the East.

One thread that runs through all these narratives is that the Pinkerton figure's Orient is a feminized, infantilized, and aestheticized construct. This perspective is particularly prominent in the founding text by Loti, but it is apparent in every one of the Madame Butterfly stories. Of course, it is in the very nature of the Butterfly story that the central character is an Oriental woman, and that her feminine (and in most cases girlish) nature embodies the very essence of the Orient for the Western man. In each of the stories the two principal Oriental characters are women, while the two principal Western characters are men. Each text has another Oriental woman associated with Butterfly: the Suzuki figure, who is Butterfly's maid-companion Suzuki in Long, Belasco, and Puccini, and who takes the form of the landlady Madame Prune in Loti and of Comrade Chin in Hwang and Cronenberg (see **Melinda Boyd**). And in each text there is a man who goes along (in various senses) with Pinkerton: the Sharpless figure, who is the American consul Sharpless in Long, Belasco, and Puccini, and who takes the form of the narrator's close friend Yves – with strong homoerotic suggestions – in Loti (see **Joy James**), and Gallimard's school friend Marc in Hwang. In Cronenberg, Marc has been excised along with all the flashbacks, but the film opens with Gallimard and a male fellow-diplomat working together in the French embassy in Peking and then walking together to a recital at the Swedish embassy. In each Butterfly narrative the West is mainly male, the Orient mainly female, and in the Hwang-Cronenberg representations of the story Western constructions of the Orient as feminine are particularly conspicuous in that Gallimard's ideal Oriental woman is a doubly constructed figure: '[I]n China,' Gallimard tells the audience in act 2 of Hwang's play, 'I once loved, and was loved by, very simply, the Perfect Woman (*Song enters, dressed as Butterfly in wedding dress*)' (Hwang [1989] 76–7), and earlier in the act there is a memorable exchange between Song and Comrade Chin.

SONG: Miss Chin? Why, in the Peking Opera, are women's roles played by men?
CHIN: I don't know. Maybe, a reactionary remnant of male –
SONG: No. (*Beat*) Because only a man knows how a woman is supposed to act.
 (ibid. 63)

'Woman' is a role designed by men and performed for their benefit, and in *M. Butterfly* (both play and film) this applies particularly to the Oriental woman, because of the Western construction of the Orient as woman (see **Kate McInturff**).

In the nineteenth-century[7] representations of the Butterfly story, the Western man constructs the Orient as *girl*, and the Pinkerton figure emphasizes the childlike (and often childish) nature of Asia. Loti's narrator is the most conspicuous of all the infantilizers: 'I really make a sad abuse of the adjective *little*, I am quite aware of it, but how can I do otherwise? In describing this country, the temptation is great to use it ten times in every written line. Little, finical, affected, – all Japan is contained, both physically and morally, in these three words' (1887/1985, 242). Near the end of *Madame Chrysanthème* the narrator reflects that '[a]t the moment of my departure, I can only find within myself a smile of careless mockery for the swarming crowd of this Lil[l]iputian curtseying people' (328), and in Long's story not only does the Pinkerton figure infantilize Japan but we are told by the narrator himself, when Butterfly (Cho-Cho-San)[8] first catches sight of a 'blonde woman' with Pinkerton, that '[h]er little, unused, frivolous mind had not forecast such a catastrophe' (55). Butterfly's little, unused, frivolous mind is painfully evident in Belasco's play in the embarrassing pidgin dialect she is compelled to use as speech – as she is in Long's story, but the dialect is much more prominent in the play. In both story and play, Pinkerton's American wife refers to Butterfly as a plaything: 'How very charming – how *lovely* – you are, dear! Will you kiss me, you pretty *plaything*?' (Long, 'Madame Butterfly,' 57; italics in original). In Belasco's play Butterfly rejects the appellation, but her very mode of speech confirms it:

KATE: ... Why, you poor little thing ... who in the world could blame you or ... call you responsible ... you pretty little plaything.
(*Takes* Madame Butterfly *in her arms.*)
MADAME BUTTERFLY (*Softly*): No – playthin' ... I am Mrs. Lef-ten-ant B. F. – No – no – now I am, only – Cho-Cho-San, but no playthin' (Belasco, 'Madame Butterfly,' 635; ellipses in original)

Puccini's Kate says to Sharpless after the equivalent of this scene (in a passage added in the 1906 Paris revision) 'Povera piccina!' (Poor little one) (Puccini [John ed.] 122), and to Puccini's Pinkerton, as to Long's and Belasco's and to Loti's narrator, Butterfly is a *piccina* – little and feminine – throughout each of the texts.

When Pinkerton explains to Sharpless in act 1 of Puccini's *Madama Butterfly* the nature of his attraction towards Cio-Cio-San, he emphasizes her small, fragile body, and her innocent charm, and also her status as an aesthetic artefact:

> Certo costei
> m'ha colle ingenue – arti invescato.
> Lieve qual tenue – vetro soffiato
> alla statura – al portamento
> sembra figura – da paravento
> Ma dal suo lucido – fondo di lacca ...   (Puccini 73)

Pinkerton says that Butterfly, with her innocent charm, has entranced him: 'Almost transparently fragile and slender, / Dainty in stature, quaint little figure, / She seems to have stepped down straight from a screen. / But from her background of varnish and lacquer ...' This image of a painted screen (*paravento*) is also to be found in all of the predecessor texts. Here is Loti's narrator talking about his first experiences of Nagasaki: 'At times we passed by a lady, struggling with her skirts, unsteadily tripping along in her high wooden shoes, looking exactly like the figures painted on screens, tucked up under a gaudily daubed paper umbrella' (30). Loti's narrator repeatedly sees Japanese women in such aesthetic terms, as figures painted on screens or on vases, fans, or teacups. In chapter 3, on his visit to M. Kangourou the marriage broker, he reflects that he is not really encountering this quaint Japanese world for the first time (see **Maria Ng**):

At this moment, my impressions of Japan are charming enough; I feel myself fairly launched upon this tiny, artificial, fictitious world, which I felt I knew already from the paintings of lacquer and porcelains. It is so exact a representation! The three little squatting women, graceful and dainty, with their narrow slits of eyes, their magnificent chignons in huge bows, smooth and shining as boot-polish, and the little tea-service on the floor, the landscape seen through the verandah, the pagoda perched among the clouds; and over all the same affectation everywhere, in every detail. Even the woman's melancholy voice, still to be heard behind the paper partition, was so evidently the way they should sing, these musicians I had so often seen painted in amazing colours on rice-paper, half closing their dreamy eyes in the midst of impossibly large flowers. Long before I came to it, I had perfectly pictured this Japan to myself. (42–3)

Then when M. Kangourou has produced Mlle Jasmin as a possible bride, the narrator exclaims in the next chapter: 'Heavens! why, I know her already! Long before setting foot in Japan, I had met with her, on every fan, on every tea-cup – with her silly air, her puffy little visage, her tiny eyes, mere gimlet-holes above those expanses of impossible pink and white which are her cheeks' (56). It is proleptic Orientalist expectations of just this kind that cause Hwang's Gallimard to misread China so completely, and this specifically aesthetic nature of a representation that has already been acquired in the West figures in Puccini (as we have seen) and very much in Long and Belasco. When in Long's story Butterfly's family comes to remonstrate politely with Pinkerton over the marriage he flippantly brushes them off: '"Do you know," he continued to the spokesman, "that you look exactly like a lacquered tragedy mask I have hanging over my desk?"' (27). Then, after Pinkerton's departure Butterfly comforts her baby with a lullaby:

> 'Rog-a-by, bebby, off in Japan,
> You jus' a picture off of a fan.'
> This was from Pinkerton. She had been the baby then.   (Long 32)

In Belasco's play this lullaby, identified as an American song entitled 'I call her the Belle of Japan,' is sung by Butterfly just before and just after Pinkerton's return (Belasco 633–4).

Pinkerton's song, along with the screens, vases, and other aesthetic artefacts[9] we have been looking at, confirms the apparently outrageous assertions made by Vivian in Wilde's dialogue *The Decay of Lying*. For the Pinkerton-figures in our group of texts, and to some extent for their authors as well, the whole of Japan is a pure invention.[10] Loti's novel explicitly draws attention to questions of representation in passages that we have cited, in which the Japan the narrator encounters is 'so exact a representation' of what he had known in France beforehand from paintings. In chapter 45 there is an account of a visit to a Nagasaki photographer by the narrator, Yves, and Chrysanthemum, with disappointing results: '[W]e look like a supremely ridiculous little family drawn up in a line by a common photographer at a fair' (252), and in chapter 51 the narrator, as he prepares to leave Nagasaki, makes a sketch of his lodgings there while three Japanese ladies look on 'with an astonished attention.' 'Japanese art being entirely conventional, they have never before seen anyone draw from nature, and my style delights them ... I have been taught to draw things as I see them, without giving them ingeniously distorted and grimacing attitudes; and the three Japanese are amazed at the air of *reality* thrown in my sketch.' But the narrator feels that his representation has failed to convey the appearance of the place. 'If the ladies are satisfied with my sketch, I am far from being so. I have put everything in its place most exactly, but as a whole, it has an ordinary, indifferent, French look which does not suit' (298–300). The narrator has formed his impressions of Japan before arriving there, and once there he cannot accurately represent what he sees. Thus, Loti's readers are warned that what they are getting is very much Japan under Western eyes, that 'the Japanese people are the deliberate self-conscious creation' of this French artist-sailor.

In David Henry Hwang's 'Afterword' to his *M. Butterfly*, he recalls hearing the story of the hapless French diplomat Bernard Bouriscot, the original of Gallimard. Hwang concluded that Bouriscot 'must have fallen in love, not with a person, but with a fantasy stereotype,' and that he 'probably thought he had found Madame Butterfly.' But like Gallimard at the beginning of the Cronenberg film, Hwang did not know Puccini's opera.

> The idea of doing a deconstructivist *Madama Butterfly* immediately appealed to me. This, despite the fact that I didn't even know the plot of the opera! I knew Butterfly only as a cultural stereotype; speaking of an Asian woman, we would sometimes say, 'She's pulling a Butterfly,' which meant playing the submissive Oriental number. Yet, I felt convinced that the libretto would include yet another lotus blossom pining away for a cruel Caucasian man, and dying for her love. Such a story has become too

much of a cliché not to be included in the archetypal East-West romance that started it all. Sure enough, when I purchased the record, I discovered it contained a wealth of sexist and racist clichés, reaffirming my faith in Western culture. (Hwang 95)

This is a remarkably interesting comment on a play about ways in which preconceived expectations can affect perception. What are we to make of the vision of the Occident that Hwang says he had, and that was so precisely confirmed by *Madama Butterfly*? The assured ironies of the speaker here are usually quoted with tacit agreement by people who write about Hwang's play and Puccini's opera, but can the politics of this opera be so smoothly and confidently encapsulated? Does the opera really consist of a wealth of racist and sexist clichés that are neatly subverted by Hwang's version of the story? *Madama Butterfly*, as we have been emphasizing, is – along with the other texts we are considering – indisputably a Western construction of the Orient, but there are two elements in it that distinguish the opera from all the other works. One is its resistance to an Orient essentialized in a single, female character, a resistance that is connected with the opera's reduction of the *West* to a monolithic ideological identity; and the other is the genuinely tragic elevation of Butterfly at the end (see **Vera Micznik**). Loti's narrator refers to his narrative as 'my little Japanese comedy' (214), and in Long's telling of the story readers' attention is once again drawn to issues of literary genre and modes of emplotment. When his Sharpless has to confront Cho-Cho-San's optimism about Pinkerton's return to her, he 'remembered the saying of the professor of rhetoric that no comedy could succeed without its element of tragedy' (Long 50).[11]

One of the themes of the opera, which it partly shares with its immediate sources (Long and Belasco), has to do with cultural identity and assimilation. The opera, much more than any of the other texts (including Hwang and Cronenberg) puts before us a *variety* of 'Oriental' characters.[12] Whereas Pinkerton himself does indeed essentialize the Orient in the person of his child-bride, the opera as a whole deliberately avoids doing so. The opera's Cio-Cio-San is surrounded by Japanese characters who represent a continuum running from the highly assimilated (i.e., Westernized in this treaty port) and the unassimilated. The most assimilated is Goro, and the least is the dead father of Cio-Cio-San, who is not exactly a character but is, it could be argued, ideologically the most important figure in the drama. So the continuum would look like this:

Goro → Yamadori → Cio-Cio-San's family → Suzuki → Officials at wedding (the Imperial Commissioner and the Official Registrar) → the Bonze → Cio-Cio-San's father

All of these characters are present in either Long or Belasco (or both), but their musical expression in the score of Puccini's opera, and to some extent the way they are delineated in the libretto, gives them much greater prominence than in the other works. One good example would be the Goro figure, who is transformed into a significant character in the opera from an relatively incidental character in the predecessor texts (and then is restored in importance as the Engineer in *Miss Saigon*). Goro is an especially interesting case in the context of assimilation, in that he is the most Westernized character in the opera – much more so than Butterfly herself in her pathetic assimilationist efforts in act 2.

In Puccini's *Madama Butterfly* it is not Japan that is essentialized but rather the West, embodied as the American Pinkerton who declares, in a brash musical idiom that draws in a few bars of the American national anthem:

> Dovunque al mondo lo yankee vagabondo
>   si gode e traffica
>   sprezzando i rischi.
> Affonda l'ancora alla ventura   (Puccini 72)

'The whole world over, on business or on pleasure / the Yankee travels / and scorns all danger. / He casts his anchor wherever he chooses,' and Pinkerton's aria concludes 'America for ever' (in English, with the appropriate American music). This aria is in the tradition of the Duke's 'Questa o quella' or 'La donna è mobile' in Verdi's *Rigoletto*: in each of these three tenor arias one finds a deliberate musical vulgarity that contrasts with the delicacy of the soprano, Gilda in Verdi and Cio-Cio-San in Puccini. In *Madama Butterfly* the crudeness of Pinkerton's sexual imperialism is not shared by the other two American characters, but the point is that Sharpless and Kate, though more refined personally, are ideologically indistinguishable from Pinkerton and fully complicit in his activities. Kate, the 'vera sposa americana,' has one dramatic imperative in the opera, and that is to persuade Cio-Cio-San to give up her child to the West. It is significant that Puccini avoids what seems a dramatically obvious scene between the two women,[13] a scene that might humanize

Kate and make her a more sympathetic character. But all that we get is a very brief encounter between the two women, which prevents Kate from being developed as a character in the way she is in Long's story. Sharpless is, of course, in his professional capacity the official representative of the American imperialist ideology – that is, the system that treats Cio-Cio-San as a commodity to be purchased for the pleasure of 'lo yankee vagabondo.' The American consul, in spite of his personal misgivings, is totally complicit at every step of the way; he is convivially drinking whisky with Pinkerton during the 'Dovunque al mondo' aria in act 1, and he joins with Pinkerton in the line 'America for ever.' In act 2 he re-enacts the role of Giorgio Germont in Verdi's *La traviata* in urging that the woman should sacrifice herself to the dominant ideology that makes her a victim. Sharpless's plea to Suzuki ('Io so che alle sue pene') is strongly reminiscent of the earlier baritone aria that is similarly earnest and moving (Germont's 'Pura siccome un angelo') in its exhortations on behalf of the values of the dominant ideological force – French middle-class conventional morality in *Traviata* and American imperialism in *Madama Butterfly*. Thus, all three American characters are fully united in their national cause in the opera, whereas the Japanese characters represent a wide range of cultural attitudes.

The principal dramatic action of *Madama Butterfly* is Cio-Cio-San's movement across this spectrum of Japanese cultural attitudes. She is the deracinated character, like Hardy's Tess (to take just one late-nineteenth-century English example), who has been destabilized socially and who searches for a secure identity – and finds fulfilment only in death. Cio-Cio-San enters the action of the opera as a dignified figure who is being sold to Pinkerton by the Westernized go-between Goro, and then in the first scene of act 2 she herself has become a liminal figure, a mimic person[14] who tries, with painful ineptitude, to act the part of an American wife. But the second, final scene of act 2 constitutes her rejection of this cultural betrayal, for here she moves furthest from Goro and closest to the cultural values of her father, the samurai soldier of the emperor (see **Joshua Mostow**). The father, with his code of honour, is at the furthest possible remove from the manipulative, amoral Goro, and also from the man who lacks any sense of honour, Lieutenant Benjamin Franklin Pinkerton.

Catherine Clément has influentially drawn a parallel between the two penetrations of Cio-Cio-San: the phallus in act 1 and the sword in act 2 (see **Susan McClary**). But each of these penetrations signifies something quite different in the opera. In the ecstasy of the love duet that concludes act 1, she gives herself to Pinkerton while being swept away by her own sexuality and by her submissive sense of cultural, national inferiority to him. In the ritual suicide that concludes act 2 she performs an autonomous act of authentic choice. She chooses not to live except on her own terms:

> Con onor muore
> Chi non può serbar vita con onore.   (Puccini 124)

'To die with honour / Who cannot keep life with honour,' or, it is better to die with honour than to live without it. This is a vocabulary, and an attitude, that lies beyond anyone else's perceptions in the opera (apart from the dead father). Cio-Cio-San does not die for her love for Pinkerton. She has rejected Goro's values of a Western, commercial, commodifying civilization in which a woman is to be bought, and acts on the samurai values of her father. The inscribed sword signifies austere, noble, feudal values that stand in contrast to both Goro and Pinkerton. Not that there is necessarily anything 'authentic' about the opera's concept of samurai values, any more than Shakespeare's *Antony and Cleopatra* embodies authentic Roman or Egyptian values. The concept of a traditional Japanese aristocracy is no more authentic in Puccini than it is in a work like Yeats's 'Meditations in Time of Civil War,' but dramatically Puccini's ending places the opera in a class of its own as a telling of the Butterfly story. In the immediate predecessor texts – Long and Belasco – some of the same words are present, but without anything of the resonance that Puccini's score gives to them. Puccini's opera is the first of the Butterfly texts to give Cio-Cio-San a *voice* – a woman's voice that is silenced at the end, as in so many operas, but a woman's voice that finally achieves a personal autonomy and a dignity that are absent in both the predecessor and the successor works.

Hwang's *M. Butterfly* concludes with a deliberate travesty of Cio-Cio-San's suicide (see **Sherrill Grace**). Instead of a full orchestra playing Puccini's score, we have the music played on a tape recorder,[15] and it is the *wrong* music: in the play itself the love duet from Puccini's act 1, and in the film 'Un bel dì' from the first part of act 2. The relationship between the respective endings of the two works is revealing about the whole nature of Hwang's play as a response to Puccini's opera. The play has reversed the roles of the opera so that it is now the Western man who is Madame Butterfly (see **Rachel Ditor and Jan Selman**) and the

Oriental ex-woman who has Pinkerton's final words, now given an interrogative inflection: 'Butterfly? Butterfly?' (Hwang 68–9). In the film this final touch is for some reason omitted, but the last scene is nevertheless an ingenious reworking of Cio-Cio-San's suicide at the end of Puccini's opera. And that is just what Hwang's play is: an ingenious reworking of the opera, and of the Butterfly story generally. The play takes the materials of the Butterfly narrative and puts them together in a way that expresses late-twentieth-century attitudes towards Western imperialist ambitions and male sexuality. Whereas Puccini's opera represents Western imperialism as something powerful and destructive to the colonized East, Hwang's post-Vietnam play is set in a world in which the West has become a paper tiger and Gallimard's imperialist fantasies are only *self-destructive*. In the late-nineteenth-century incarnations of the Butterfly story Western imperialist power was unquestionably strong (see **Richard Cavell**), and male sexuality was powerful and (apart from Loti) heterosexually stable; and in Puccini's opera these two forces are made identical, so that international and sexual politics are merged in the site of Pinkerton's penetration of the Orient. In the 1980s play – and the 1990s film – both Western political power and male sexuality have been undermined, and the changes over the preceding century are brilliantly suggested by the use of the Butterfly myth.[16]

It is highly appropriate to construct a travesty of the Butterfly narrative, for the story itself is in a way a myth of travesty. The word 'travesty' derives from the Italian verb 'travestire,' to disguise, which literally means to trans-clothe (tra vestire), and thus 'transvestism' is etymologically identical to 'travesty' and preserves its original sense. Now here is the original Goro figure, from chapter 3 of Loti's *Madame Chrysanthème*: 'At this moment enters M. Kangourou, clad in a suit of grey tweed, which might have come from *La Belle Jardinière* or the *Pont Neuf*, with a pot hat and white thread gloves' (Loti 46). In the cross-cultural Butterfly story, cross-dressing of various kinds is always present. Most notably Cio-Cio-San trans-dresses – travesties herself – in the first part of Puccini's act 2. Productions can clothe her in American-style dress, as in Jean-Pierre Pannelle's film, and the libretto itself has her welcoming Sharpless to her American-style house: 'Benvenuto in casa americana' (Puccini 99). Then, in the second part of act 2, after the night vigil, her travesty-shrine with its Christian and American artefacts has been replaced by an image of Buddha as she re-assumes her ancestral culture and values. Thus, the literal cross-dressing in Hwang's play, in which Song performs the role of a woman, really derives from early versions of the narrative.

There is another form of trans-dressing, too, that pervades our book. One of the fascinating characteristics of the Butterfly story is that it is a modern myth that has expressed itself in such a variety of media. It began in the dress of prose fiction and then changed to that of theatre, and then to opera, and then to early films (see **Bart Testa**), and then to drama, and then to more recent films (see **Brian McIlroy**). The media keep changing, and so does the shape of the narrative itself. Take the ending, for example. 'Alone in this cell,' Hwang's Gallimard tells us near the beginning of *M. Butterfly*, 'I sit night after night, watching our story play through my head, always searching for a new ending' (4). That is what we see when we look at all the various tellings of the story together: the constant search for a new ending. One may consider Butterfly's death to be a *sine qua non* of the myth, but that is not at all what happens in the foundation text, Loti's piece of travel fiction. 'What will the last act of my little Japanese comedy be like?' the narrator of *Madame Chrysanthème* wonders (275), slightly anticipating Gallimard's line, and Loti's last act is truly of the world of comedy. For one thing, the relationship between the narrator and Yves, which is the main issue of the narrative, remains intact; Chrysanthème has not come between them – for the very good reasons that Yves respects the fact that she is married to his friend and the narrator himself despises her. The parting between the narrator and Chrysanthème could hardly be more different from subsequent versions of the story. The narrator, before his departure from Nagasaki, makes one last visit back to the dwelling he has shared with his temporary wife. He tiptoes up the stairs, and hears singing. 'It is undoubtedly Chrysanthème's voice and the song is a cheerful one!' And there is another sound too, mingled with her song: '*dzinn! dzinn!* a clear metallic ring as of coins being flung vigorously on the floor.' He then walks into the room unobserved.

> On the floor are spread out all the fine silver dollars which, according to our agreement, I had given her the evening before. With the competent dexterity of an old money-changer she fingers them, turns them over, throws them on the floor, and armed with a little mallet *ad hoc*, rings them vigorously against her ear, singing the while I know not what little pensive birdlike song which I daresay she improvises as she goes along.
>
> Well after all, it is even more completely Japanese than I could possibly have imagined it – this last scene of my married life! I feel inclined to laugh. How simple I have been, to allow myself to be taken in by the few clever words she whispered yesterday, as she walked beside me, by a tolera-

bly pretty little phrase embellished as it was by silence of two o'clock in the morning, and all the wonderful enchantments of night. (318–20)

This is exceedingly remote from the attempted suicide at the end of the Long story, which in turn is distinct from the achieved suicide in Belasco and Puccini, an ending that is of course radically reworked by Hwang and then Cronenberg. The dress of the story keeps being changed: from one medium to another, and from one mode of emplotment to another, from comedy to tragedy to ironic farce. In studying widely varied expressions of the Madame Butterfly story, one can gain insights into ways in which the tellings and retellings of this powerful modern myth can shift and take new shapes, in response to different media and different social and political contexts – as the essays that follow will demonstrate.

Notes

1 In his notes to *M. Butterfly* David Henry Hwang writes: 'I use the term "Oriental" specifically to denote an exotic or imperialistic view of the East' ([1989] 95). So do we, throughout our volume.
2 For this political context of Puccini's operas see Jeremy Tambling's *Opera and the Culture of Fascism*, including his account of 'Italy's African adventure' (76ff.) in his chapter on Verdi's *Otello*.
3 And this Canadian connection has a nineteenth-century counterpart, in that David Belasco spent part of his childhood in Victoria, British Columbia.
4 Quoted in Kaori O'Connor's introduction to Laura Ensor's 1985 English edition of *Madame Chrysanthème*, p. viii.
5 Nagasaki was one of the treaty ports imposed on Japan by the United States in the years following Commodore Matthew Perry's landing in Tokyo Bay on 8 July 1853. Here is another Western sailor penetrating Japan, and in a way Commodore Perry is the original Pinkerton. And this might be the place to mention a particularly sinister later political enactment of the Butterfly narrative: Naval Lieutenant Pinkerton, one could say, returned to Nagasaki on 9 August 1945 in the person of Air Force Major Charles W. Sweeney of the B-29 Superfortress 'Bock's Car.'
6 This source is carefully examined in Arthur Groos, 'Madame Butterfly: The Story,' and see also Jan van Rij's *Madame Butterfly: Japonisme, Puccini, and the Search for the Real Cho-Cho-San*.
7 For our purposes here, 1904 can count as 'nineteenth-century.'

8 This is the spelling in Long and Belasco – as opposed to Puccini's Italian version of the name.
9 And the Cronenberg film has painted screens, a fan, a mask, and other paraphernalia of *japonaiserie* as the background to its opening credits.
10 One useful context in which to place *Madama Butterfly* is the late-nineteenth-century European *japonaiserie* that is reflected in this passage from Wilde, and in the confession of Bunthorne, who is supposed to be partly based on the early Wilde, in Gilbert and Sullivan's operetta *Patience* (1881), that 'I do *not* long for all one sees / That's Japanese.' Some other musical examples of this fascination with – and fashion for – all one sees that's Japanese would be Gilbert and Sullivan's own *Mikado* (1885), Saint-Saëns's *La Princesse Jaune* (1873), Messager's *Madame Chrystanthème* (1893), and Mascagni's *Iris* (1898); and the Messager and Mascagni operas are in different ways obvious predecessors of Puccini's Japanese opera. Then there are many other operas in the second half of the nineteenth century that have Oriental-like (though not Japanese) settings and can be fruitfully compared to *Madama Butterfly* in a variety of ways. These include Meyerbeer's *L'Africaine* (1865), Verdi's *Aida* (1871), Bizet's *Carmen* (1875), Saint-Saëns's *Samson et Dalila* (1877), Massenet's *Hérodiade* (1881), Delibes's *Lakmé* (1883), Verdi's *Otello* (1887), Mascagni's *Cristoforo Colómbo* (1892), and Strauss's *Salome* (1905).
11 Puccini's opera, which carries the subtitle 'Tragedia giapponese in 2 atti,' is the only representation of the Butterfly narrative that can be described as tragic. Loti's narrator explicitly excludes tragedy as a possibility in the Japanese context: 'It is true that a complete imbroglio, worthy of a romance, seems ever threatening to appear upon my monotonous horizon; a regular intrigue seems ever ready to explode in the midst of this little world of mousmés and grasshoppers: Chrysanthème in love with Yves; Yves with Chrysanthème; Oyouki with me; I with no one. We might even find here, ready to hand, the elements of a fratricidal drama, were we in any other country than Japan; but we are in Japan, and under the narrowing and dwarfing influence of the surroundings, which turn everything into ridicule, nothing will come of it all' ([1985] 214).
12 Another work of 1904 that dramatizes imperialist/colonialist relationships is Bernard Shaw's play about relations between England and Ireland, *John Bull's Other Island*. This work is explicit in its rejection of essentialist ethnic stereotyping. The familiar stage Irishman appears in the first act, which is set in London, and he is revealed as an imposter; the subsequent acts, set in Ireland itself, bring onto the stage a great variety of 'real' Irish characters.
13 Illica and Giacosa had in fact written such a scene, in an act of *Madama Butterfly* that was deleted at Puccini's insistence during the composition of the

opera; manuscript versions surfaced a few years ago in Milan. See Arthur Groos, 'The Lady Vanishes.'

14 See McClintock 223: 'Incapable of themselves actually engendering change, African men are figured only as "mimic men," to borrow V.S. Naipaul's dyspeptic phrase, destined simply to ape the epic white march of progress to self-knowledge.'

15 In the Cronenberg film this bit of Western mechanism is very evident in the suicide scene. In the text of the Hwang play the music '*blares over the speakers*' (see Hwang 93), but in his opening speech Gallimard refers to the contents of his cell: 'I'm responsible for the tape recorder, the hot plate, and this charming coffee table' (Hwang 2), and in scene 3 in the first act '*He turns on his tape recorder. Over the house speakers, we hear the opening phrases of* Madame Butterfly' (4). In a production of the play there is much to be said for drawing an audience's attention to the tape recorder as a mode of reworking, diminishing, and commodifying the Puccini opera.

16 Two dramatists who might come to mind here, as one thinks about this play by the Chinese-American David Henry Hwang, are the Anglo-Irish Bernard Shaw and the Anglo-Czechoslovakian Tom Stoppard. Shaw's *Candida* is a travestying reversal of Ibsen's *Doll's House*, in which (as Shaw himself pointed out) it is the man who is the doll; the gender roles are reversed. Shaw's *Caesar and Cleopatra* is a travesty of Shakespeare's *Julius Caesar* and *Antony and Cleopatra*, taking the historical-Shakespearean figures and reworking their stories in order to interrogate the values of the Shakespeare plays. And Stoppard's *Rosencrantz and Guildenstern Are Dead* reworks the materials of Shakespeare's *Hamlet*, while his *Travesties* travesties Wilde's *The Importance of Being Earnest*. Stoppard's *Travesties* is an especially interesting work to set beside the Hwang play.

PART TWO

Texts

Mounting Butterflies

SUSAN MCCLARY

Midway through her love scene with Lieutenant Pinkerton, Puccini's Cio-Cio-San suddenly recoils with trepidation: 'They say that abroad, every butterfly – if it falls into a man's hands – is transfixed with a pin and fastened to a table.' Pinkerton does not entirely allay her fears when he patiently explains that this practice prevents the butterfly from flying off. Then clasping her to him, he sings: 'I have caught you. I hold you trembling. You are mine.' Following this exchange, the lovers move into the scene's climactic consummation, which we have been nudged to understand (not to put too fine a point on it) as Pinkerton mounting his newly acquired specimen with his pin. Nor is this the only scene that concludes with an impaled Cio-Cio-San; her sexual initiation foreshadows thematically her final self-annihilating act of ritual suicide. She does not flutter away at the end of the opera.

If one knows the opera, one may be struck by the absence of this portentous symbolism in John Luther Long's story on which it was based.[1] Long's Pinkerton always calls his bride Cio-Cio-San; only the narrator refers to her as Madame Butterfly. This appellation follows the custom in *fin-de-siècle* literature of naming Japanese objects of desire after small creatures or flowers – witness Pierre Loti's Madame Chrysanthème.[2] Moreover, the European-language stage names of Ki-Hou-San (Loti's character) and Cio-Cio-San mark both women as geishas, who were conscripted to entertain foreign troops.[3] Most obviously, however, the name 'Butterfly' recalls the image of a dazzling kimono with its wing-like sleeves.

It seems to have been Puccini and his collaborators who spun the web concerning mounted insects for symbolically trapping their hapless heroine, and they wanted to be sure their listeners didn't miss their point. In the words of Catherine Clément: 'The female butterfly is impaled, and the opera draws out the metaphor to its most simplistic application: first a man's sexual member, then a dagger in the body' (45). Already in his first conversation with the American consul, Pinkerton explains that Cio-Cio-San 'is like a figure on a painted screen; but from her glittering background of lacquer, with a sudden movement she frees herself, like a butterfly fluttering, and comes to rest with such silent grace that a sudden madness seizes me and I must pursue her, even though I damage her wings.' Sharpless, the justly named impotent bureaucrat who merely wrings his hands as the events unfold, cautions him that 'it would be a great sin to pluck off those delicate wings.' Thus, even before Cio-Cio-San appears on stage, the fateful implications of her pet name have been spelled out for us in flashing neon lights.

Like García Márquez's *Chronicle of a Death Foretold*, Puccini's *Madama Butterfly* presents a well-oiled narrative-machine that pursues its relentless course towards a destiny announced right at the outset.[4] When Cio-Cio-San enters into her love duet with Pinkerton, he knows, she knows, and we in the audience know where this union must lead. Not content with simply combining the lovers' voices in close harmony, Puccini compels Cio-Cio-San to participate in her own undoing: each time she commences her expression of love, Pinkerton breaks her off with an unsettling augmented triad. This device forces her tonality a step higher – and a step higher – until her series of modulations has traced an irrational whole-tone scale.

Pop songs often attempt to simulate ecstasy by jacking up the key in this manner once. Occasionally it occurs twice, but such repetition calls attention to the device as rhetorical hyperbole: it is then understood as self-parody rather than sincere expressive intensity, and it usually provokes laughter.[5] Puccini, however, defiantly performs this move four times in a row – arousing, frustrating, and ratcheting up desire by mechanical increments. Recall that Cio-Cio-San had already sung this music as she mounted the hill towards Pinkerton's house; she thus repeats her arduous climb, now within the confines of the bridal chamber. Only when she has reached a nearly excruciating height of vocal vulnerability and self-exposure does her bridegroom deign to join her for their rapturous conclusion.

Neither Long's story nor the play by David Belasco that brought it to Puccini's attention includes a scene of seduction and deflowering: their narratives focus on the vigil of the married Cio-Cio-San as she awaits Pinkerton's return and on her subsequent discovery of his betrayal.[6] Given the stakes of this cross-cultural affair, Puccini's literal upping of the ante during the wedding-night sequence could well be heard as sadistic. And to the extent that listeners desire that multiply deferred gratification – a desire produced and exacerbated within the music itself – we become complicit in Pinkerton's demand for satisfaction. The composer Ferruccio Busoni stormed out of the theatre at this point in the opera because he heard it as 'indecent.' A later commentator, A.K. Holland, explains: 'It was indecent to wrap all this up in music of the most voluptuous character, to seek to intoxicate the senses with this mixture of eroticism, sentimentality, and cruelty.'[7] But one might ask those of us who sit through the remainder of the opera, who watch this doomed butterfly flutter around the false consciousness that has fixed her in our gaze, what pleasures we derive from this story – one of the most successful, indeed one of the most *beloved*, in the history of opera.

Allow me for the moment to mount a defence of *Madama Butterfly*. Imagine a situation similar to the one described by Borges in 'Pierre Menard, Author of the *Quixote*' (36–44), in which a young Japanese-American female artist decides to produce a devastating indictment of Western attitudes towards Asian women. She could scarcely do better than to reiterate Puccini's opera word for word, note for note – except that she would risk being accused of political shrillness.

As virtually all commentators have observed, Puccini constructs Lieutenant Pinkerton as an unambiguous lout. Moreover, the other characters tell him he is a lout, and he eventually confesses his loutishness himself. He resorts to the most shameless expressions of American patriotism and even wraps himself in 'The Star-Spangled Banner' to legitimate his imperialist exploitation of the Japanese in general and Cio-Cio-San in particular. If anything, we might urge our imaginary postcolonial artist to develop a more nuanced personality for Pinkerton so that her opera doesn't come across as mere agit-prop, as the vengeful bashing of both men and the West. Gustav Kobbé wrote in his *The Complete Opera Book* in 1919: 'The use of the "Star-Spangled Banner" motif as a personal theme for Pinkerton always has had a disagreeable effect upon me, and from now on should be objected to by all Americans.'[8] For Pinkerton is a cartoon – a crudely concocted blend of nationalist jingoism and predatory sexuality.

Cio-Cio-San, by contrast, carries the dramatic, emotional, and musical weight of the opera. Although she finds herself in the role of victim, she also manifests qualities such as nobility, loyalty, and heroism. Indeed, she alone in the opera exhibits that most precious of Western properties: namely, interiority. And, to be sure, this aspect of Cio-Cio-San's characterization invites us to eavesdrop on her exquisite suffering: her protracted martyrdom allows listeners to experience cathartically what they often take as their own deep subjective feelings.[9]

Yet unlike the heroines of Long's story and Belasco's play, who speak in a broken pidgin English, the opera's Cio-Cio-San displays remarkable powers of self-expression in the 'universal' mode. Narrative and lyrics aside, hers is the voice of a wilful individual. Puccini's collaborators urged him to interview Japanese women so that he could obtain 'an authentic impression of the timbre of a female Japanese voice, with its peculiar high twitter.'[10] Yet after the disastrous premiere, he cast Cio-Cio-San as a dramatic soprano, and he has her sing forcefully throughout the opera.[11] Thus, if the character passively accepts her fate, the woman who sings the part of Cio-Cio-San gives passionate voice to recognizably Western ideals and feelings. As film historian Nick Browne puts it: 'Puccini's combination of theatricality and singing drew famous divas to the piece, challenged by the possibility of bringing a realistic interpretation to the subjectivity of the character through vocal performance' (231).

Recall, for instance, Cio-Cio-San's deservedly celebrated aria 'Un bel dì' – One Fine Day. Without question, the lyrics express her tragically deluded hopes, her childlike timidity, even her masochism – but not the music, which actually sounds quite incongruous with the simpering text that serves as the verbal vehicle for her remarkable vocalization. Indeed, the pleasures of *Madama Butterfly* largely derive from this music, which delivers larger-than-life representations of emotions many of us think we harbour within us, regardless of the social constraints that require us to keep them tucked away out of sight. It is this music that produces the goose bumps, sometimes even in the most unwilling of listeners.

Cio-Cio-San starts high in her register, accompanied primarily by solo violin, harp, and clarinet, which double her melody rather than offering the dialectical support a bass line would grant. Her melody contains hints of the pentatonic scale that aligns her with *japonaiserie*; yet those elements had so permeated the artistic vocabulary of *art nouveau* and Impressionism that they can be found in the arias of Puccini's Parisian characters as well. Minimal harmonic filler comes from tremolo strings ('like a distant murmur') and tentative woodwinds. Along with her the instruments trace a graceful descent through the G-flat major scale; only when the ship appears in her imagination is the fantasy grounded with a solid arrival in the bass. Up until that point, she seems to exist in a kind of suspended animation, waiting – we might say – to exhale.

As she continues to narrate her vision of Pinkerton's return, she occasionally pushes through the limits her own melody would seem to dictate. At 'Vedi? E venuto!' for instance, where she claims to see him, she strains upward to G natural – thereby transcending the reality of her implied key. This grasping at transcendence reaches its culmination, however, in her recapitulation, her most heroic sequence.

Cio-Cio-San explains to Suzuki how she will hide from Pinkerton, thus fulfilling his expectations of her childish behaviour, but also so as to conceal the surge of passion she will experience – a surge so powerful that it threatens to kill her. Suddenly, with the unanticipated word 'morire,' she seizes the G-flat with which she started her aria, but now with the entire orchestra thundering in unison with her. The lyrics, which then describe how Pinkerton will chuck her under the chin and call her pet names, bring on a short invasion of 'diminutive twittering' before she returns to her steeliest statement yet: 'All this will happen, I promise you. Stay your fear – I wait for him with unshakeable faith!' Here the supporting harmony that has been in such short supply bears her up. Over a sombre B-flat minor chord, she pushes repeatedly up to that same G natural, then finally hurls herself up to her climactic concluding pitch on a high B-flat. Yet Puccini harmonizes that pitch with G-flat – the pitch that grounds the aria as tonic but that now sounds in context like a flat VI chord: a key relation identified in nineteenth-century music with retreats into fantasy.[12] But even if the plot and bass line remind us that her triumphal moment is sheer delusion, Cio-Cio-San enacts her arrival in the promised land with the power of a Verdian hero singing 'Vincerò!' – I will conquer!

I have undertaken my Borges experiment in order to consider more carefully some crucial debates circulating now concerning the interpretation of music. Until about fifteen years ago, musicologists rarely addressed the content of works. Any negative comments usually had to do with formal or stylistic issues: Puccini's music may have been criticized for structural imbalances or for indulging in vulgar effects (recall Joseph Kerman's description of *Tosca* as 'that shabby little shocker'),[13] but not for its ideological resonances. Before Catherine Clément's *Opera, or the Undoing of Women* (published in English in 1988), few had noticed that dead female characters littered the opera stage; even fewer asked why.

But a funny thing happened with the development of music criticism after Clément. In contrast to most other humanities disciplines, which have undertaken a thorough examination of misogyny and imperialism in art, film, and literature, most musicologists have chosen to present apologetics for the great works in the repertory. As it turns out (or so it would seem), all the important composers of the European tradition were always already feminists and postcolonials inasmuch as they gave women and ethnic Others the power to sing on the stage – to perform their alternative subjectivities in a world that otherwise insisted on their silence and invisibility. It has thus become possible within musicology to maintain the same canon, but now to bestow upon it the laurel wreaths of 1990s ethical wisdom relating to class, race, and gender.[14]

As we have seen, it takes no great effort to reread *Madama Butterfly* as a text that empowers women and condemns imperialism. One can, in short, have one's cake and eat it too – bring the latest cultural theory to Puccini and use it to justify getting goose bumps during 'Un bel dì.' I might add – in case there was any doubt – that contributing a laudatory feminist reading of a mainstream text stands to increase one's disciplinary capital.

I do not deny the legitimacy of such recovery projects: the works of the canon are not likely to disappear any time soon, and we need strategies for opening them up to interpretations congenial to contemporary sensibilities. Indeed, if I were cast in the role of Cio-Cio-San, I would work hard to project precisely this kind of subversive reading, to cause it to speak forcefully against the patriarchal and imperialist assumptions that frame the character.[15]

And yet I have difficulty imagining that Puccini in 1904 had this kind of cultural critique in mind as he penned his score. This is not to suggest that Puccini and his collaborators owned the meanings of their text or that earlier readings must prevail over newer ones. Nevertheless, there are reasons for interrogating original contexts and the history of reception that have made *Madama Butterfly* such a popular opera among audiences for nearly a hundred years. What kind of cultural work has it performed along the way from its inception to the present?

Alas, history often baulks at divulging its pleasures verbally, and a search of the standard literature actually yields more documentation for sustaining a negative view of the opera than for arguing its value. Those writing publicly about versions of Madame Butterfly have frequently adopted a defensive stance. They freely concede possible objections to the story, then abruptly change the focus of their discussions: they either offer excuses understood in advance to be lame or else sidestep content altogether to concentrate instead on purely formal concerns.

To cultural critics today, those excuses may appear even more problematic than the story itself, which does – as we have seen – allow for multiple readings; by contrast, many of the attempted justifications often reveal only too clearly their cultural biases and priorities.

In a famous response to Belasco's play, for instance, a reviewer for the *London Times* commented that 'in any other than an exotic setting this dramatic episode would be intolerably painful. Redeemed as it is by delicate grace and, above all, by strangeness of detail, the little play proves by no means as distressing as a bald recital may suggest, but tear-compelling merely. A tragedy to be sure, but a toy tragedy.'[16] Mosco Carner, Puccini's indefatigable biographer, refers admiringly to 'the melting softness and insinuating feminine grace of *Madama Butterfly*,' and he claims (in words calculated to guard him against charges of personal racism) that, '*Butterfly recaptures* the quaintness, daintiness, the childlike innocence and humility which the West at one time associated with Japan and its *diminutive* people.'[17] Indeed, some critics have read Cio-Cio-San's predicament as the very paradigm for Puccini's female leads: the author of a celebratory guidebook to the opera waxes rhapsodic as he explains that 'those frail and fragile little women who are the heroines ... of nearly all his operas, and whose whole *raison d'être* is to love and suffer ... are all butterflies of varying hues, all destined to be caught and crumpled in the web of fate.'[18]

Even Pinkerton comes in for whitewashing. William Ashbrook writes: 'If [Pinkerton] is made totally crass, completely selfish, then Butterfly's devotion becomes incomprehensible ... [B]ut if we consider his words in the love duet as *she* hears them, then his ardent outbursts have a ring of sincerity.'[19] And as to the theory that *Madama Butterfly* means to operate as cultural critique, Carner explicitly ridicules what he calls a Communist production of the opera, in which Pinkerton's imperialism was emphasized.[20] 'The theatre is not a moral institution,' he claims, 'and no matter what kind of subject is brought on to the stage, its sole criterion is its dramatic propriety and its artistic handling.'[21] Along the way, he defends Puccini's taste for 'tragic little women' and for the exoticism that serves merely to spark his imagination. Indeed, in response to Busoni's disgust with the opera, A.K. Holland explains how stupid it would be to pursue such a critique, even though he freely acknowledges the sordidness of the story. With friends like this, Puccini scarcely needs enemies.

In other words, if I were to try to push my politically correct reading of *Madama Butterfly* – in which Puccini and his collaborators deliberately planted devastating attacks of patriarchy and imperialism – I would have to fly in the face of those who have supported the piece over the course of the last century and who have guaranteed its centrality in the opera repertoire. Those responsible for its longevity have apparently derived other pleasures from it than those I might want to offer at this late date in its history. I can claim the right to my self-empowering feminist, postcolonial reading, but I cannot argue very productively that the opera has always been understood in this fashion.

But at least Carner and others grapple with the problematic parts of Puccini's opera, if only to reject potential criticisms in advance as inappropriate. Another approach involves bracketing the content and luxuriating in the technical details of the score. Although music theorists have long applied such formalist projects to Wagner, Richard Strauss, and other German composers who might otherwise seem problematic, they have only recently come to Puccini studies. This is because music theorists typically expend their energies on music that presents new syntactical challenges, and Puccini has always been heard as entirely transparent – even tacky. But on the heels of an extremely successful scrutiny of Verdi's operas has come a surge of interest in his most popular successor.

I do not question the importance of paying attention to Puccini's musical choices: indeed, to the extent that his scores manage to jerk tears from even the most resistant of listeners, they demand the careful attention of cultural critics. I have tried in my discussions of the love duet and 'Un bel dì' to account for how Puccini creates some of his effects. But if the past history of formalist projects can be used to predict the probable course of Puccini studies, it would suggest that attention will focus not on the rhetorical manipulation that sways the hearts of opera-goers, but precisely on details that only the connoisseur can savour after intensive score-study. And the greater our investment in such details – say, the ways Puccini marks the incompatibility of Cio-Cio-San and Pinkerton through long-term key relations – the greater our resistance to violating the internal integrity of the piece with the irrelevancies of public meanings and cultural work.[22]

Okay, so why bother with this century-old opera, long dismissed as vulgar by arbiters of taste in classical music? Well, largely because musicologists don't own meanings and cannot police the consequences music has in the real world. As the work of Asian-American cultural critics such as Karen Ma and Dorinne Kondo reminds us, the myth of *Madama Butterfly* has had a pernicious effect on the ways Asian women are viewed and treated in the West: far from regarding Pinkerton as an insidious cad, Caucasian males have frequently aspired to inhabit his subject position, to acquire a docile Asian plaything all their own.[23] Exploitative gender relations in the Pacific theatre following the Second World War and during the Vietnam War, a booming business in mail-order brides from Thailand, and a particular form of cross-cultural sexual harassment in Pacific Rim universities bear witness to the ongoing devastation fuelled by versions of the Butterfly fantasy, among which Puccini's opera still stands as the most prominent and most prestigious.

Moreover, *Madama Butterfly* continues to spawn cultural progeny. Avant-garde composer John Zorn recently released a couple of albums (*Torture Garden* and *Naked City*), the covers of which were festooned with the tortured and dismembered bodies of Asian women and men. He thereby collapsed the metaphors through which Cio-Cio-San expresses her fears – that she will have her wings pulled off, that she will be mounted on display as a specimen – and presented graphic realizations of precisely these acts. In response to protests from the Asian-American community (inspired by the courageous work of music theorist Ellie Hisama), Zorn offered the same excuses long thrown up in defence of Puccini's opera: exoticism and Asian women inspire his art, which ought to be sufficient justification. After boycotts and picketing, he yielded an apology of sorts, but needless to say, many musicologists perceive Hisama – not Zorn – as the bad guy in this dispute.[24]

So long as the discussion remains within musicology, the longstanding barriers that protect classical music from social criticism will continue to deflect the serious scrutiny of *Madama Butterfly*. Note that the principals involved in the composition of the opera itself never came out and said explicitly that they were engaged with ideological tensions. Nor did they talk about why they were taking a complex set of international political problems and rewriting them within the economy of a ill-fated love affair. What they *did* squabble over endlessly was whether to present the opera in two acts or to break the second part in half. They also worried a great deal about whether or not they should give Pinkerton more music to sing – a crucial consideration if they wanted to attract major opera stars to the part. If 'history' entails merely the documentation of what people actually stated as intentions, *Madama Butterfly* remains sealed up as a formal entity.

Of course, the documents also bear witness to the guilty consciences that evidently have always accompanied *Madama Butterfly*, for all those defensive statements declaring critiques of exoticism and gender representation out of bounds raise those very issues, even as they attempt to erase them from consideration. And the fact remains that *Madama Butterfly* emerged from a complex cultural world that has always engaged in dialogue with the opera: that world – its fears and anxieties, its notions of exotic Others, gender, the body, emotions, erotic pleasures, and so on – also constitutes part of the historical picture.

Above all, we have to be willing to read the score itself as a historical document. Indeed, musical scores are among the most invaluable yet neglected sources of potential historical information we possess. Puccini's music, for instance, traces with matchless precision the sadistic quality of the wedding night, the complicated negotiations between Japanese identity and Italian musical style that form Cio-Cio-San's discourse, the rhetorical ploys designed to engage and manipulate the passions of listeners, all of which rely on specific historically based cultural assumptions.

Fortunately, historians from other disciplines have taken up the task of interrogating the opera, in the absence of responsible accounts within music studies. Jeremy Tambling's book *Opera and the Culture of Fascism* examines how operas from Wagner through the Second World War contributed to the habits of thought and feeling that made fascism possible. In his chapter on *Madama Butterfly*, Tambling (long a professor of comparative literature at the University of Hong Kong) sets out the political tensions between Asia and the West at the turn of the century that helped ignite the Orientalist fantasies of Long, Belasco, Puccini, and others. Strange to tell, for all the talk of the diminutive, quaint, and childlike Japanese people, Japan had just emerged as a major player on the world stage of military expansionism. And although the United States was in the process of coming out as an imperialist power at this same moment, it – and the rest of the West – needed assurances of its innate superiority. By presenting to itself fantasies of its ability to dominate the feminized East, the West could weep copious tears over its victims, yet retain its sense of divine right.[25]

To be sure, accusations of 'fascism' circulate rather widely in musicology today. They are hurled, however, not at pieces of music, but rather at those who would interrogate meanings. Cultural critics such as myself are regarded as the Pinkertons of the discipline, as we dissect poor helpless artefacts such as *Madama Butterfly*.[26] Unfortunately, critics from other fields rarely address the music, except to mention it as the lubricant that helps us swallow the story. With the music itself exempted from criticism, opera companies continue to stage productions of Puccini's beloved tragedy. And most of them continue to milk the score down to the very last drop of sentiment. Why does this piece still work?

Frankly, I'm not the one to ask. When I saw a newspaper advertisement for Frédéric Mitterand's film, I actually thought it said 'Puccini's immoral opera,' and I breathed a sigh of relief – until I realized that (of course) it said 'immortal.' And as I sat squirming through the film, I became painfully aware of the gap between my own outraged reaction and that of those around me who had brought ample quantities of tissues in eager anticipation of their leaky responses. I considered doing some on-the-spot ethnography: that is, turning to the blissfully weeping people around me and questioning them. But it didn't seem like the right thing to do, somehow. Is it possible to perform Puccini's music – to mount *Butterfly* – without reproducing its immortal/immoral message?

Not surprisingly, the most effective critiques of *Madama Butterfly* have come from within the arts themselves, from those canny enough to restage the music itself. For instance, in his 1984 album *Fans*, Malcolm McLaren – the Andy Warhol of music, producer of the Sex Pistols – produced a postmodern version of 'Un bel dì.' McLaren himself recites Pinkerton's side of the story with a grotesque imitation of a good-old-boy Southern accent, in language only slightly more crude than the original. In dialogue with this, Cio-Cio-San sings a cheesy pop torch song – an English line-for-line paraphrase of 'Un bel dì,' which resorts at the end to

> Call me fool! call me stupid!
> Bend this arrow kill this cupid.
> I have faith I'll always pray
> My white honky's here to stay.

Meanwhile, a soprano sings the aria, tattered reminiscences of which flutter in the background over a whiplash disco beat. The disco backdrop refuses to support Cio-Cio-San's rhetorical moves in this arrangement: the harmonies that compel the listener to identify with her delusion in the opera fail to materialize. Her melody is left twisting in the wind, in an alienation effect worthy of Bertold Brecht. If somewhat heavy-handed, McLaren's version lays bare the sado-masochistic basis of this sordid story.

But by far the most brilliant deconstruction of the opera is David Henry Hwang's play *M. Butterfly*, in which a gullible Caucasian male takes the Butterfly myth so literally that he is easily duped into accepting a female-impersonating spy as a demure Asian maiden. According to his own account of the play's genesis, Hwang began formulating his scenario when he read a news story concerning the real-life Rene Gallimard.

> The idea of doing a deconstructivist *Madama Butterfly* immediately appealed to me. This, despite the fact that I didn't even know the plot of the opera! I knew Butterfly only as a cultural stereotype; speaking of an Asian woman, we would sometimes say, 'She's pulling a Butterfly,' which meant playing the submissive Oriental number. Yet, I felt convinced that the libretto would include yet another lotus blossom pining away for a cruel Caucasian man, and dying for her love. Such a story has become too much of a cliché not to be included in the archetypal East-West romance that started it all. Sure enough, when I purchased the record, I discovered it contained a wealth of sexist and racist clichés, reaffirming my faith in Western culture. ([1989] 95)

Those who know Hwang's play only from the film version by Cronenberg may not know the extent to which he draws on Puccini's music to unmask itself. All the highlights of the opera appear: 'Un bel dì,' the death scene, the jingoistic duet between Pinkerton and Sharpless, but most of all the love duet, which occurs no fewer than five times – including the occasion of Gallimard's own suicide. Earlier in the play, Helga, Gallimard's wife, offers two very important comments: she insists that the power of *Madama Butterfly* resides not in the story, but only in the music, and she scoffs at Asians who object to the opera: 'Politics again? Why can't they just hear it as a piece of beautiful music?' (19)

But as Hwang positions Puccini against his highly ironic, ultimately devastating critique, he insists that his audience realize the lethal seductiveness of this 'beautiful music.' As the play indicates over and over again, the cruelty of the Caucasian male is a crucial component in the myth, which is why pointing up Pinkerton's loutishness – far from undermining the story – only reinforces it. What truly undoes the opera here is that Hwang's Asian woman fails to play the role of victim. Instead, the Pinkerton-figure ends up hoisted on his own petard, as a mounted butterfly in his own right.

However it might be accomplished, the only way of breaking the spell this opera has cast over the West's notions of Asian women is to take it apart limb from limb. To borrow Pinkerton's words: '[A] sudden madness seizes me and I must pursue [Butterfly], even though I damage her wings.' Sharpless, you will recall, counters that 'it would be a great sin to pluck off those delicate wings.' Far better, however, to damage the delicate wings of this score than to reinscribe over and over the poisonous fantasies it perpetuates. I look forward to the day when we can pin this opera up in the museum of strange cultural practices of the past, when we can mount Puccini's *Butterfly* once and for all as a historical exhibit. But until that day – 'un bel dì,' we might call it – this odd cluster of story, play, opera, films, and postmodern spin-offs will demand our serious critical attention.

Notes

1 John Luther Long, 'Madame Butterfly,' *Century Magazine* (January 1898); reprinted in a collection also including 'Purple Eyes,' 'A Gentleman of Japan and a Lady,' and 'Kito Glory' (New York: The Century Co., 1904).
2 Pierre Loti, *Madame Chrysanthemum* (1887). The female character in *Madame Chrysanthème*, Ki-Hou-San, is referred to variously as a plaything, a dog, a cat, a doll, and an insect. The narrator asks: 'What can take place in that little head? ... I'll bet one hundred to one that nothing takes place there. And even if it did, I wouldn't care.' Quoted in Szyliowicz 76. Similarly, Cio-Cio-San is called a squirrel, a doll, a little baby, and a plaything.
3 See Karen Ma 19–20.
4 Joseph Kerman uses much the same image when he writes concerning all Puccini's heroines: 'What a shame (we are to feel), what a shame that butterflies are broken on this excellently oiled wheel' (20).
5 See, for instance, Bon Jovi, 'Living on a Prayer,' on *Slippery When Wet* (1986), and the discussion of the device in this song by Robert Walser, *Running with the Devil: Power, Gender, and Madness in Heavy Metal Music* (Hanover, NH: Wesleyan University Press, 1993), 123. See also Boyz-II-Men, 'On Bended Knee' (*Boyz-II-Men II*, 1994), by Jimmy Jam and Terry Lewis, which modulates twice in a bid for rhetorical overkill.
6 David Belasco, *Madame Butterfly* (premiere: Herald Square Theater, New York, 5 March 1900; London premiere: Duke of York's Theatre, April 1900); published in Belasco, *Six Plays*.
7 Holland 36. Holland goes on to dismiss Busoni's reactions, however, which he regards as inappropriate.
8 Gustav Kobbé, *The Complete Opera Book* (New York, 1919), as quoted in Osborne 165. Osborne goes on to write: 'I have yet to meet an American who finds Puccini's use of "The Star-Spangled Banner" offensive. (It would not be

surprising, surely, if Japanese were to find the entire opera offensive, but that is another matter.)'

9 For a discussion of race and representations of interiority, see Walser, 'Deep Jazz: Notes on Interiority, Race, and Criticism.'
10 Mosco Carner, *Puccini: A Critical Biography*, 3rd ed. (New York: Holmes and Meier, 1992), 138.
11 William Ashbrook credits the casting of two dramatic sopranos (Salomea Krusceniski and Emmy Destinn) in performances following the ill-fated premiere with deepening the role: 'The prominence given these two dramatic sopranos suggests that Puccini later modifed his original view of Butterfly as a sort of Japanese doll and came to stress more and more the tragic aspects of the role' (114).
12 For a discussion of flat VI excursions, see my 'Pitches, Expression, Ideology: An Exercise in Mediation,' *Enclitic* 7.1 (Spring 1983): 76–86.
13 Kerman 254. Kerman has been widely castigated, of course, for this callous dismissal of *Tosca*.
14 See, for instance, the discussion of Strauss's *Salome* in Abbate 225–58.
15 I performed such an against-the-grain reading of Alessandro Stradella's seventeenth-century oratorio *La Susanna* in my *Susanna Does the Elders* (Minneapolis, 1987).
16 *London Times*, as quoted in Carner, *Puccini* 134–5.
17 Carner, *Puccini* 309 and 295; emphasis added.
18 Holland 36–7.
19 Ashbrook 117: 'On the whole, the librettists are more successful than one might expect with Pinkerton. If he is made totally crass, completely selfish, then Butterfly's devotion becomes incomprehensible. Pinkerton states his easy-going philosophy tersely in his Act I scene with Sharpless. There is bitter irony in Pinkerton's drinking a toast to a real marriage with a real American wife, just as Goro comes hurrying in to announce Butterfly's imminent arrival. Seeing this side of Pinkerton, we realize he is merely infatuated with Butterfly, but if we consider his words in the love duet as *she* hears them, then his ardent outbursts have a ring of sincerity. The plot does not, of course, contain the scene of Pinkerton's departure from Butterfly, but we get her side of it. She was convinced he smiled to conceal his deep feeling when he told her he would come back "when the robin makes his nest again." That Pinkerton is momentarily – if not like Butterfly, permanently – capable of real feeling comes across in his remorse as he learns the true nature of Butterfly's attachment to him. We come to see that Butterfly's tragedy is not just that she is Pinkerton's victim; rather, her faithfulness is an anomaly even in her own culture. Her attitude is incomprehensible to Goro and to Yamadori.' Original emphasis.

20 Carner, *Puccini* 430: 'Communism has in fact seized on Butterfly as propaganda against "colonial imperialism." As reported in *The [London] Times* of 14 October 1957, in a production given in Bucharest's new opera house, Pinkerton appeared complete with pipe and white flannel trousers suggesting a sort of composite Anglo-American colonial type, for whom it was difficult not to feel intense dislike. In addition, in order to impress the supposed Marxist moral of the plot on the audience, the programme book explained that the naval lieutenant's attitude was "repulsive because it is the result of an odious conception of morals." The morals were those of *bourgeois* society, that is, of the "ruling class of the United States." According to the writer of the programme book, "Puccini had been a realist belonging to a movement which mirrored the hard life of the people, though like other members of the movement, he was unable to understand the laws of class struggle in the resolution of social conflicts." This is on a par with the fact that, when in the early years of the Soviet régime, the libretto of *Tosca* was rewritten, Cavaradossi painting his Attavanti-Magdalene was replaced by Delécluze painting a picture of the Triumph of the Commune.'

21 Carner, 'In Defence of Puccini' in *Puccini's* Madame Butterfly, 24.

22 See, for example, Atlas 186–96. To be fair, Atlas does address some of the ideological concerns raised by the piece, but he also tries to salvage the piece by locating an enlightened attitude in its structural apparatus. See also Powils-Okano.

23 Ma, *The Modern Madame Butterfly* and Kondo, '*M. Butterfly*: Orientalism, Gender, and a Critique of Essentialist Identity.'

24 See Ellie Hisama, 'Postcolonialism on the Make: The Music of John Mellencamp, David Bowie and John Zorn,' *Popular Music* 12.2 (1993): 91–104. A useful summary of the controversy appeared in Denise Hamilton, 'Zorn's "Garden" Sprouts Discontent,' *Los Angeles Times*, Calendar section, 15 August 1994: 9.

25 Film historian Nick Browne argues along similar lines in his remarkable study of the spate of silent films based on the story of 'Madame Butterfly,' which gained cultural prestige through their connections to the opera. See Browne, 'The Undoing of the *Other* Woman.'

26 See Treitler 23–45, who regards the *discussion* of gender and racial stereotypes in music as responsible for these pernicious binarisms. He concluded the first version of this essay with a comparison between critical musicologists and those who murdered Jews in Auschwitz.

Cio-Cio-San the Geisha

VERA MICZNIK

Most critical writings (including many in this volume) view the tragedy of the Madame Butterfly story as an epitome of the clash resulting from the stereotypical racial encounter between the submissive Oriental woman and the cruel white man. The tragic outcome of the story is seen as an example of Western domination, in which the Oriental woman sacrifices everything for the unscrupulous American and dies as a martyr 'destroyed by Western values' (Marchetti 78–89).[1] Such (feminist, postcolonial) approaches are valuable in that they reprehend ideologically works of art that have enjoyed a long-standing success despite their use of this problematic plot. Yet, like any ideologically charged interpretation, they emphasize only one of the many possible critical readings of the story, offsetting other perspectives reachable according to different critical positions. I would like to move away temporarily from the emphasis on the tragedy and victimization of Butterfly, and to start by pointing out that, from a narrative point of view, no attention has been given to the contradiction between Butterfly's behaviour in the story and her alleged social position as a geisha before the beginning of the plot, and as a 'temporary wife' in her relationship with Pinkerton. The psychological traits of Butterfly's character – her incomprehensible blindness to the reality of her situation, her self-deception to a point of ridicule – do not correspond to the expectations one would have from geisha or hired wives.[2] An interrogation of this contradiction and of the verisimilitude of Butterfly's dramatic behaviour would have normally diminished the credibility of the story, yet despite such flaws, critics and audiences alike are still swept away by the ominous tragedy that, like any myth, seems beyond the need for questioning.

On a woodblock print of a geisha from circa 1900 is inscribed the text of a 'kouta' – a song usually sung by a geisha accompanied by the shamisen[3] – which reads: 'Parting, regretting, reuniting again. Left waiting, still meeting – such is life' (Dalby 75). There is perhaps no better way to summarize what seems to be the image of a geisha's psychological make-up and view of life: acceptance and patience, moments of loneliness mixed with hopes for opportunities for new encounters, without which a geisha could not support herself. An overwhelming feeling of resignation underlines this state of mind, yet with an implication of a self-knowledge and self-control enabling geisha to accept such a life to which, by choice or lack of choice, they dedicate themselves.

This essay is an attempt to explore the transformation/distortion of these defining characteristics of the geisha/hired wife in the *myth* of Madame Butterfly. How did she become the woman who, in response to her American husband's desertion, committed *seppuku* or ritual suicide? Was it in the name of traditional Japanese honour that she chose this way of defying her fate? Was it just out of love? Or as an acceptance of defeat? Was the mere intervention of Pinkerton – the foreigner, the 'colonizer' – the only reason that changed the 'willow[-like] resilience of the geisha' and her ability 'to bend gracefully in many different directions depending on the winds of fortune' (Dalby 175)? Or, put another way, how did Cio-Cio-San the ex-entertainer become one of the West's favourite fantasies – the submissive Oriental woman as victim who sacrifices herself as a result of the Western imperialist ruthless exploitation of her situation? Does the popularity of the myth confirm what Song Liling in David Henry Hwang's *M. Butterfly* observed in his/her cynical demystification of Butterfly's appeal: '[B]ecause it's an Oriental who kills herself for a Westerner – ah! – you find it beautiful' (Hwang, sc. 6: 18)? And, most importantly, which view did Puccini embrace about his main character, and in which ways did his opera contribute to, or subvert, the Butterfly myth?

The incarnations of the Madame Butterfly myth preceding Puccini's opera, and the opera itself, suggest with various degrees of clarity that before her marriage to the Westerner, the main character has had some connection with the profession of a geisha.[4] Brief allusions to Butterfly's former occupation occur in John Luther Long's short story *Madame Butterfly*: for example, the American consul greets Butterfly with the words: 'You used to dance, did you not?' (Long, 'Madame Butterfly,' 42), and she tells the consul that after her father had died, 'I go an' dance liddle, so we don' starve. Also, ... if somebody wish me I git married for while ...'

(47). David Belasco, basing his play partly on Long's short story, makes this information even more explicit, as Butterfly fondly reminisces about her pleasant time with Pinkerton: 'Then I'll dance like w'en I was Geisha girl' (Belasco, 'Madame Butterfly' 628); and so does the libretto of Puccini's opera: '[W]e had to go as geisha to earn our living' (*Madama Butterfly*, libretto [John ed.] 76).

Most critical readings ignore, or are not bothered by, the discrepancy between Butterfly's geisha past and her suicidal behaviour in these stories. Yet, attempts to trace biographically the possible model for the Butterfly character through documentary sources have shown that in 'real life,' geisha and such behaviour do not necessarily coalesce, and that, therefore, Butterfly should either not have been a geisha, or not have committed suicide. Having researched the lives of geisha, Cecilia Segawa Seigle found that the Long and Belasco stories use the term 'liberally,' and expressed doubts as to whether the term 'geisha' in the sense of a profession can strictly be applied to Butterfly, despite her comment that she could go back to entertaining people with her singing ('Samurai's' 10). It may also be added that given her young age at the time of her marriage (18 in Loti, 17 in Long, 15 in the opera), if she had, at all, attempted to pursue the career of a geisha before the moment when the stories begin, she could have only been at the beginnings of her apprenticeship.

A piece of evidence in the genesis of the Butterfly story that sheds doubts on the authenticity of Madame Butterfly's past as geisha comes from the research of Arthur Groos, who has identified the actual characters in the allegedly real-life story reported to Long by his sister (who was living in Japan as a missionary at the time), on which his short story is based. According to Groos's research, the model for Madame Butterfly was a tea-house girl who lived with a lover who deserted her and their child (there is no mention of a 'temporary marriage') ('Butterfly' 130). Whether or not the story is authentic (apparently Long's sister received the information second hand, 'related to her by a Nagasaki tradesman' [Seigle, 'Samurai's' 10]), it becomes clear that in the process of fictionalization several Oriental female character types have been collapsed together: geisha, 'rented' temporary wife, tea-house Oriental girl with child deserted by her foreign lover, and the Oriental woman who, betrayed by her Western husband, commits suicide to save her honour.

Indeed, in all these representations, the term 'geisha' may have been used generically by the authors in part because they had no first-hand knowledge of Japan, but also because already at that time, within the export of cultural Orientalism, the 'trope' of the geisha (as well as of the manner of death by *seppuku*) had become 'markers of Japanese identity' (Kondo 9). As will become clearer, the association of Butterfly with the class of geisha served best the interests of these authors in presenting the Western public with a commodity to whose background and inner nature they could have related. My present argument does not hinge on whether she was technically a geisha or not, because, in the narrative representations under discussion, she *is* fictionalized as a geisha. Yet while it is understandable why these authors would collapse together the socio-economical, spiritual, or psychological conditions of most women 'for hire' or working for money in tea-houses or the entertainment business into the notion of geisha, it is important to attempt a historical reconstruction of those social categories, insofar as this helps us to understand the process of fictional representation.

In order better to highlight the tension between what Butterfly (or someone like her) might have been in the real world and her fictionalized representation, we first need to know more details about the profession of geisha. A geisha belonged to a special category of female entertainer allowed to work in tea-houses and other designated entertainment areas, populated also by various other categories of entertainers, such as prostitutes and courtesans. Described as early as the 1750s as 'good at playing the shamisen and singing' (Seigle, *Yoshiwara* 172), they were recognized as of 1779 as practising a distinct profession, and achieved a professional status as entertainers (ibid. 174). Eventually they had to register with the government to get a licence; their wages were standardized, and they had to pay taxes (Dalby 66–7). Unlike prostitutes, geisha were trained as professional dancers and singers, specializing in tea-ceremony and etiquette, flower and table arrangements, and, to distinguish their higher professional status from that of the other women in the entertainment industry, their appearance was characterized by less adorned hairstyle, and by a certain simplicity in their kimono (Seigle, *Yoshiwara* 170). They were hired to amuse and entertain guests at dinners, or parties, or in public tea-houses, and they were inseparable from the three-stringed instrument called 'shamisen.' Acting as 'hosts,' not as 'maids,' they had an obligation to 'make the guest feel comfortable and relaxed'; they had to know how to move the conversation in order to keep their customers interested, and generally they held 'pampering the male ego' to be one of their most important skills (Dalby 8 and 174). Unlike the other categories of tea-house entertainers, the geisha's 'engaging in sex with customers was officially prohibited' (Dalby 54),[5] yet while they had no sexual obligations as part of their 'job description,' many geisha and entertainers accepted the financial and sexual patronage of rich men. Not all had to become prostitutes, although the West often makes this assumption. In fact, men's attraction for geisha was not for their eroticism, but rather for their social graces.[6] Partly because of their professional class position, geisha inspired in their customers more respect and, therefore, more reticence to enter a sexual relationship (Dalby 111).

Officially, most women did not enter the profession with the idea of finding a husband. At best, they expected to find a good patron who would provide continuous financial support, so that they could either leave the tea-house and live as kept women, or continue to live as geisha while enjoying a mainly continuous relationship. Getting married was the exception rather than the norm. But, as Liza Dalby has documented, during the Meiji period (1868–1911), when a geisha 'found a patron [she] could stop working ... [O]f course, if something happened to your patron then you were in a fix, ... [Y]ou could always come back to the geisha life' (197–8). She also gives other examples of geisha returning to their previous life after having been married and divorced, and even having had children, and maintains that this was not regarded as dishonourable among the Japanese.[7]

A different direction in the strong Japanese tradition of treating women as commodities consists of the practices of buying and selling or renting women, which began at least as early as the mid-eighteenth century, and were legally institutionalized under the government's attempt to control and regulate the entertainment industry. As early as the 1760s 'live-in geisha' in Yoshiwara were available for hiring out (Seigle, *Yoshiwara* 173), and '[w]omen could be rented by the month at the [Pontochō] inns' (Dalby 60). A new category of 'women for rent' named 'rashamen' appeared, specifically designated for foreigners. 'Term marriages' through contractual agreements between such women and foreigners, especially naval officers, were recognized by the authorities, and were common especially in places where the traffic of foreigners was high, such as in the harbour of Cio-Cio-San's Nagasaki. The practice is described very clearly in Loti, who was even surprised by the casual attitude of the mother of such a girl sold for money, who accepts the transaction as 'an act perfectly admissible in their world' (Loti [1985] 58). References to the practice and monetary aspects of the institution of 'rashamen' survive in Long, in Belasco, and even in Puccini's libretto.[8]

Groos cites additional personal testimonies from various people, such as the Great Duke Alexander of Russia, stationed in Nagasaki in the mid-1880s, and a doctor in 1868–9, both of whom describe the matter-of-fact, mercantile way in which these relationships were regarded (Groos, 'Butterfly' 151–2).

The documentation presented so far concerns mostly the background and context of what we may call the *public*, official, image and place that geisha and, in general, 'women for hire,' occupied in Japanese society. Yet there is another side of these women, one that we may call the *private*, inner, image, not much talked about even in Japan. These inner voices were constantly suppressed by the institutions that ruled their professions, or by the women themselves, whose preservation of their public image was essential in order to for them to work. While the documentation on these private aspects is scarce, the inner side of a geisha's life can be inferred from the few extant testimonies, as well as from a psychological reading of the human experiences such a woman goes through, and their consequences for their lives.

The difficult inner life of a geisha has been explored by Aisaburo Akiyama in the 1937 book *Geisha Girl*. He points out that '[t]he lives of the Geisha-girls are very trying in many respects and keep them nervous day and night' (26). The constant efforts to please everybody, the tea-house customers as well as the tea-house mistresses on whom they depend financially, the constant task of pretending to like the company of guests they do not particularly care about – all these take a toll on these women's mental health and well-being. 'A conflict between *giri* and *ninjō* [duty versus human feeling] was built into a geisha's life' (Dalby 197), in which most of the time the former takes over, transforming her life into a continuous frustration. And despite the 'sisterhood' that develops among the geisha, they are mostly lonely, with no system of support except for their own self-sufficiency. Falling in love under these circumstances is a very dangerous thing, which most of them avoid at all costs.

Considering that most geisha during previous centuries entered the profession either sold by their families or forced by financial circumstances, it can be argued they suffered some kind of interior trauma that lingered throughout their lives, despite the constructed appearance of self-contained assuredness required by their professional behaviour; as Dalby points out, '... the geisha's actions are the required façade for their work' (157). This statement seems to be corroborated by evidence such as Segawa Seigle's that '[t]he high rate of suicide among the women of the pleasure quarter reflects their fragility and the tenuousness of their existence ... [T]hey were ... vulnerable in spite of their high spirit and pride' (*Yoshiwara* 197). Similarly, among the women offered for rent for temporary marriages, especially with foreigners, many resented this condition and would occasionally commit suicide rather than abide by the orders to receive foreign clients (Seigle, 'Samurai's' 12).

An apt conceptualization of this condition of deep loss and vulnerability, of a depressed self repressed throughout life under a fake facade, can be found in Julia Kristeva's theory of abjection, according to which geisha or rented wives are potential 'subjects of abjection.' The abject, writes Kristeva, can be experienced 'at the peak of its strength when that subject, weary of fruitless attempts to identify with something on the outside, finds the impossible *within*; when it finds that the impossible constitutes its very *being*' (*Powers* 5). The abjection of the self is experienced when the subject discovers that her entire surrounding world, whatever constitutes the basis of her life, consists of an 'inaugural loss' (ibid.). Clearly, a woman sold or rented by her parents early in life will bear the 'inaugural loss' of her subjective identity for the rest of her life.

Deprived of the parental shelter, the abjected subject will live with a continual 'want' of replacing this loss, which will become a subliminal obsession. '[A]ll abjection is in fact recognition of the *want* on which any being ... is founded' (ibid. 5). The 'object of the want' – the Other – is thus fetishized to the point that it 'settle[s] in place and stead of' the abjected self (ibid. 10). In other words, in the process of fetishization, without necessarily identifying with the other, the abjected subject perceives her existence only as a result of being possessed by the other (ibid.). The Other, in turn, having become an alter ego, sets a frontier that alienates the abjected subject, but the abject finds in that sublime alienation an enjoyable existence (ibid. 9). This creates a situation of balance, in which the subject is 'swallowed up in a certain jouissance,' but through which the Other, in return, keeps the subject from breaking down' (ibid.). Thus, through fetishism, 'fantasy and acting out replace the denial of psychic pain' (Kristeva, *Black* 45).

As Anne McClintock also points out, fetishes can be seen as the displacement onto an object or person of contradictions that the individual cannot resolve at a personal level: 'The contradiction is displaced onto and embodied in the fetish object, which is thus destined to recur with compulsive repetition. Hence the apparent power of the fetish to enchant the fetishist. By displacing power onto the fetish, then manipulating the fetish, the individual gains symbolic control over what might otherwise be terrifying ambiguities' (184). Through the lens of Kristeva's and McClintock's theories of abjection and fetishization it is easier to understand the process through which a geisha or a hired wife, having to reconcile constantly her facade with the original loss felt throughout her life as a projection of her 'personal and historical memory,' could 'displace' her own 'contradiction onto an object or person, which becomes the embodiment of the crisis' (McClintock 185). Such an interpretation might allow us to alleviate the discrepancy between the historical reality of geisha and the fictionalization of character development, especially in Puccini's opera, where the musical treatment of the story conveys deep psychological subtleties not always available in language.

This review of the historical and psychological background of the geisha and, more generally, of women 'for hire,' enables us to articulate how Western authors manipulated the historical reality of what they might have known about Japanese women to create the fictionalized world of their narratives. The historical 'evidence' of Japanese customs reveals a discrepancy between the historical Japanese reality and these fictional interpretations. As we have seen, first, a geisha could have easily entered a temporary marriage; second, neither a geisha nor a 'rashamen' would have expected an arranged marriage with a foreigner to last;[9] and third, it would not have been so unusual for a geisha to enter a temporary marriage, get out of it, and go back to geisha life. Therefore, in terms of historical accuracy, the story ultimately used by Puccini and his librettists for the opera is flawed and Butterfly's suicide implausible. It is through Western eyes, particularly the American ones of Long and Belasco, followed by Puccini and his librettists, that Butterfly's situation was made into a catastrophe. Indeed, as Liza Dalby, who has lived in Japan as a geisha in order to better understand geisha lives, has stated, 'The notion of the geisha as a simpering slave to male whim is an absurd stereotype formed outside Japan' (173).

It is likely that these writers' stories may constitute sincere reactions to their fantasized view of Japan, and thus may in fact articulate implicit judgments/condemnations of Japanese institutions and customs seen through the eyes of the industrial modernized, 'democratic' American observer. It is also probable that Belasco, the first to construe a Butterfly who commits suicide, might have obeyed in part the requirements of tragedy and melodrama; at the same time, this tragic ending would have also served to heighten the moralizing 'Western' condemnation of the extreme, pitiful situation resulting for a Japanese woman from the custom of 'renting' wives, which would have been so foreign to Americans. Under the derisive treatment of Butterfly's naivety, despite the pity that her character might have drawn from Western audiences, this interpretation of the Japanese reality brings with it a statement of the moral superiority of the American system, where allegedly such a catastrophe could not have happened. Implicit in this fictionalization and misreading is a criticism of Japan, of Butterfly's foolishness, but *not* of the American officer; this explains his fleeting appearance in both Long's and Belasco's stories. Pinkerton is a foil for bringing to American and Western audiences a 'slice of Japanese folklore,' populated by naive Oriental women who, in their 'need' to be dominated, worship the Western male hero whose desertion is unbearable for them. The documentary inconsistency – the discrepancy between the geisha or rashamen concepts and this woman's behaviour – did not matter in the creation of the myth of betrayal and tragedy of the Oriental woman. The Western fascination with this archetype can be only intuited in Belasco, but it is captured and demystified much later by David Hwang's Song Liling in his insidious statement in *M. Butterfly* that 'because it's an Oriental who kills herself for a Westerner – ah! – you find it beautiful.'

The progressive construction of the myth can be followed through the various versions of the story, through its gradual distancing from the Japanese documentary reality that might have informed the earlier versions. Leaving aside for now the racist attitudes of the authors, Pierre Loti's novel, although fictional, has some documentary credibility. The young girl Chrysanthème was 'rented' by the French naval officer as a temporary wife directly from her family, through the negotiations of Mr Kangourou, 'interpreter, washerman, and matrimonial agent' (Loti 1887/1985, 36). She does not seem to have been employed at the teahouse with which Mr Kangourou was associated. And although her constant playing of the 'long-necked guitar' (the shamisen), which 'exasperated' her French temporary husband, is a sign that she might have been raised with this profession in mind (ibid. 78), the differentiation between geisha and the girls sold for temporary marriages seems quite distinct in Loti: Pierre sees a dancer and a singer in the tea-house and asks whether he can have one of those for a wife, to which Kangourou replies, 'No, sir, no! Those are only geisha, sir!' (48). Loti's comment that later on, when he understood Japanese affairs better, he realized that 'one would really suppose I had talked of marrying the devil' shows that, at least in Loti's perception, geisha might have been thought of socially as much worse than the girls sold for temporary marriages. Thus, Loti's novel is closest to the documented reality in terms of the institutionalized mercantile relationship that binds the Oriental woman to the Western man – Pierre does not pretend that he loves her, she does not fall in love, they live according to the contract. She is, indeed, treated as an object by the male, but she keeps her strength and can easily survive his departure.

John Luther Long, in light of his sister's report of a real story read through American missionary eyes, already mythologizes the power relationship between Butterfly and Pinkerton by presenting derisively her lack of English skills and her blind faithfulness and adulation, but in the end he allows for the possibility that Butterfly finds the strength to survive. Belasco is the one who, by ending the play in tragedy, definitively establishes the over-determined myth of domination, by totally fictionalizing the reality of what a woman in Butterfly's situation – geisha or teahouse girl – might have done. Yet, Belasco's fictionalization, his distortion of the public image of 'willow[-like] resilience' of the geisha, and his betrayal of the spirit of survival that would have characterized such women can be interpreted, paradoxically, as his subtle reading of the most intimate subtext subliminally underlining the life of such women – what I described above as their 'private,' hidden, 'abject' psychological make-up.

Thus, Belasco brings out from underneath the geisha's facade, and maps onto her 'public' image of strength her psychological 'private' reality never officially acknowledged – the subconscious death-drive that rules the abjected subjects she represents. Pinkerton fulfils the role of agency through which these two sides – public and private – otherwise separated, could be collapsed together. That the hidden psychological misery of such a woman is brought out through the intervention of a Westerner undeniably marks the point where the myth of the Oriental naive and submissive woman falling victim to the evil Westerner begins, as a Western concoction that satisfies the colonial impulse to assert superiority and domination of the West. Yet while this 'vision of the Orient' might, indeed, serve as an example of purposeful misreading of the Japanese realities, Belasco's subtle reach into a woman's damaged psyche caught in the conflict between the ancestral societal impositions and the betrayal of the foreigner, even if based on historically inaccurate facts, acquires an authenticity credible both on a universal psychological basis and according to Western sensibility.

Again, viewed through Kristeva's and McClintock's theories of abjection and fetishization, Cio-Cio-San's unrealistic attachment to Pinkerton is not completely fictional, but, rather, a projection of the 'personal and historical memory' of her previous life, structured by various recurring features, by the 'displacement of the contradiction onto an object or person, which becomes the embodiment of the crisis' (McClintock 185). This could explain the contradiction between Butterfly's social past and her compulsive ritual waiting for Pinkerton's return, as well as her exaggerated identification with his values as a symptom of an abjected subject that has already been victimized by society long before the encounter with Pinkerton – the 'object' that became her fetish and that she was doomed to imagine as her salvation. Indeed, it is precisely this mixture in the character of Butterfly of two diametrically opposed psychological traits – the conventionally polite, obedient, patient, 'public' facade of the geisha / hired wife and the 'private' subconscious drive of abjection brought into actualization in her encounter with the American officer – that attracted Puccini to Belasco's play in the first place, and that ultimately saved the play and the opera from the embarrassments of an inaccurate historical construction.

In this line of justification, Butterfly already enters into the marriage with the traumas of an abjected subject as part of her past, due both to the impoverishment of her family and death of her father and to the demands of her previous profession. Like other subjects of the abject, she refuses to see reality, and even seems to delight in abasing herself. It is thus not surprising that she projects the 'lack,' or 'void,' she experiences as a result of the societal and institutional contradictions responsible for her present situation, against which it is too late (if at all possible) to rebel, onto another person, who becomes the object of her fetishistic displacement. Her surrender is to fetishize the other, Pinkerton, with all his values, as she understands or misunderstands them, to let herself be possessed by them so that she can live. While these forays into the private, subconscious life of Butterfly the geisha – her self-victimization, predilection for suffering, and fetishization of Pinkerton – may still be figments of the fictional fantasy about the East that informs the Western construct of the plot, these features also correspond best to those belonging to the pantheon of plots of dying women in the nineteenth-century tradition of Italian opera. It is, therefore, not surprising that this self-sacrificial plot interested Puccini, although, as we shall see, having at his disposal the means of music, he manages better than any of his predecessors to bring to the surface precisely the conflict in Butterfly between her geisha facade and her inner abjected self.

Butterfly's references early in the opera to her life as geisha and rented wife serve as pointers that her doomed ending is inscribed already before the beginning of the staged plot. Through the opera's libretto there is a clear progression in Butterfly's behaviour from the required 'public' geisha/wife politeness, which she manages to maintain through her fetishization of Pinkerton, to her tragic ending caused by the disappearance of the fetish. These can be seen as stages in the process of gradual manifestations and the ultimate taking over of the abjection caused by the trauma from her previous life.

It seems to me that Puccini manages to capture and outline this process musically, through means that the previous discourses did not possess. At first the musical means concentrate on her past as a geisha, mixing obedience with sensuality, and her repetitive formulas and lack of her own Oriental idiom underline her fetishization of Pinkerton and America. But in the last sections of act 2, once these support mechanisms fail, she is left alone in her abjection, which eventually leads to suicide, expressed in her much more personal musical language.

Puccini's 'vision of the Orient' goes deeper than the surface musical differences between Japanese and Western music, and beyond ridiculing the Americans by blasting their national anthem to underline their boasting. While in the earlier stages of the opera he provides musical signs that in an almost tongue-in-cheek style lampoon both Butterfly's geisha stereotypical protocols and Pinkerton's values that she fetishizes, he already brings in signs of doom. In a very subtle touch, when the American anthem appears for the first time, announcing Pinkerton's aria 'Dovunque al mondo,' it takes a turn from a major into a minor key, which cannot be explained in any other way but as a foreshadowing of the tragic result of Butterfly's over-infatuation with (fetishization of) what this tune stands for (example 1).

While setting up musically the demarcation between East and West, Puccini's *Madama Butterfly* is much less concerned with representing the Orient than with following the trajectory of the abjected subject in its encounter with the other, which results in what the musicologist Allan Atlas calls Puccini's 'Crossed Stars' (187–8). This trajectory seems to me to be best represented by the course followed throughout the opera by a seldom mentioned motive that appears in the most crucial moments, and which, like many leitmotifs in Wagner, has the ability to gradually

Example 1. *Madama Butterfly*, act 1

change its meaning in relation to its context (example 2). In what follows I shall outline the course of this motive and its musical/dramatic role in the crucial moments of the opera, during which, I believe, it embodies, first, the remnants of Butterfly's public condition as a geisha/rented wife, then her fetishization of Pinkerton, including her unsolicited adoption of his religion, and, finally, her doom. This discussion will hopefully show how Puccini, through his subliminal reading of the connection between the Butterfly character and her past, makes the music tell us more about the historical drama of Butterfly than the text manages to suggest.

Called by Powils-Okana the 'young Butterfly' motive, this eight-bar-long melody has some very special features: it has symmetrical conventional 2+2 measure phrasing, with simple, traditional harmonies and cadences, and on the whole sounds like a chorale or hymn, or an aphorism or maxim meant to convey some deep meaning (example 2). In addition, while it has some pentatonic features, and therefore can be associated with Butterfly's ethnic background, it also contradicts that quality because it behaves like a tonal tune, starting in a major and end-

Example 2. *Madama Butterfly*, act 1, reh. 41

ing in a minor mode. Again, the minor ending gives it a pensive, lyrical twist, denying the more optimistic simplicity of its beginning.

The melody appears for the first time, wordless, in the orchestra, and passes almost unnoticed, yet structurally it fulfils the important role of marking the arrival of Butterfly and her friends at the top of the hill (act 1, rehearsal no. 41 in the score, beginning before Butterfly's words 'Siam giunte' ['we've arrived'], which it then accompanies; see example 3). Soon afterwards, this same melody becomes part of the background in the first interchange between Pinkerton and Butterfly, during which they carry on a polite conversation, he trying to compliment her, she answering, and in exchange showing off her knowledge of protocol formulas (act 1, rehearsal no. 43; see example 4). In the score Puccini gives a relevant stage direction: [Butterfly] 'wanting to show off her repertory of compliments,' an allusion, of course, to her professional skills. A detailed unravelling of the text here is helpful for understanding Puccini's musical choices. Just before the appearance of this melody, Butterfly and her friends, freshly arrived at the top of the hill, bow ceremoniously in front of Pinkerton, who, slightly embarrassed by such treatment, greets them with a courteous question as to whether their climb was tiring. Butterfly responds with an ostentatiously polite versified formula that sounds as if taken straight from a 'Book of good manners for a bride-to-be': 'A una sposa costumata / più penosa è l'impazienza' ('to a well-behaved bride, impatience is even more difficult to bear'), yet the phrase contains an openly sexual allusion to Butterfly's impatience to consummate her marriage, which only a geisha, not a young innocent girl, could have intimated. Pinkerton's remark that 'this is a very pretty compliment' incites Butterfly to make an offer: 'I know even prettier ones ... if you'd like to hear some now,' which, however, is received by Pinkerton with a flat 'No, thank you!' The rules of the game are already set: he is not interested in playing the 'well-mannered geisha' (or any) game, no matter how inciting – it is too foreign to him. The geisha parlor relationship is reproduced, together with the first hint that her feelings will not be spared any more than in her previous life, and that the facade must be kept to hide the 'inaugural loss.'

Musically the entire polite chattering is set in square phrases, filled

Example 3. *Madama Butterfly*, act 1

Example 4. *Madama Butterfly*, act 1

with conventional cadences, reminiscent of the motive in example 2, which I will call the 'geisha motive.' Even Pinkerton mimetically adopts the musical signs of conventional conversational formulas, but gets tired of them very quickly, whereas Butterfly is at ease in her routine learned as a professional geisha to please her clients. Puccini's introduction of this motive just under Butterfly's text 'If you'd like to hear some [more compliments] now' makes clear the connection between her cliché behaviour and this motive.

The next appearance of this melody, this time sung by Butterfly herself, seems to unveil even more fully its true meaning. In a private moment between Butterfly and Pinkerton during the wedding, after confessing to him that she secretly converted to Christianity, she tells him: 'I am following my destiny, / and full of humility / I bow before the God of Mr Pinkerton' (reh. 80, example 5). What was suggested all along through the musical characteristics of this melody – the square traditional phrases, its maxim-like, hymn-like ritualistic quality, its modal quasi-pentatonic sound – comes now in the words with which it is associated: Butterfly's submission to her fate, her humility, and her passive-aggressive repudiation (transgression) of her ancestral customs in the fetishistic embrace of Pinkerton's Christianity, all done with the calm and dignity required by the geisha/wife facade.[10] It seems that Puccini has so far captured musically the public, professional image of the hired wife.

Most relevantly, this same music reappears as a closing for the love duet at the end of act 1. Towards the end of the duet we see Butterfly for the first and only time through the opera happy, and in total communion, with Pinkerton. It seems that in the throngs of erotic attraction all boundaries between them have been forgotten, and Butterfly comes into her own, lets her sexuality show freely. The fetishization works, and helps her suppress, at least temporarily, the void of her previous existence. The music's extreme chromaticism portrays the sensuousness of the interaction. Following more or less the traditions of the operatic duet, the two characters sing first separately, then together at times, their voices entangled. At first Pinkerton seems to have the lead, as he brings in his melody on the words 'è notte serena,' yet immediately afterwards, the power is hers: during the last section of the duet when, on the same melody, she sings the words 'dolce notte,' not only does Butterfly have the main melodic line, while Pinkerton only accompanies, but the music and its harmony are 'Butterfly's music' – the music supported by the augmented chords that accompanied her and her girl-

Cio-Cio-San the Geisha 53

Example 5. *Madama Butterfly*, act 1

friends as they were climbing up the hill.[11] It is only after a while that Pinkerton joins in, and they end the duet in the perfect union symbolized by their singing in unison. Just after the climactic ending, however, right after her words 'Tutto estatico d'amor ride il ciel' ('The sky smiles down full of the ecstasy of love'), and after his 'Ah, vien, sei mia!' ('Oh, come, be mine'), the submissive geisha motive mentioned earlier (now bearing the shadow of doom) reappears (see example 6). As the obedient geisha motive pounds obsessively, the music reminds us that the

Example 5 (continued). *Madama Butterfly*, act 1

doom of Butterfly's past, her abjection, although absent and forgotten in her momentary entrancement with Pinkerton, is there to stay. The same motive appears only once more, in the prologue to the second part of act 2: after Pinkerton's desertion, the geisha subservience seems to disappear. As she grows through the opera, as she gradually has to accept reality, Butterfly gives up both the hopes and strength – the facade of the geisha in her and the fetishistic borrowing of the language, customs, and music of the foreigner – that served as her life support until then. Her language matures, the music becomes more and more her own, filled with anxiety and dissolution, and that of her ancestors, thus signalling the danger that once she lets go of her fetish, she can no longer live.

Indeed, in the last scene of the opera, from Butterfly's last entrance when she sees Kate and finally understands that she has to let go of her fetish Pinkerton, the musical language is entirely a representation of her abjection. Aside from a short continuous arietta in which she gathers her forces to address her son ('O a me, sceso dal trono dell'alto Paradiso' – 'My son, sent from the throne of Paradise'), her phrases are short, incoherent, almost shrieking, as if she was strangled by pain. The composure of the 'Butterfly geisha' motive that once signified her public strength is gone. The orchestra's ritualistic pedals and unisons after her speech act as signs of the doom that finally engulfs her. And even

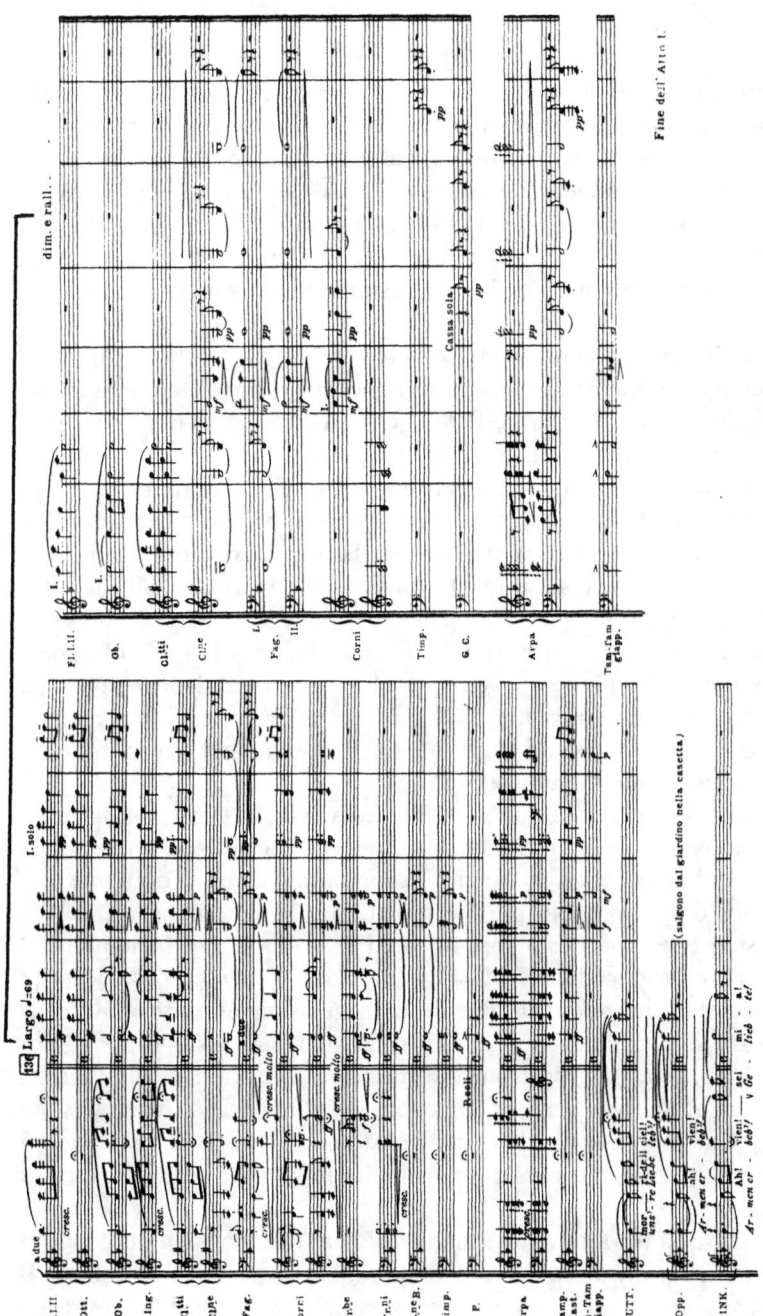

Example 6. *Madama Butterfly*, end of act 1

the pentatonic 'Japanese' hymn of the closing measures, often thought of as representing Butterfly's redemption by having finally returned to her original faith, does not, in fact, belong to her consciousness, since, by then, she is no longer alive. Rather, the nobility of the Japanese hymn is a projection imparted by what was going on in the heads of the two men, Pinkerton and Sharpless, as they were watching Butterfly die, once again misconstruing her demise as a result at her 'Japanese condition.'

There are other subtle ways in which Puccini portrays musically the incompatibility between the two characters, and Butterfly's faithful yet inverted appropriation (as fetishization) of the other. Allan Atlas shows that the two main key areas, G-flat major and A major, represent by association exactly the opposite for Pinkerton and for Butterfly: Pinkerton's G-flat major stands for the negative values of his 'renunciation and rejection of both Butterfly and her culture' (187). His 'Dovunque al mondo' and many of the Star-Spangled Banner quotations are in that key, as well as his music when he talks about marriage 'all' uso giaponese' (ibid.), while for Butterfly the same key, G-flat, represents acceptance and affirmation (her famous 'Un bel dì' – her aria of hope – is in that key). For Pinkerton A major is associated with lyrical eroticism, while Butterfly uses this key when, in her 'selfless sacrifice,' she renounces her own gods and culture (Atlas 188; this can be seen in example 5, with her 'geisha' motive).

If, indeed, the victimization of Butterfly is a Western construction resulting from a desire to dominate the East, Puccini's opera materializes through music a very particular vision of that construction, one that succumbs only in part to the Western desire to dominate, yet on the other side accomplishes a sophisticated critique of the socio-political reality that produced the transformation of women into subjects of abjection. Puccini does not give us any signs suggesting that Butterfly dies because of Pinkerton. Nor is it clear that she dies because of her love, or honour. Judging from the music's description of the gradual unfolding of the symptoms of abjection, she dies because death was the natural outcome inscribed in her condition. Thus, Puccini's reading brings to the plot the missing verisimilitude and supplants its lack of credibility.

The cultural work of music digging beneath stereotyped perceptions of reality is lucidly articulated in Ping-hui Liao's observation that '[a]s an instrument of understanding, of organizing the world, of constituting the audible as well as visible waveband of the vibrations and signs that constitute society, opera is very subtle, for it produces the unconscious "sound form of knowledge"' (36); yet I would add that beyond 'serving the West's cultural dominion,' in this case the 'sound form of knowledge' provides information and insights otherwise unavailable to Western modes of knowledge. Puccini's 'Vision of the Orient' is one of pity for the woman victimized by society, of sympathy for her condition, and perhaps it is for this reason that his opera has remained universally appreciated.

Notes

1 For similar views and subtle reinterpretations see, among many others, Clément 45, Liao 32, Browne 242–9, and Kondo 6.
2 As Ping-hui Liao, for example, notices '[t]he dramatic irony of Butterfly's complete self-deception and ignorance of her fate, whereas everybody else around her has no difficulty guessing at the final result of her love' (32).
3 Traditionally the name of this instrument is spelled 'samisen' in English; however, Dalby and Seigle, who both know Japanese and whose books are relatively recent, spell it 'shamisen,' and the same spelling is given in the *Grove's Dictionary of Music and Musicians*. The shamisen is a long-necked plucked lute with three strings, and it has become the quintessential 'instrument of the geisha world' (Dalby 252).
4 I am referring here to the known sources, Loti, Long, and Belasco.
5 Unless specified otherwise, most of the information about the geisha is taken from Dalby, Seigle, and Akiyama.
6 Dalby mentions that '[g]eisha generally know more about sex than housewives do, but a man who thinks of the geisha's gei [art] as rampant eroticism will be disappointed' (111). Her further discussion on this subject is on the same page.
7 For instance, a geisha who quit the tea-house in her twenties, when she had found a patron, returned to geisha life when, after his death, she was left penniless and with a child (Dalby 7). Similarly, a modern geisha married for seventeen years obtained a divorce after her children grew up and came back to the Pontochō tea-house (Dalby 127).
8 In Loti (1887/1985), pp. 36–67 describe in detail the process of selection through which Pierre finally chose Chrysanthème as his rented wife. E.g.: 'It is ten o'clock when all is finally settled, and M. Kangourou comes to tell me: "All is arranged, sir: her parents will give her up for twenty dollars a month, – the same price as Mlle. Jasmin' (62). In Long ('Butterfly' 47), Butterfly describes how her family wished she 'got married for a while' to bring money

home. In Belasco ('Butterfly' 629–30), Butterfly talks about the pressure her poor family put on her to take 'the beas[t]'; '"He's got moaneys." So I say for jus' liddle while, perhaps I can stan'.' And in Puccini Butterfly says: 'For me you paid a hundred yen' (84) and 'I used to think: if anyone should want me, Then perhaps for a while I might have married' (94). Even Pinkerton's statement that 'in this country, the houses and contracts are elastic' (72) refers to the same flexibility of marriage contracts. The practice of rashamen is described in Groos, Powils-Okano, and Seigle.

9 This statement is corroborated by the study of Osman Edwards, *Japanese Plays and Playfellows*, of 1901, cited by **Joshua Mostow** in his essay here. Edwards found Belasco's plot unrealistic: 'But most of all I doubt the verisimilitude of the alleged motive for self-destruction ... [W]hat [Madame Chrysanthème] would not do is what Madame Butterfly does – namely, consider that she has suffered a dishonour expiable only by death. The Western sentiment of honour is out of place in such a connection, for she had been party with open eyes to a legal, extra-marital contract, sanctioned by usage and arranged by her relations' (Edwards 65).

10 Powils-Okano also mentions this motive and rightly notices its child's-song quality, as well as its power of suggesting of 'a modest, charming and very young Japanese girl' (150). While the tune presents some resemblances with the Japanese song Hana saku haru, I agree with Powils-Okano that it seems better to qualify it as Puccini's own composition inspired by such an authentic Japanese song, rather than a quotation (see Powils-Okano 61–2).

11 A comparison between the early – La Scala – version of the opera and the later versions shows that Puccini has increased Butterfly's strength here, by enlarging the part where she sings alone, and thus, for the only time in the opera, she dominates in her relationships with Pinkerton (CD set Voxa 7525, which reproduces the original 1904 La Scala version of the opera, as well as the revisions for Brescia and Paris). Also, it is interesting to compare my interpretation of this duet with **Susan McClary**'s, where she sees the balance of powers between the two characters in the opposite position from mine: she hears Butterfly's interaction with Pinkerton as manipulated entirely by Pinkerton, whose interruptions compel Butterfly to ascend chromatically higher and higher, as a reflection of her advancement towards irrationality.

'Re-Orienting' the Vision: Ethnicity and Authenticity from Suzuki to Comrade Chin

MELINDA BOYD

In only a few lines from his closing monologue, Rene Gallimard – the fictional 'unhero' of David Henry Hwang's *M. Butterfly* – summarizes the pervasive element that lies at the heart of the matrix of texts constituting the Butterfly myth. According to Gallimard, 'There is a vision of the Orient that I have. Of slender women in chong sams and kimonos, who die for the love of unworthy foreign devils. Who are born and raised to be the perfect women. Who take whatever punishment we give them, and bounce back, strengthened by love, unconditionally. It is a vision that has become my life' (Hwang [1988] 68). Gallimard's 'vision of the Orient' is carefully preserved through the transmission of a putative and enduring set of cultural values, beginning with Pierre Loti's novel *Madame Chrysanthème*, and ending, one might say, with David Cronenberg's cinematic version of *M. Butterfly*. Despite the constant metamorphoses in the various media, from America to France, Japan to China, or male to female, one thing is certain in the story of Madame Butterfly. There is always a Pinkerton and always a Butterfly. These two figures represent the two extremes of the East-West binary, thus commanding the bulk of our critical attention. However, the same cannot be said of the supporting cast, which remains a fluid, albeit underexplored entity in which characters are reinvented, expanded, elided, and ignored. I propose, therefore, to shift the focus of inquiry away from the central characters to the margins, specifically to the figures of Suzuki and Comrade Chin. As the narrative re-inscribes its set of cultural boundaries, Suzuki and Comrade Chin perform an analogous dramatic function. I suggest that these characters 're-orient the vision,' so to speak, in that they function as a cultural yardstick of gender, ethnicity, performativity, and voice – the mark of authenticity against which Butterfly's border-crossings may be measured. Yet as essentialist constructions of the 'authentic,' Suzuki and Comrade Chin are by their very natures as much a fabrication as Butterfly. By way of parody and caricature, they represent a different, more pernicious 'vision of the Orient' – the vision of the 'undesirable.'

The characters of Suzuki and Comrade Chin evolve somewhat slowly throughout the Madame Butterfly texts. In the preface to his travelogue *Madame Chrysanthème* (1887), Pierre Loti asserted that 'although the most important role may appear to devolve on Madame Chrysanthème, it is very certain that the three principal personages are *myself, Japan*, and the *effect* produced on me by that country' (Loti [1985] 5). The 'effect' is that of a palpable repugnance and fear. As Endymion Wilkinson, and others, have noted, in Loti's book 'the Japanese are mercilessly caricatured as an inferior yellow people – they are small, fragile, and feminine. They are decadent, dangerous, and contradictory; full of trickery, superb imitators like comic, aged monkeys' (115). While seeking a temporary bride among these grotesqueries, Loti is afraid 'now lest she be like them' (20).

At first glance, there appears to be no room in Loti's corner of Japan for a character analogous to Suzuki or Comrade Chin. Yet the seeds for both of these characters are already sown in the form of the landlady, Madame Prune. According to Loti, 'Madame Prune is eagerly attentive, obsequious and rapacious, her eyebrows are closely shaven, her teeth carefully lacquered with black as befits a lady of gentility, and at all hours, she appears on all fours at the entrance of our apartment, to offer us her services' (108). Despite Madame Prune's class – she is a member of the gentility and therefore not 'typical' Japanese – in Loti's eyes she is clearly a servant. Moreover, even though Madame Prune is not formally engaged as Chrysanthème's servant, she, like Suzuki, is imbued with an eagerness to please. Her uncanny ability to appear, uninvited, at any given moment, further marks her as something of a spy, an early yet unmistakable counterpart to Hwang's Comrade Chin.

Suzuki is officially introduced into the narrative by way of John Luther Long's short story *Madame Butterfly*. Long assures his readers that Butterfly has 'only one small maid to command' (John 26),[1] but Suzuki is a formidable, albeit primarily silent, presence throughout. When Pinkerton banishes Butterfly's relatives from the house, Suzuki becomes her one remaining link to her Japanese heritage. Like her mistress, Suzuki is caricatured through her garbled pidgin English. Yet one aspect of Long's story is frequently overlooked, one that is crucial to the

Example 1. Suzuki's introduction, overture motive a third higher

Madame Butterfly myth. At the end of Loti's version, Chrysanthème shows little interest in the departure of her 'husband,' much less in taking her own life. Although Long introduces the idea of suicide, Suzuki takes matters into her own hands and binds Butterfly's wound. Thus, 'when Mrs. Pinkerton called next day at the little house on Higashi Hill it was quite empty' (John 59). Long's ambiguous ending leaves open the possibility that Butterfly has survived.

Suzuki's actions at the end of Long's story may grant her something of hero status, but that status is withdrawn in David Belasco's stage play *Madame Butterfly: A Tragedy of Japan* (1900). When Belasco decided to base his play on Long's *Madame Butterfly*, he preserved aspects of the story's language, but made certain changes in the plot. Belasco dispensed with almost the entire first half of Long's story, but maintained the crudely drawn caricatures and pidgin English of Butterfly and Suzuki. Moreover, Suzuki's rescue was also elided; thus, Belasco's Butterfly became the first in a long line of heroines who succumbed to a tragic death, whereas in the preface to the sixth edition of the play, editor Arthur Quinn notes that in Long's version, 'Madame Butterfly lets her mother-love conquer, and, after attempting suicide, decides to live' ('Butterfly' 624).

Although the elision of the rescue leaves Suzuki with little to contribute to the plot, her almost constant presence in both Long and Belasco provides a necessary counterweight to Butterfly. However, it is not until Puccini's opera *Madama Butterfly* (1904) and Hwang's play *M. Butterfly* (1988), that the figures of Suzuki and her counterpart, Comrade Chin, become crucial to the story. In the opera, Suzuki's voice is, importantly, the first female solo voice we hear following the opening exchange between Pinkerton and Goro. Goro introduces her to Pinkerton not as 'Suzuki,' but as the more exotic 'Miss Nuvola Leggiera' ('Miss Light Cloud'), just before the opening motive from the overture returns (now a major third higher, in G major versus E-flat in the overture, see Example 1).[2] Launching into a speech intended to welcome Pinkerton, Suzuki

Example 2. Overture motive in sequence

invokes the ancient Japanese wisdom of Ocunama, while the light staccato accompaniment underlying her recitative serves as an 'Orientalist' signifier. The textual signifier is coupled with a further recurrence of the overture motive punctuating the midpoint of her speech, thus furnishing a satisfactory 'Oriental' atmosphere, or, as **Susan McClary** would put it, negotiation 'between Japanese identity and Italian musical style.' Yet one can speculate that Puccini has gone further than merely providing 'atmosphere.' In the overture, the music of example 1 serves as the subject for an elaborate four-voice fugue: a compositional device representative of the 'learned,' intellectual style. However, the musical 'frame' provided for Suzuki is devoid of this fugal treatment. What is more, when the motive returns at the midpoint of her speech, it is treated in a descending sequence over an open fifth B–F-sharp that is sustained for a total of five measures (14/4/2 to 15/2/1, see example 2). Suzuki's musical identity is therefore 'fixed' as both 'Oriental' and 'lower' (that is, unlearned) class. Not surprisingly, Pinkerton is unimpressed by Suzuki's welcome, noting that, 'a chiacchiere costei, mi par cosmopolita' ('by her chattering, she seems just like all women the world over').

Act 2 begins with an exchange between Butterfly and Suzuki; for the first time, the two figures are directly juxtaposed. At this particular moment in the plot, Pinkerton has already been gone for three years. Despite his apparent promise to return, 'Quando fa la nidiata il pettirosso' ('when the robins nest again'), Butterfly is near the breaking point. According to Puccini's stage direction, Suzuki 'prays in front of the image of Buddha, from time to time she rings the prayer bell, while Butterfly stands rigid and motionless near a screen' (Groos, 'Return' 174). As Arthur Groos has pointed out, the Buddhist details are problematic, since the deities are those of Shinto, invoked inaccurately to the tune of 'Takai yama,' a 'popular song of the late Edo-period, which

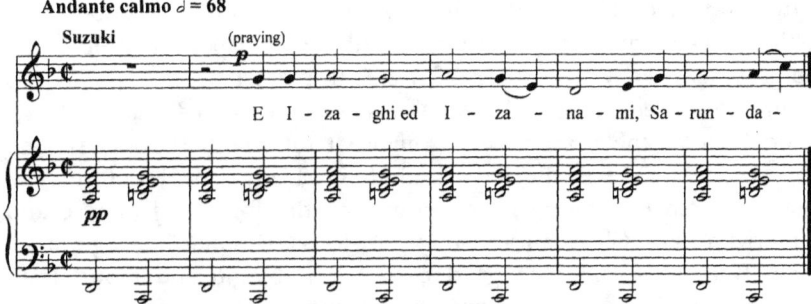

Example 3. Suzuki's prayer, act 2

evokes the blossoming of cucumbers and eggplants' (ibid. 175–6).[3] Puccini underscores the futility of Suzuki's prayer with an incessant tonic-subdominant repetition in the bass, keeping her firmly tied to her Japanese roots (169/1/1 to 170/2/3, see example 3). Suzuki has, in fact, uttered the same prayer in act 1, but the incantation goes by practically unnoticed and unseen, in the form of unaccompanied recitative. Only Pinkerton notices that someone is 'muttering' inside the house ('Chi brontola lassù?'). Although his comment comes across as yet another example of his loutish attitude towards Japanese culture, in the latter scene the conflation of sacred and secular elements, coupled with the interruption 'Oh! la mia testa!' (O, my head!), paints Suzuki as a somewhat cartoonish figure. Yet, for the uninitiated Western audience, the Japanese text and pentatonic melody of the second prayer – incorporated in a recognizably religious (that is, Christian) chorale setting – provide an appropriately Japanese ambience, thereby effectively marking Suzuki as ethnically 'authentic.'

However, issues of ethnicity and authenticity are most clearly marked in visual representations of the prayer scene. In a 1974 video production of the opera, directed by Jean-Pierre Ponnelle, the scene is clearly divided into East and West. On the right is mezzo-soprano Christa Ludwig, our 'authentic' Suzuki, kneeling in prayer before a statue of Buddha placed on a low table. In contrast, Butterfly (soprano Mirella Freni) has constructed her own Western shrine: attired in a middle-class Victorian-style dress, she stands in front of Pinkerton's tall wooden armoire, adorned with the American flag and a picture of Jesus; all appropriately Western and Christian iconography. On the floor nearby, Butterfly's young son plays with an Uncle Sam doll. The separation of cultures is a transparent facade; co-mingling and contamination of cultures and ideologies – East versus West, low versus high, Buddhist/ Shinto versus Christian – is prevented only by the paper-thin walls of the shoji, which, like Butterfly herself, are easily pierced.

In a more recent cinematic version (1995), director Frédéric Mitterrand handles the prayer scene somewhat differently; here, East and West are not as clearly divided. Suzuki (Ning Liang) kneels before a single shrine incorporating both cultures in the form of Japanese and American flags, Christian and Buddhist icons. Despite the stage direction, Butterfly (Ying Huang) does not 'stand rigid and motionless.' Instead, she sits at a sewing machine, actively pursuing her transformation by creating what later proves to be her version of a Western-style dress. The sewing machine is a powerful symbol of Western industrialization and modernization, underscoring Butterfly's statement 'Pigri ed obesi son gli dei giapponesi!; ('The gods of Japan are fat and lazy!'). Recalling Butterfly's words from the act 1 love duet, 'Dicon ch'oltre mare se cade in man dell'uom ogni farfalla d'uno spillo è trafitta ed in tavola infitta!' ('They say that overseas if it should fall into the hands of man a butterfly is stuck through with a pin and fixed to a board!'), the mechanized repetition of the sewing machine's needle, like the father's sword, becomes a dominant phallic symbol, metaphorically 'mounting' the Butterfly over and over again.

There is no prayer scene for Suzuki in Hwang's *M. Butterfly* when Gallimard, in a series of flashbacks, summarizes the plot of *Madama Butterfly*. But, while Puccini's opera – by way of the Italian libretto – erases the crude pidgin English found in the earlier texts, Hwang restores it, in part, through Suzuki's vulgar indictment of Pinkerton:

> SUZUKI: Girl, he's a loser. What'd he ever give you? Nineteen cents and those ugly Day-Glo stockings? ... I mean, the guy was a woofer! He tried before, you know – before he met you he went down to geisha central and plunked down his spare change in front of the usual candidates – everyone else gagged! These are hungry prostitutes, and they were not interested, get the picture? ... Now, what about Yamadori? ... What do you mean, 'But he's Japanese?' What do you think you are? You think you've been touched by the whitey god? He was a sailor with dirty hands! (Act 1, scene 5)

Although Suzuki cuts to the heart of the matter, 'telling it like it is,' her presence in Hwang's play goes virtually unnoticed. She does not rank among the three secondary female characters (Helga, Renee, and Comrade Chin), who, as Colleen Lye has noted, 'are all in some sense caricatures' (276). Because Suzuki is also a caricature, the subversive potential of her explicit critique of the Butterfly myth is effectively dissipated.

Following her outburst, Suzuki vanishes – or does she? Not until much later in the play does the audience realise that Hwang has reinvented her role. One actress performs three roles: as Suzuki, servant to Butterfly; as Shu-Fang, servant to Song Liling; and as Comrade Chin, loyal servant to Chairman Mao and Communist China. Shifting from the stage to the screen, under Cronenberg's direction, Suzuki is elided from Hwang's *M. Butterfly* screenplay while the roles of Comrade Chin and Shu-Fang are redistributed among two actresses. Whereas the bit player performing multiple roles addresses the matter of theatrical convention, there may be more here than the simple economic reality of staging live theatre versus cinematic realism. As cultural yardsticks, Suzuki and Comrade Chin are crucial to the story. When Chin makes her first entrance in Hwang's play, the author has Song Liling put the matter quite succinctly: 'Rene, be sensible. How can they understand the story without her?' (2.3). As Song Liling's government contact, Comrade Chin's role is small but essential to the development of the espionage storyline. Nonetheless, it is the visual and vocal presence of these supposedly authentic characters that is of interest here.

Although there is no 'prayer scene' in either the stage or screen versions of *M. Butterfly*, there is a scene in which the issues of ethnicity and authenticity are enacted no less explicitly. Here Rene Gallimard's 'Butterfly' (Song Liling) is juxtaposed against Suzuki's *doppleganger*, Comrade Chin. Unlike her alter ego, Suzuki, Chin makes no pretense at prayer. Although one might argue that Chin 'worships' at the altar of Chairman Mao and Communist China, she is concerned only with the more practical matter of collecting information about American troop movements in Vietnam in a scene that 'unveils' Song Liling's role as spy. But the conversation between Chin and Song, as Marjorie Garber has noted, also 'addresses the question of cross-dressing and the essence – or construction – of womanhood' (Garber, *Vested* 248):

CHIN: How do you remember so much?
SONG: I'm an actor.
CHIN: Yeah. Is that how come you dress like that?
SONG: Like what, Miss Chin?
CHIN: Like that dress! You're wearing a dress. And every time I come here, you're wearing a dress. Is that because you're an actor? Or what?

SONG: It's a ... disguise, Miss Chin.
CHIN: Actors, I think they're all weirdoes. My mother tells me actors are like gamblers or prostitutes or –
SONG: It helps me in my assignment.

Chin is presented as an androgynous figure, attired in a generic Mao tunic and cap.[4] The uniform effectively erases gender as well as class difference. Our only clue to Chin's 'true' gender identity is the title 'Miss.' According to the play's costume plot, Song, who remains in character even when Gallimard is not present, nonetheless epitomizes his 'vision of the Orient' by wearing a purple cheong sam, purple pumps, and cloisonné earrings (Hwang 80). When Chin reminds Song that 'there is no homosexuality in China,' Song acknowledges the fact before turning to the audience and commenting ironically, 'What passes for a woman in modern China.'

What 'passes for a woman,' or for a Japanese or Chinese, for that matter, is entirely the point. However, this scene seems to imply not so much a clash between East and West as a significant gap between the old order and the new within Chinese culture itself. Garber suggests that 'in Hwang's play cross-dressed men are emblematic of cultural crisis (or even of the 'human condition'), but the cross-dressed woman is a risible sign of failed "femininity"' (Garber, *Vested* 249). Failed according to whose standards? Certainly not Comrade Chin's standards. Her views are made clear a few scenes later (2.10), when she orders Song to renew the relationship with Gallimard in Paris. Song protests, telling Chin, 'You don't understand the mind of a man.' But Chin replies, 'Oh no? Then how come I'm married, huh? How come I got a man?' From Chin's perspective, it is she, not Song, who epitomizes not just the 'successful Communist,' but, more importantly, 'successful' femininity, at least in her own culture. Jan Wong, a self-professed 'Montreal Maoist' who lived and studied in China in the early seventies, writes:

> Spinsterhood or bachelorhood was a horrible fate in China. A single person was a social misfit, doomed to a life sentence in a collective dormitory with smelly latrines and no kitchens. Even gays, who had no choice but to remain in the closet because homosexuality was, and still is, illegal, married the opposite sex, often without revealing their secret to their spouses. They did this partly for camouflage and partly because staying single was socially unacceptable. (181)

In a society struggling to come to grips with the Cultural Revolution, both cross-dressers (Song and Chin) may be said to be 'emblematic of cultural crisis.'

When this scene from *M. Butterfly* is transferred from the stage to the screen, the issue takes on a global perspective. Arriving at Song's apartment, Chin is greeted by another kind of spy, the servant Shu-Fang, who hands her a bundle of women's magazines. As the camera zooms in on the Chinese version of *Hollywood* magazine, the image of Western decadence becomes the focal point of the conversation:

CHIN: (*Throwing magazines at Song*) Trash! Decadent Trash!
SONG: Forgive me, Comrade. I didn't expect you ... He's begun to tell me about Vietnam. The Americans plan to increase troop strength to 170,000 soldiers, 120,000 militia, 11,000 advisors.
CHIN: Don't you understand how degrading those images are to women? And why do you behave like this when he's not even here?
SONG: Comrade, in order to better serve the Great Proletarian State, I practice my deceptions as often as possible. I despise this costume. For our Great Helmsman, I will endure it. Along with all the other bourgeois Western perversions.
CHIN: I am still not convinced that this will be enough to redeem you in the eyes of the party.
SONG: I am trying my best to become somebody else.

Although Song has traded her cheong sam for a pair of slacks and a colourful tunic, she remains in character as a woman, and thus is ultimately more feminine than Chin, whose unisex title 'Comrade' now compounds the androgyny of her Mao suit. The pen, clicking furiously in Chin's hand, substitutes for the missing phallus. But, Chin's homophobic comments are excised from the screenplay, along with the biting satire of Song's 'passing for a woman.'

Whereas Chin's marriage (also cut from the screenplay) is enough to redeem her in the eyes of the party, her representation as an 'authentic' Chinese woman in a play and film that propose to dismantle negative Asian stereotypes remains problematic. It is worth noting that in the film version, the role of Chin is performed by a *Japanese* actress, Shizuko Hoshi, whose other credits include four guest appearances on *M*A*S*H* in the 1970s where she played various *Korean* characters.[5] In other words, whether Chinese, Japanese, or Korean, any Asian will do (see **Maria Ng**). James Moy asserts that if 'Hwang's hope is to offer a truer view of what it means to be Asian ... Comrade Chan [*sic*] (and the other characters played by the same actor) is perhaps even more stereotypical and cartoonish than the worst of the nineteenth-century stereotypes' (54). Like her operatic counterpart, Comrade Chin comes across as a laughable caricature. Moy further contends: 'Thus marginalized, desexed, and made faceless, these Asian characters constitute no threat to Anglo-American sensibilities. Instead, they provide a good evening's entertainment and then float as exotic Oriental fetishes articulating Anglo-American desire, now doubly displaced into the new order of stereotypical representations created by Asian Americans' (55). While Chin's words 'offer a clear indictment of the cultural hegemony of the west,' as the butt of the joke her representation as a buffoon undermines the force of that indictment (ibid.).

The 'real' Asians in Hwang's drama may be trapped in the author's own double background. As an Asian American, Hwang 'obviously incorporates a cultural and ethnic identity which has its own specific parameters'; however, his 'Western half and his male perspective prohibits a true understanding of the East-West, Male-Female paradigm and only exacerbates traditional misunderstandings' (R. Ma 1055, 1057). A 'true understanding' may be impossible, but the film, in particular, invites us to view and measure the squalor and poverty of Beijing through the lens of the Western camera. *M. Butterfly* may, on some level, deconstruct Puccini's opera, but the film itself returns to Loti in its portrayal of the Chinese as small, shrivelled, toothless, and monkey-like. The scene in the Chinese opera house serves as a useful example. Gallimard's description of the scene could be quoted directly from Loti: 'The room was hot, and full of smoke. Wrinkled faces, old women, teeth missing – a man with a growth on his neck, like a human toad. All smiling, pipes falling from their mouths, cracking nuts between their teeth, a live chicken pecking at my foot – all looking, screaming, gawking ... (1.8). As **Bart Testa** has noted, 'the Chinese opera itself hardly resembles the *Madama Butterfly* performance,' but what the scene brings into sharp relief is the clear distinction between high (that is, Western) culture and low (Eastern) culture. By inverting the stereotype of the opera audience (see **Kate McInturff**), Hwang and Cronenberg emphasize that it is Gallimard who looks out of place.

Clearly outnumbered by the 'Other,' Gallimard's discomfort is no doubt enhanced by the shock of self-alienation, the realization of his own 'whiteness' and the implicit knowledge that *he* is as much an object of the gaze as the actors on the opera stage. Although the 'inter-racial looking relation' is momentarily inverted, the power structure of the gaze remains intact (see Kaplan 56–93). By imaging and racializing the Chinese audience as animals who do not know how to behave in the supposedly 'civilized' opera house, the film exploits an all-too-familiar Hollywood trope. Moreover, while the true viewing subject (the film's audience) recognizes Gallimard for the fool that he is, their sympathies nonetheless lie with him.

Certain adjustments had to be made to the opera house scene when *M. Butterfly* was staged in Singapore in 1990. According to Colleen Lye, the 'Peking Opera performance was significantly condensed,' because, as director Krischen Jit noted, 'you can't fool an Asian audience with the Peking Opera. There are people out there who really know it. So we decided to cut down on that scene and use the Chinese audience as a distraction.' The 'distraction' came from placing the Chinese audience onstage, to provide 'noisy comic relief.' Hence, while the Singapore production 'seemed to be registering signs of discomfort with the play's implication in certain techniques of Orientalist seduction,' it sacrificed one trope (the 'authentic' Peking Opera) for another (the 'ethnically authentic' onstage audience) (Lye 267). The Singapore audience was thus invited not to identify with Gallimard's subject position, but to laugh at the onstage audience, and themselves.

Whereas the Singapore production avoided a certain degree of verisimilitude by distancing itself from the Peking Opera, the opposite situation obtains for Puccini's opera, with 'attempts at realistic casting, by using Japanese singers in the lead, a practice that began early on' (Groos, 'Return' 182). Yet such attempts to address larger issues of ethnicity and authenticity have not always been appreciated or successful. In 1915, Tamaki Miura of Tokyo made her London debut as Cio-Cio-San, and was subsequently engaged for the lead role in a New York production. According to Nick Browne, the Japanese diva's reception was mixed. One critic conceded that, 'though there is an ethnographic truth in some details, Mme. Miura had to divest herself of most of the artistic traditions of her own land before she could *impersonate* the character imagined by an American novelist and set to music in Italy' (Browne 232). Perhaps most importantly, for our purposes here:

> In Finck's account, the quality of voice, as distinct from acting and gesture is the site of cultural contradiction: At the lower end of the register, the

voice hints at an impurity – an Oriental residue – which gradually disappears with increasing volume and warmth in the higher end. He concludes that though it would be interesting to hear her in a Western role, no part 'could suit' her as Butterfly does. (ibid. 232)

Miura's portrayal of Butterfly was highly regarded in Japan (Groos, 'Return' 182–3), but clearly, in Finck's time, the *Western* world was not yet ready for a 'real' Madame Butterfly. Stanley F. Kaye reinforced the point in his comparison of Miura and Geraldine Farrar:

> Miss Farrar is undoubtedly the supreme impersonation of this role ... It was not long ago that this city heard Butterfly sung by a Japanese *prima donna*, and at that time a Japanese effect was made that no occidental could hope to equal. But the thrill of a dramatic voice was absent then, and the welcome visit of Mme. Tamaki Miura serves as a standard of comparison by which Miss Farrar's enacting of the geisha may be more fully appreciated than ever before. (Quoted in Groos, 'Return' 182 n. 43)

In light of such attitudes, it is worth noting that in Mitterrand's 1995 film version the roles of Butterfly and Suzuki are filled by Chinese singers, Ying Huang and Ning Liang respectively. Reviewer Janick Beaulieu regards this casting as a refreshing take on operatic convention: 'Mitterrand rejuvenated this work by having the role of Butterfly played by a young Chinese singer, who gives the impression of being the same age as Puccini's heroine, if one can trust her waistline and her face' (Beaulieu 45).[6] For Beaulieu, the *impression* of 'visual' realism is central. But, like Hwang's fictional Rene Gallimard, Beaulieu (and Mitterrand) conflates Japanese and Chinese ethnic identity: any young, slender, ethnic 'Oriental' is more believable than 'so many huge women in bad makeup' (Hwang 1.6).

As participants in the semiotic encoding of the 'Orient,' the figures of Suzuki and Comrade Chin are no less caught up in the conflation of binaries. Yet the 'ethnographic truth' that these characters are purported to represent is displayed as empty caricature, buffoonery, and cultural crisis. Loti's Madame Prune, with her laquered teeth, is repulsive despite her gentility. In John Luther Long's short story, Suzuki has a brief heroic moment, binding Butterfly's wound and thereby preventing her death, but in Belasco's play Butterfly's suicide attempt is successfully immortalized as the only 'acceptable' ending. The operatic Suzuki is unable to avoid the tragedy of Madame Butterfly's death, while Comrade Chin's manipulations seem to ensure the same result in *M. Butterfly*. The only 'true' Orientals in the Butterfly narrative may be the 'extras' in Cronenberg's film, who fare no better than Loti's 'comic, aged monkeys.' Myth, not truth, lies at the heart of the Madame Butterfly narrative. Therefore, Gallimard's 'vision of the Orient,' aestheticized and fetishized, remains intact.

Notes

1 The version of Long that I cite here is reprinted in Nicholas John, ed., *Madama Butterfly*, English National Opera Guide 26 (London: John Calder, 1984), 25–59.
2 All references to the score are to the Ricordi edition (1907, 1990), in the format page number / system number / measure number.
3 The conflation of Buddhist and Shinto details may stem from a misappropriation of Loti. Loti, however, makes it clear that Madame Prune worships the Shinto gods, while Chrysanthème is Buddhist (Loti [1985] 145–8).
4 In China, however, a Mao suit 'was called not a Mao suit but a Yat-sen suit, apparently because Dr. Sun Yat-sen had originated the fashion craze.' See Wong 61.
5 What little information there is available on Hoshi can be found on the Internet Movie Database, at http://www.IMDb.com.
6 'Mitterand rajeunit aussi cette oeuvre en faisant jouer le rôle de Butterfly par une jeune chanteuse chinoise, qui donne l'impression d'avoir l'âge de l'héroïne de Puccini, si on se fie à sa binette.'

That Old Familiar Song: The Theatre of Culture in David Henry Hwang's *M. Butterfly*

KATE McINTURFF

[T]he gap between opera and the people, which was nowhere wider than in America, has been closing from two sides: opera has been moving towards Broadway and Broadway has been moving towards opera.

Graf, *Opera for the People* 149

Contemporary stereotypes catalog opera as the most elitist of all art forms. It is perceived as a plaything of the rich and the stamping ground of cultural snobs.

Zelechow, 'The Opera' 261

Many critics of David Henry Hwang's play *M. Butterfly* have focused on the extent to which the play is successful in interrogating the Orientalist elements of the opera's plot,[1] although **Susan McClary** and **Bart Testa** raise important questions about this project here. Critics Kathryn Remen, Colleen Lye, and **Melinda Boyd** have extended discussions of the play's deconstructive strategies by drawing attention to the importance of the physical and cultural-geographical locations of the theatres in which the play has been performed. I would like to further expand this argument by insisting that the relative success or failure of the play's deconstruction of *Madama Butterfly* also depends upon the extent to which it addresses itself to perceptions of the operatic institutions that occupy the same urban and, arguably, the same cultural milieu as the Broadway theatre in which *M. Butterfly* has had a long and successful run.[2]

The material spaces in which *Madama Butterfly* and *M. Butterfly* are performed are themselves shaped by pre-existing notions of the opera and the theatre. Bernard Zelechow, like opera historians Herbert Graf and John Dizikes, argues that the American stereotype of opera as 'an elitist museum' bears little relation to the actual practices and histories of operatic institutions in America (265). Rather than focusing on the demographics of opera audiences, I would like to argue that the stereotype of the opera as the pinnacle of high social and aesthetic culture works in support of internal stereotypes of racial and sexual otherness. This stereotype effectively constructs the audience's perceptions of their place and of the status of opera, regardless of whether or not they perceive themselves to be a part of the 'elitist museum' or the exception that disproves the rule.[3]

The first Metropolitan Opera House in New York was funded by wealthy opera patrons who bid for particular reserved boxes within the new structure in advance of its construction. It was described by a critic of the period as 'a semi-circle of boxes with an opera house built around them, a private club to which the general public was somewhat grudgingly admitted' (quoted in Dizikes, 218). As Kathryn Remen has argued of the Broadway theatre, the opera house also forms something akin to a Foucauldian panopticon: 'distributing individuals in a space in which one might isolate and map them' (Foucault, quoted in Remen, 391). While Remen posits that the invisibility of the audience during a performance is a sign of their privilege, I would argue that, in the Metropolitan Opera House at least, the audience's ability to visibly display themselves to one another has also been perceived as a signifier of privilege. The role of the box seats as a space in which to display one's wealth and privilege was not lost on the opera patrons who dictated the details of their composition. During the construction of the first Metropolitan Opera House, the *New York Times* reported, '[a] change is contemplated in the decoration of the boxes, the pale colour of which does not show off the brilliant costumes of the ladies to advantage' (quoted in Eisler, 18). Another criticism of the first home of the Metropolitan Opera was that the view from the upper balcony – the location of some of the least expensive seats – was often completely obstructed. Not only were the wealthy opera patrons assured of their own privilege by the image that they presented to themselves, but simply the ability to see – to survey all that was before them – became an inscription of privilege and power.

The role of the boxes as signifiers of privilege continues to shape critical and sympathetic visions of the opera house throughout the history of both the late nineteenth-century structure and the modernist hall at Lincoln Center. Peter Conrad comments that '[t]he new Met virtually doubled that number [of box seats] ... The auditorium too is a galactic version of the old jewel casket' (254). While the *Dramatic Mirror* may have characterized opera boxes as 'cages in a menagerie of monopolists' in 1883 (quoted in Preston, 13), the power of those monopolists to shape the structure in which they displayed themselves is borne out by both the increased number of boxes in the new Metropolitan Opera House and in the successful struggle of the Metropolitan Opera's decorating committee to cover the modernist interior of the new building in red velvet, much against the protests of the architect, Wallace Harrison.

At first glance the self-conscious exoticism of some of the images presented on the stage of the opera house appeared designed to take the audience away from its setting. In her evaluation of Foucault's discussion of representations of race, however, Ann Laura Stoler has suggested that those images of racial and colonial distinction served an important and necessary role in reinforcing and even naturalizing social divisions *within* Europe and, I would argue, North America: 'Foucault clearly identifies a process that has become central to contemporary colonial studies and European history more generally: namely, the observation that external colonialism provided a template for conceptualising social inequities in Europe and not solely the other way around' (75). The representation of the power of the colonizer over the colonized supported the power that the wealthy industrial class held over the working class. In this way the representation of imperialist race relations on the stage of the Metropolitan Opera House only served to underscore the inscription of class relations made apparent in its spatial relations – the privilege to see delivered a vision of privilege, no matter which way you looked.

Distinctions between opera houses and their repertories have created another, internal, layer of social stratification. They have also created a space within the European configuration of class relations, of which Stoler and Foucault speak, for the representation of a self-consciously populist middle class. Opera critic and historian Herbert Lindenberger suggests that 'in New York today the older European distinctions between "high" and "low" persist in the division of activities between the Metropolitan Opera, with its more rigorously classical repertory ... and, only a stone's throw away, the less pretentious, more popular-minded New York City Opera' (212). In an American context, the perceived distinction between a 'classical' repertory and a 'popular-minded' one is inscribed with a unique social significance. The popular is itself represented as a position of privilege within an American nationalist iconography that equates populism with democratic power relations. Without disturbing the class structures inscribed in the space of the Metropolitan Opera, the New York City Opera provides an apparently democratic space from which to view some of the same stereotypes of 'globally powerful Americans' using and 'discard[ing] people (and especially women) from less powerful, and less cynical societies' (Arblaster 250–2). The celebration of a populist cultural space does not mean that social inequities do not exist or that the Metropolitan Opera has ceased to be a space in which power and privilege are displayed. Rather, the New York City Opera provides opera in New York with something of a populist alibi. Whether or not its repertoire is actually very distinct from that of the Metropolitan Opera, the perception that opera can be presented in a 'more popular-minded' venue suggests that opera is not elitist in itself.

The representation of the New York City Opera as 'popular-minded' brings it into close, if not identical, association with the world of the Broadway musical. John Dizikes points out that George M. Cohan 'dismissed Rodgers and Hart's songs as "Gilbert and Sullivan"' (503), that is to say, as belonging to the realm of light opera. Dizikes goes on to suggest that the distinction between Broadway musical and uptown opera was purely nominal: 'These American dramas-by-means-of-music were something else. What to call them? *Operetta* or *comic opera* were terms too tied to the European past. *Musical comedy* had adherents, but best of all was *musical* ... An opera by any other name sounds as sweet' (502).[4]

Setting aside the generic musical classifications that might distinguish between different forms of musical theatre, Dizikes' comment directly addresses the desire to escape a 'European past' and the elitism that it implies. Within this configuration the Broadway or New York City Opera audience preserves the illusion of its own internal equality by locating elitist European values and class structures *over there* in the Metropolitan Opera House. In this context, David Henry Hwang's decision to confront the Broadway audience with one of the standard titles in the Metropolitan Opera's repertory is in itself an act that brings into question the perception that Broadway theatre is exempt from the social structures displayed in the Metropolitan Opera House.

The currency of stereotypes of the opera as 'a plaything of the rich and the stamping ground of cultural snobs' (Zelechow 261) is further borne out by the countless images of opera singers (usually in the form of the colloquial 'fat lady' or the Valkyrie) and opera audiences (usually peering haughtily through opera glasses) deployed in film and on television in North America. One example of this kind of stereotype is a sequence in the popular American film *Pretty Woman* in which Julia Roberts's character causes a scene at the opera when she is unable to use her opera glasses correctly. This character's subsequent enjoyment of the opera is set against the 'cultural snob[bery]' of those around her, who seem to be interested in the exterior trappings of opera-going – in opera's role as high (social) culture – and not in the emotional truth and beauty of the opera itself. A similar play on the stereotypes of opera is made in the film *Meeting Venus*, in which the trappings of an elaborate stage production and the histrionics of European opera singers are set in contrast to the puritan austerity and emotional sincerity of the American singer played by Glenn Close.

What both of these invocations of the opera reveal through the introduction of a sincere, unpretentious (and American) figure is that the stereotype does not preclude an affinity for opera-going. A distinction is made in each example between the pleasure derived from the insincere world of cultural snobbery and the pleasure that is derived from a sincere appreciation of the beauty and emotion of an opera production. It is opera's role as a marker for high *social* culture that is made ridiculous rather than its role as high aesthetic culture. The claim made by countless critics, fans, and historians of Western European opera, that opera contains and conveys to its audience universal aesthetic and emotional truths, is left unchallenged by the stereotypes of cultural snobbery and dramatic excess. The insincerity of both the stereotypical audience and the stereotypical singers and designers (in the case of *Meeting Venus*) are figured as screens that conceal the *real* operatic truth.

This stereotype fails to be a threat to the perpetuation of the racial and gender stereotypes contained within an opera like *Madama Butterfly*. Rather, it works in support of an opinion like the one expressed by a critic contemporary to Puccini, who wrote: 'Though the scene of "Madame Butterfly" is laid in Japan, the story is not essentially Japanese, any more than the plot of "Faust" is essentially German. It is, in fact, a presentation of a universal theme – "Man's love is of his life a thing apart; 'Tis woman's whole existence"' (Hadden 200).

From the stage of a Broadway theatre *M. Butterfly* attempts to undermine these structures of stereotype and the truth claims that they produce by manipulating the audience's perceptions of and potential pleasure in the opera. While the beginning of act 1 does gloss the narrative of *Madama Butterfly* for the audience, the parodic nature of this gloss is only clear to an audience familiar enough with opera conventions, if not this particular opera, to understand that Gallimard and

Marc are exaggerating the colloquial form of the opera's dialogue and undermining the opera's relatively serious tone.

The fact that *M. Butterfly* literally and metaphorically contains elements of the opera suggests that an audience that has taken pleasure (however unpretentious and sincere) in an operatic performance might also take pleasure in Hwang's play – in so far as it contains elements of an opera. Hwang notes in an interview that he 'assumed that many in the audience would be coming to the theatre because they hoped to see something exotic and mysterious' (quoted in Lye, 267). Critics Lye and Chang both suggest that Hwang's use of a 'glamorous Oriental spectacle' to critique the Orientalist structures of that spectacle is in danger of 'simultaneously ... perpetuat[ing] it by making the Oriental exotic elements – costume, music, dance – the play's major market attractions' (Chang 747). **Rachel Ditor and Jan Selman**, in this volume, also note the importance of staging in shaping the audience's awareness of the critique being presented in the play. The use of operatic elements, within a play critical of those elements, runs the risk of using the operatic as the spoonful of aesthetic sugar that makes the political medicine go down. This tactic is one that would leave the division between pleasure, aesthetics, and politics unquestioned, allowing the audience to separate one from the other – taking their aesthetic pleasures where they find them and leaving the politics behind. However, the play does not simply present a scene from the opera and follow it with a critique. *M. Butterfly* deconstructs the distinctions drawn between high (elitist) and low (democratic) culture and between the political, social, and aesthetic elements of opera.

SONG: 'Vieni, vieni!'
GALLIMARD: 'Come, darling.'
SONG: 'Ah, dolce notte!'
GALLIMARD: 'Beautiful night.'
SONG: 'Tutto estatico d'amor ride il ciel!'
GALLIMARD: 'All ecstatic with love, the heavens are filled with laughter.'

(Hwang [1989] 41)

In act 1, scene 6, Gallimard encounters Song for the first time. Hwang places Gallimard in the position of the sincere and unpretentious opera lover of the two examples mentioned earlier.[5] In this scene Gallimard addresses the audience directly, confessing his own ignorance and opposing himself to the 'they' who make (pretentious) claims about opera: 'They say in opera the voice is everything. That's probably why I'd never before enjoyed opera. Here ... here was a Butterfly with little or no voice – but she had the grace, the delicacy ... I believed this girl. I believed her suffering' (15–16). Gallimard goes on to explain to Song that he has always liked *Madama Butterfly* but that the 'huge women in so much bad makeup' got in the way of 'the beauty of the story' (16–17).

Up to this point in the play Song has appeared on stage in the costume of Cio-Cio-San, acting out the part of the operatic heroine silently, as Gallimard tells the theatre audience the story of the opera. Before act 1, scene 6, Song has not disturbed Gallimard's construction of the opera and his pleasure in its 'beautiful story.' Gallimard has attempted to take the audience into his confidence over the course of act 1 by speaking directly to them, by flattering them and appealing for their sympathy ('you – my ideal audience ... who come to understand and even, perhaps, to envy me' [4]), and by playing on traditional Western models of gender and heterosexuality ('the sad truth is that all men want a beautiful woman' [14]).[6] While Gallimard's self-confessed social ineptitude might undermine the audience's interest in empathizing with him at this point in the play, his lack of pretension and the arrogant and caddish behaviour of Marc make Gallimard the more appealing of the two. As Gallimard says in act 1, scene 3, if he 'played Pinkerton, the womanising cad [in the preceding dialogue] and my friend Marc from school ... played Sharpless, the sensitive soul of reason,' in life '[their] positions were usually – no always – reversed' (7). This formulation of Gallimard's leaves him in the position of being the sensitive soul of reason, in spite of his apparent self-deprecation.

In the latter half of scene 6, Song starts to undermine the construction of opera, and of *Madama Butterfly* in particular, as a beautiful and universal story. She begins by reminding Gallimard, and the audience indirectly, of the cultural and geographic specificity of her own position and her relation to the character Cio-Cio-San: 'Convincing? As a Japanese woman? The Japanese used hundreds of our people for medical experiments during the war, you know. But I gather such an irony is lost on you' (17). Song's comment points to the violent results of racial prejudices and to the irony of their mutability. In Song's terms the 'Japanese' are able to construct Song's 'people' as so distinct from themselves, so totally other, that they become the appropriate subjects of medical experiments. Gallimard does not distinguish between Song's Chinese identity and the ostensibly Japanese identity of the character

Cio-Cio-San. His attempt to discuss the beauty of the story of *Madama Butterfly* in general, even universal, terms renders invisible the racial demarcation that supported the material violence of the Japanese medical experiments to which Song refers. Song further undermines the notion that *Madama Butterfly*'s beauty and truth are universal by reversing the cultural locations of the central characters in the opera:

SONG: [W]hat would you say if a blonde homecoming queen fell in love with a short Japanese businessman? He treats her cruelly, then goes home for three years, during which time she prays to his picture and turns down marriage from a young Kennedy. Then, when she learns he has remarried, she kills herself. Now, I believe you would consider this girl to be a deranged idiot, correct? But because it's an Oriental who kills herself for a Westerner – ah! – you find it beautiful. (17)

Song steps out of the character and milieu of an opera to critique the part she has played and the pleasure with which she has provided her audience.[7]

M. Butterfly goes on to both exploit and critique the divisions made between elitist and democratic pleasures. Song's suggestion, at the end of her first exchange with Gallimard, that he 'come to the Peking Opera sometime [and] expand [his] mind' allows Gallimard a way to protect what Song has characterized as his 'favourite fantas[y]' (17). Act 1, scene 7 finds Gallimard characterizing Chinese culture (including, presumably, the Peking Opera) as a sort of decrepit museum and Chinese people (including, presumably, Song) as elitist:

HELGA: What is it that Madam Su says? 'We are a very old civilization.' I never know if she's talking about her country or herself.
GALLIMARD: I walk around here, all I hear every day, everywhere is how *old* this culture is. The fact that 'old' may be synonymous with 'senile' doesn't occur to them. (18)

Gallimard reduces Song and her culture to artefacts in an 'elitist museum' in order to deny the validity of her critical analysis of Gallimard's fantasy and of the opera that embodies it. Within this framework, the imprecation to 'expand your mind' or to consider an alternative cultural and social perspective is reduced to social pretension. Gallimard and Helga further reduce Song's political analysis to a fit of pique, ironically recasting Song as the self-abnegating Cio-Cio-

San (in Helga's version) and as a Chinese man (in Gallimard's version):

HELGA: She hated it, but she performed it anyway? Is she perverse?
GALLIMARD: They hate it because the white man gets the girl. Sour grapes if you ask me.
HELGA: Politics again? Why can't they just hear it as a piece of beautiful music? So, what's in their opera?
GALLIMARD: I don't know. But, whatever it is, I'm sure it must be *old*. (19)

The division that exists in the example of American stereotypes of opera culture, between pretensions to high social culture and the unpretentious pleasures of low culture, is rewritten as the division between Song's position and Gallimard's in act 1, scene 6. While members of the play's audience may be wholly sympathetic to Gallimard's characterization of Song's analysis and to the role of politics, they come to see Gallimard's position as an increasingly untenable one as the play progresses.

Gallimard's next encounter with Song and his first encounter with the Peking Opera undermines the characterization of 'old' Chinese culture as elitist. It is Gallimard, in this scene, who finds himself viewing the appearance and behaviour of his fellow opera-goers with what might be characterized as an elitist distaste: 'All smiling, pipes falling from their mouths, cracking nuts between their teeth, a live chicken pecking at my foot – all looking, screaming, gawking ... at her' (20). It is precisely Gallimard's attempt to distance himself and his pleasure in watching Song from 'the masses' (21) that Song encourages as she begins to play the part in her relationship with Gallimard that he has admired in *Madama Butterfly*: 'I love them for being my fans, I hate the smell they leave behind. I too can distance myself from my people ... Be a gentleman, will you? And light my cigarette' (21). Song makes Gallimard feel that she has singled him out – as a 'gentleman' – and wishes to play only to him, unlike the fantasy woman in the pornographic magazine who is there for anyone to see or the girls who populate the sexual 'grab bag' (8) of Marc's adolescent sexual adventures. Song's performance is an exclusive one and the pleasures Gallimard derives from it turn out to be neither purely democratic nor purely aesthetic.

The role that power and sexual desire play in the construction of the opera audience's pleasure is emphasized through the development of Gallimard's relationship with Song, in his desire to watch the 'Chinese diva,' and in his attempts to control her performance (20). As their sexual relationship commences Gallimard speaks his desire for Song through the libretto of *Madama Butterfly*. In one sense the opera has taught Gallimard how and whom to desire and he now attempts to teach Song, and the audience, the same lesson. Gallimard puts the words of *Madama Butterfly* into Song's mouth, following her apparent capitulation to his demands that she declare openly that she is his 'Butterfly' (40). In this scene Song not only impersonates the character of Cio-Cio-San but also speaks the insistent 'Vieni, vieni' of the impatient Pinkerton who calls Cio-Cio-San into their bedroom on their wedding night. In her mouth both the object of Gallimard's desire and the desire for that object meet. The lines Song speaks are then translated from Italian into English by Gallimard, for the audience – in an attempt to include them in the scene and gain their complicity with his desires:

GALLIMARD: Yes, Butterfly?
SONG: 'Vieni, vieni!'
GALLIMARD: 'Come, darling.'
SONG: 'Ah, dolce notte!'
GALLIMARD: 'Beautiful night.'
SONG: 'Tutto estatico d'amor ride il ciel!'
GALLIMARD: 'All ecstatic with love, the heavens are filled with laughter.' (41)

This scene confirms Gallimard's inability to follow Song's twice-repeated advice that he 'expand his mind,' despite several visits to the Peking Opera (17, 22). Gallimard's vision of 'Butterfly' blinds him to both the Communist context in which Song performs 'art for the masses' (21) and the cultural tradition of an opera in which all of the female characters are played by men. The Western opera acts as a screen to the truth of the cultural and political location of Song's performance and the Peking Opera – as Hwang represents them.

Hwang continues to play on the traditional critical claims to 'universal' truths embodied in *Madama Butterfly* as the play develops. The notion of the 'globally powerful' West/man dominating the 'less powerful and less cynical' East/woman is supported by Gallimard's apparent success with Song and in politics simultaneously (Arblaster 250–1). Gallimard describes his promotion at work as an 'initiat[ion] into the way of the world' (38), linking his public and private success to the knowledge he has gained from the power structure embedded in *Madama Butterfly*. His success with Song has given him the 'new aggressive confiden[ce]' (38) that inspires Toulon to promote him, and the first three scenes of act 2 continue to establish the link between Gallimard's understanding of the way of the sexual world and his knowledge of the way of the cultural-political world. Toulon and Gallimard interpret Gallimard's sexual and emotional relationship with Song as the source of an 'insider's knowledge' about what 'the Chinese think' (45). The translation of Gallimard's relationship with Song into a comprehensive knowledge of 'the Orient' (46) mirrors the notion often found in opera criticism that an understanding of and empathy with the emotional relationship depicted onstage can be translated into a universal understanding of 'the way of the world' (38).

As act 2 progresses, sympathy for Gallimard's dismissal of the role of politics in art and for his apparently naive and unpretentious pleasure in both Song and her operatic counterpart is undermined by the explicit link that is made between the reasoning that Gallimard employs in order to justify his treatment of Song and the reasoning he employs in order to justify the power that he exercises in the realm of diplomatic politics. On the assumption that the majority of a Broadway audience would be familiar with the events of the Vietnam War, it is made clear to them that Gallimard's knowledge of Song has not left him with anything like an accurate political insight into 'the Orient':

TOULON: I don't see how the Vietnamese can stand up to American firepower.
GALLIMARD: Orientals will always submit to greater force. (46)

The audience's awareness that Gallimard is not as worldly as he thinks is amplified by the revelation that immediately follows this exchange. The audience's growing understanding that Gallimard has failed to 'know' something about the politics of South-East Asia provides the framework against which Gallimard's failure to 'know' Song is dramatized. At the play's midpoint the audience begins to see that the object of Gallimard's desire is nobody's old familiar Song. This 'Chinese diva' hits her own high notes, and what shatters is Gallimard's favourite fantasy.

Divas were treated like goddesses and, as such, were exempt from many of the constraints that other women faced. And, like the Greek gods, their behaviour was often highly unconstrained. Lavish life-styles and promiscuity were not uncommon.
(Plaut 74)

True, there were signs reading 'No dogs and Chinamen.' But a woman, especially a delicate Oriental woman – we always go where we please. Could you imagine otherwise?
(Hwang 22)

While Hwang finds the representational content of the opera's narrative to be rich with 'sexist and racist clichés' (Hwang 95), the same is also true of some of the language used to describe the vocal qualities of a female singer's voice and the appearance and behaviour of the singer herself. The sound of a Western opera singer's song is often described in terms of its tones, hues, and colours. Those tones range from light to dark and, in the words of one vocal training manual, 'a high light women's voice suggests girlishness, innocence and fragility,' while a 'darker quality' is 'sometimes associated with sexiness, but more often with evil' (Rushmore 30). The association of vocal hue with race is evident in **Melinda Boyd**'s discussion of comparative reviews of the performance of the lead role in *Madama Butterfly* by Miura and Farrar. Boyd quotes Browne's comment about the Japanese singer's performance: '[T]he voice hints at an impurity – an Oriental residue.'

Opera historian Wayne Koestenbaum argues that those racialized and gendered terms that are invoked in the description of the tonal qualities of the opera singer's voice are, in some cases, translated into a description of the personality and appearance of the opera singer: '[D]ivas, though usually white, have been linked to racial otherness, darkness, exoticism, and "blood"' (106). Robert Rushmore's guide to the singing voice makes this connection between vocal and physical characteristics quite literal: '[J]ust as the soprano *acuto sfogato* is most often doll-like and petite, and the bass tall and commanding, the shape of the face is one more guideline to vocal identification' (220).

A less explicit version of this connection can be found in Rupert Christiansen's history of prima donnas, in which he repeatedly describes opera singers such as Kiri Te Kanawa and Rosalind Plowright as possessing an 'irregular but exotic beauty' (333) and 'a strikingly attractive appearance, tall, dark, and slim' (340) respectively. It is, however, in relation to descriptions of Maria Callas that the work of critics like Christiansen and Conrad conforms most remarkably to both Koestenbaum's argument and Robert Young's suggestion that 'the "primitive" animal vitality and emotionalism of the lower races was reassigned its Romantic role as an object of value to be retrieved for the benefit of the regeneration of a tired, degenerate, vulgarized, mechanical European civilization' (52).

The opera diva in the person of Maria Callas is both the haughty and demanding performer and the 'primitive' soul whose life is not always distinguished from the roles she plays on stage. Conrad devotes a chapter to Callas that he entitles 'The Black Goddess' and proclaims that she 'took an art enfeebled by sophistication and demonstrated the savagery in it' (324). Christiansen describes the quality of Callas's voice in much the same terms as Conrad: 'Callas's natural vocal colour ... can be heard on any Greek island when the peasant women start shouting at each other. Peremptory, black, strident but *vibrato*-less, it is a sound of tragic absolutes' (305). Finally, Conrad assigns Callas to the operatic role that would, in the opinion of the director he quotes, dictate the shape of the 'tragic absolutes' of her life off-stage: 'Russell believes she was Butterfly, trusting the fickle sailor Onassis who married a haughty American instead' (323). The truth of her desire and her destiny is in the colour of her song.

If, as I have argued, the performance of the opera is a lesson in the importance of hierarchical differences (between races, classes, genders), then the difference of the diva – her 'other-worldliness' – is part of that lesson. Thus, to deconstruct only the 'sexist and racist clichés' embedded in the *characters* of *Madama Butterfly* risks leaving those same clichés intact in the person of the diva (see Hwang 76).

The notion that Song is playing a role, as Gallimard's butterfly, does not necessarily undermine her exoticism, given the stereotype, not only of the opera character, but of the diva playing her. This perhaps goes some way towards explaining Gallimard's willingness to continue his affair with Song after he becomes aware that she is a spy. As a spy, the 'tragic absolutes' of Song's life remain intact. However, Hwang's characterization of Song goes some distance in interrogating the notion contained in representations of the diva who plays the butterfly. Here again, much depends on the staging of the play and the choices made by actor and director, as **Rachel Ditor and Jan Selman**'s discussion of the theatre workshop reveals.

Song follows her initial critique of *Madama Butterfly* by enacting the assumption that her dark vocal tones reveal the truth of her Butterfly/diva's passion and her masochistic character: 'Hard as I try to be modern, to speak like a man, to hold a Western woman's strong face up to my own ... in the end, I fail. A small, frightened heart beats too quickly and gives me away' (30–1). In their early courtship Song plays to Gallimard's operatic fantasy that she is a woman who cannot conceal either her self-destructive desire to 'give [Gallimard her] shame' or the 'Oriental' nature by which this desire is shaped.

This equation is one that Song brings up again in the trial scene in *M. Butterfly*. Here, in his masculine persona, Song critiques the 'rape mentality' of the West, 'her mouth says no, but her eyes say yes' (83), which allows the West to feel that it can interpret the truth of the East's desire – to be dominated by the West. It is this notion that Gallimard has enacted in his attempt to force the opera's character and the opera's words into Song's mouth. Gallimard's ventriloquism is a mirror of the ventriloquism that Puccini's opera attempts to perform – the West forcing an image of the East to sing its desire to be dominated by the West. However, the role of the singer in the production of this sound is one that Hwang's play problematizes, not least through Song's performance of both the words of Cio-Cio-San and the words of Pinkerton.

In Conrad's and Christiansen's terms the diva is both the composer's dummy – the vehicle for his or her expression – and the source of a truth revealed in her voice. The parallels that these critics draw between the diva's offstage and onstage persona suggest that the diva's performance is a revelation of her true self – the music and libretto merely allow her to better express this truth. The claim to deliver the composer's truth through the representation of a universal role is problematized if the performance turns out to be part of the diva's own act of ventriloquism. Koestenbaum argues that the figure of the diva can be read as one that 'has the power to dramatise the problematics of self-expression. One finds or invents identity only by staging it, making fun of it, entertaining it, throwing it, as the ventriloquist throws the voice' (133). The operatic character becomes the diva's tool. This reading goes against the grain of a conception of a diva who, like the characters she plays, is moved by emotions and events beyond her control.

The problematics of self-expression and identity are of course central to Hwang's play, where it is, quite literally, a diva who provokes and poses this question. Just as the diva performing in *Madama Butterfly* is not only Puccini's puppet but also the active source of the song's creation, Song turns out to be more than the doll that Gallimard and Comrade Chin thought she was. The high note she's hitting is false, or rather, falsetto – a tonal inflection that is described by a nineteenth-century writer as 'a species of ventriloquism ... an inward and suppressed quality of tone' (Nathan, quoted in Koestenbaum 164). The question of what is being suppressed or inverted in the adoption of this false voice leads Koestenbaum to connect the characterization of vocal identity to the 'cultural folklore' that 'convinces us that we can tell someone is gay by voice alone' (14). However, Song is neither simply a gay Chinese man whose desire is revealed in the performance of the part of a straight woman, nor a straight man performing the part of a gay man on behalf of Chin. Here I would see more potential for complexity in the characterization of Song than does **Bart Testa**. Where

Testa argues that Hwang is presenting us with a character whose 'real' identity is that of a gay man, I would argue that Song's falsetto enacts both her multiple desires and her multiple falsifications or betrayals. This characterization creates the potential to complicate the audience's relationship to Song, and thus the hierarchies normally established through stereotypes of the opera and the diva who performs it.

Song betrays Chin by engaging in a homosexual relationship with Gallimard and betrays Gallimard in her role as a spy. As I have pointed out above, both Gallimard and Chin come to accept these betrayals in act 3 when Chin sends Song to Paris to seduce Gallimard again and Gallimard receives Song and begins to pass information to her in order to keep her in Paris. These betrayals are acceptable to Gallimard and Chin only in so far as they treat Song's disguise as a screen that masks her true self and as one that she adopts in order to please them, not herself. In other words, Song can continue to sing as long as her song is an expression of her real desire to please her audience. The pleasure that she takes in her performance of the 'highly unconstrained ... [l]avish lifestyles and promiscuity' of the diva becomes the ultimate betrayal (Plant 74).

Song refuses to take off her 'disguise' when she is alone with Chin, provoking Chin to remind her that she must not 'gather information in any way that violates Communist Party principles' (48). Song violates more than just the prohibition against homosexuality to which Chin refers in this scene; she also appears to Chin to take pleasure in both her 'disguise' and in luxuries like the 'pastries from France and sweetmeats [on] silver trays' (70) that her espionage work has provided.

Gallimard's sense of betrayal comes when he realizes that Song's disguise was one which required that she give him her *pride* not her shame: 'And what's the shame? In pride? You think I could've pulled this off if I wasn't already full of pride when we met?' (85). Song goes on to demonstrate that her performance was not a subjection of her true self to Gallimard's fantasy, but a multivocal expression of her own pleasure as both Butterfly and the man in Armani slacks. When Song strips in front of Gallimard – a scene that might be read as the revelation of Song's true and undisguised identity – Song prefaces that act with, in the words of the stage directions, a reprise of 'his feminine character' (86). Song sings a familiar tune in both the tone of her voice and the line of dialogue from act 1 that she repeats at this point. This reprise is not, in this context, an expression of Gallimard's desire for his Butterfly but rather an expression of Song's desire for Gallimard – a desire that Song plays like the ambiguous performer that she is:

SONG: Well maybe, Rene, just maybe – I want you.
GALLIMARD: You do?
SONG: Then again, maybe I'm just playing with you. How can you tell? (*Reprising his feminine character, he sidles up to Gallimard*) 'How I wish there were even a small cafe to sit in. With men in tuxedos, and cappuccinos, and bad expatriate jazz.' Now you want to kiss me, don't you?
GALLIMARD: What makes you – ?
SONG: – so sure? See? I take the words from your mouth. Then I wait for you to come and retrieve them. (85–6)

The act of ventriloquism is transformed by Song's mouth into a kiss. What the diva performs here is not simply a parody of Western constructions of the East, of Puccini's opera, or of the audience's desires but a refiguring of the relationship of the audience and even the composer to the cultural form through her own desires and personas.

When Song ends the play with one final act of ventriloquism – speaking the lines spoken at the end of *Madama Butterfly* and the beginning of Hwang's play – 'Butterfly? Butterfly?' (93) – the words are inflected with a question mark and the audience is left to decide what kind of question Song is posing and whether or not they will retrieve Song's words with a kiss.

Notes

1 While the relationship of *Madama Butterfly* to *M. Butterfly* is not the central focus of every critical review of *M. Butterfly*, it is a component of the majority of the critiques of the play. Some examples of this trend include Robert Skloot's 'Breaking the Butterfly,' Foong Ling Kong's 'Pulling the Wings Off Butterfly,' and Hsaio H. Chang's 'Cultural/Sexual/Theatrical Ambivalence in *M. Butterfly*.'
2 The success of *M. Butterfly* reached its apex at the 1988 Tony Awards, where the play won in the category of best new play.
3 For the purposes of this article the cultural and geographical milieu of the play and opera will be confined to the limits of Manhattan.
4 The movement of different pieces and styles of musical theatre from the opera hall to the Broadway theatre was not unidirectional. *Porgy and Bess* was the first opera/musical to travel from Broadway to the Metropolitan Opera House stage. While this journey has been hailed by some opera critics as a demonstration of the democratization of opera culture, I would suggest that in some sense it conforms exactly to the traditional expectations of the opera

audience – placing its African-American characters into the same exotic milieu already occupied by the 'Japanese' characters of *Madama Butterfly*.

5 While Gallimard's nationality corresponds to the French diplomat in the story that provided Hwang with his initial inspiration, the character speaks English, employs American idioms, and was played by an American actor, with an American accent, in the initial Broadway production of *M. Butterfly*. I would argue that the combination of these elements tends to override the few references to Gallimard's French identity in the Broadway audience's perception. Those references are also often posed in the general terms 'Western' and 'modern,' which could easily apply to an American character. It is worth noting, however, that Hwang's decision not to change Gallimard's national identity and, as a result, the political context in which he operates as a diplomat, might dull some of the play's pointed criticisms of imperialism by generalizing them to the West – not America in particular.

6 While the audience may not be universally sympathetic to Gallimard in the first half of the play or consider themselves part of the straight, white male 'club' that Gallimard has attempted to implicate them in through the use of inclusive pronouns, the currency of the sort of claims that he makes cannot be underestimated. A good example of the continuing marketability of 'common sense' notions of gender distinctions and heterosexual desire can be found in John Gray's best-selling book *Men Are From Mars, Women Are From Venus*, which was produced as a successful stage show on Broadway.

7 In an earlier scene, Gallimard, Song's onstage audience, suggests a critique of the pleasure to be derived from watching an operatic performance that is less self-conscious but no less threatening to the status of opera and its audience when he links the pleasures of *Madama Butterfly* with the pleasure derived from looking at pornographic magazines. Through Gallimard the heights of high culture and the depths of low culture are brought into contact in the act of viewing and the power that that act inscribes. The notion that the audience should sit back and enjoy the show is recast in more suggestive tones.

PART THREE

Intertexts

Late Mutations of Cinema's Butterfly

BART TESTA

The focus of this essay falls on David Cronenberg's *M. Butterfly*, a 1993 film that sets out to effect mutations on Puccini's 1904 opera that Marina Heung describes as the 'prototypical Madame Butterfly myth' (174). On a first look, Cronenberg's film derives simply and directly from David Henry Hwang's Tony-winning Broadway play *M. Butterfly* (1988). The Chinese-American playwright and the Canadian filmmaker collaborated closely on the script for a production that was already set up before the director became involved (Beard 338). This essay will nonetheless suggest some deviations between Hwang's play and Cronenberg's direction of the material.

Provoked by the erotic and political 'deconstructive *Madama Butterfly*' that Hwang takes as his play's accomplishment (1989), I wish to explore, in counterpoint, Cronenberg's adaptation and the imagination of the Butterfly story that once flowed confidently through opera culture into the story's first cinematic adaptation. The essay will also develop some observations on the first period of classical American cinema, centring on 1915, the year of that first adaptation of *Madama Butterfly*, directed by Sidney Olcott for Paramount and starring Mary Pickford. I wish, in a sense, to recall some sense of the bourgeois imaginary subjectivity that was manifest at the start of this century across a range of artefacts and that was shared, despite differences, between cinema and opera.

An odd occasion for that purpose, *M. Butterfly* deliberately works mutations on the opera's Butterfly figure, especially at the level of imaginary subjectivity. The play seeks to undercut ideological supports of the opera in several ways. We might best begin with salient deviations from Puccini. Hwang's play resets the time and place of the story, inverts the power positions of the main characters' involvement, manipulates performative codes, and, with Cronenberg intervening, devises cinematic locutions like camera movement and framing and point-of-view, sound cueing and editing, to transform the story material.[1]

The play and film propose to us a fictional world in which *Madama Butterfly* is known and appreciated. Conventional adaptations of fictional works customarily presume innocence about the existence of other versions of their story so that plot elements appear to originate in the fictional world and are never part of its cultural furniture. Any film version of a biblical story, for example, will not insist that either the film or its audience be acquainted with the Bible. One sign that *M. Butterfly* is not this kind of conventional text is that Cronenberg and Hwang quickly establish that Puccini's *Madama Butterfly* is an acknowledged, even perhaps an overly familiar, European classic. It is excerpted in the first major scene. The opera's political and erotic significance is then disputed in the film's second main sequence, which shows the main characters, Song Liling (John Lone) and Rene Gallimard (Jeremy Irons), making their initial contact. This first encounter, despite their dispute – and perhaps even utilizing it – shows them beginning to inhabit, more or less consciously, the opera's personae of Pinkerton and Butterfly. They eventually, in fact quite quickly, re-initiate the opera's plot of seduction and power and play it out, initially as a latter-day rehearsal of erotic play, and then as a perversely obsessive inversion of power relations. The key difference in all this is that Song Liling is a man. Exactly in accord with the design of Hwang's play, the film recasts, with the added sense of remaking, the Butterfly figure – notorious European-made construct of Orientalist femininity – as a Chinese transvestite diva onstage and offstage alike. This Butterfly is an Asian-made feminine construct. Song is an erotically ambiguous male that Gallimard passionately embraces as a woman. The persona Song constructs enables Hwang's didactic inversion of the opera's original story. First, the point seems to be that Gallimard is so saturated with Orientalist sexism that he could confuse the image of a Butterfly with a real woman and further confuse such a woman with a man, even in the act of love. Initially we assume that Gallimard, the Western diplomat, will be the new Pinkerton and Song the new Butterfly. As events unfold, the opposite proves to be the case. While never ceasing to perform her Asian feminine stereotype, Song proves the agent of geopolitical power and Gallimard proves the hapless lover betrayed by his romantic ideal. This reversal of the opera's plotting is the heart of Hwang's 'deconstructive' critique of the opera. Hwang means to pull the Butterfly myth apart and reassemble its elements in this highly critical form of an inverted relationship between two men.

This is the first sense of a mutation of *Madama Butterfly*. As it might be bluntly paraphrased, the second sense is the thematic reversal of the opera and consists in showing Gallimard protractedly seduced and finally abandoned and then in showing him commit suicide in place of, and indeed in a grotesque parody of, the operatic Butterfly's climactic transport of sacrificial suicide. Symmetrically, Song is shown assuming the political and erotic mastery that the opera's Westerner assumes as his right and property, becoming the erstwhile Pinkerton, who abandons Gallimard to his doom.

The Cronenberg film follows the plot of Hwang's play and the film director never explicitly deviates from Hwang's thematic intent. However, as Rey Chow's 'more or less Lacanian reading' of the film shows, the film *M. Butterfly* differs in how it inflects Gallimard's embrace of a stereotype (Chow, 'Dream' 96). Subtly, Cronenberg shifts emphasis away from Hwang's anti-Orientalist defamation of the opera's symptomatically racist politics towards a 'psychoanalysis' of erotic obsession (Chow 85–7). A leading irony of Hwang's text is that it paradoxically restores to Puccini's Butterfly what she never originally possessed, namely, erotic roots in the transvestite personae and stylized performativity of Chinese and Japanese theatre. The Butterfly drama is not inconceivable in that theatre tradition, Chinese and Japanese alike, as Nick Browne observes (243–5).[2] The made-in-Europe Butterfly of Puccini's opera nonetheless did not derive from Asian sources. It was created and recreated several times in literary, theatrical, and then musical and cinematic forms. The Butterfly image should not be regarded as constantly in flux, however, for received critical opinion is correct in regarding Puccini's opera as the fixed 'classic original legend.' Specifically following Gina Marchetti, I will likewise take the opera as the canonical version. I will also restrict comparative remarks to the 1915 American film adaptation (whereas Marchetti covers other film versions), ignoring, for example, Fritz Lang's nearly contemporary German adaptation, the later Hollywood sound version, and the various adaptations made since. *M. Butterfly* does not take the opera to be a template to be adapted. Hwang's project is instead to stand the canonical version on its head and to place this inversion in harsh relief. Sharing aspects of the Butterfly figure between two men is what Hwang means by 'deconstructing' the idealized femininity of Butterfly's image.

Is the film more or something other than Hwang's subversive revisitation? This is, in the end, somewhat uncertain.[3] Despite Hwang's obvious intention implied by the term 'deconstruction,' the film's gender reversals are mediated by Oriental theatrical transvestism, so much so that the play cannot initially be considered as direct a confrontation with Puccini's opera as Hwang wishes us to believe it to be. To our contemporary eyes, Cronenberg's film highlights what we have already learned, and not from cinema alone, namely, that artistic representations of femininity are constructed in accord with codes of performance and feminine masquerade. To play on the codes of performed femininity may be rightly seen as deconstructive because to play on these codes exposes the backstage machinery of the feminine image, and finally renders femininity itself in some senses undecidable. But this is not exactly how the play or the film Cronenberg made works. I prefer the metaphor of mutation over deconstruction because the film *M. Butterfly* re-composes a seductive image of the Oriental feminine for the gaze of the protagonist, and in doing so Cronenberg constructs Gallimard cinematically to a degree the play does not attempt. Not the coming-and-going causal agent Pinkerton as in Puccini's narrative, but the punctual centre of a cinematic narration, Gallimard inhabits, in even the coarsest schema of the film, the position Butterfly holds in the opera. However odd that image of a seduced man pivoting this story may appear beside the received image of the gentle suffering martyr to love pivoting *Madama Butterfly*, the film's critique differs a bit from the play's in the privileging manner it interweaves Gallimard's seduction with Hwang's demolition of a stereotype.

To come back now to the salient points, both the play and film *M. Butterfly* do ground themselves consciously in a political critique of Orientalist feminine representation. First and foremost, it scores with broad geopolitical irony. Set in China in the 1960s and not in Japan of the opera's 1880s, the plotting boldly inverts the allegorical relationship between erotic and political presumptions that underpin the familiar Butterfly story. The opera's heroine is an allegory, critics agree, of the frail and feminine East seen through Western imperialist eyes, bending to the manly Western will in the inaugural period of America's Asian adventure. Resetting the story, whose initial phase spans 1964 to 1968, alongside the trajectory of Americans' military debacle in Vietnam, Hwang's plotting creates a dialogue with the Butterfly legend to elucidate the political ramifications of projecting a fantasy feminine onto the East. Setting his revision at the opposite end of the American imperialist arc, then, the once weak and feminine Asian now appears strong and hard; the imperialist Westerner, personified in Gallimard, appears seduced, shaky, fatally unsure. When, in a scene devoted solely to the purpose, Gallimard offers his superior, the French ambassador, his prediction that the Vietnamese will embrace the strong American conqueror, *M. Butterfly* ensures that we recognize not just his ludicrous error but also the degree that his speech is symptomatic of erotomania. Pinkerton's callous power has become humiliated over the last century. It has now become an unconscious and deluded *erotic* debility. The operatic Pinkerton was entirely unselfconscious in projecting his arrogant presumption onto the Oriental woman. It carries him smoothly, even unawares, towards sexual possession, not just of the woman but also of her child, because he rides on a current of confident political and economic power that makes his sexual sanction seem inevitable. In the opera, Cio-Cio-San's tragedy begins with her failure to recognize the reality of her fragile position or to see Pinkerton's sexual predation for what it is, her initiation into a decorous prostitution and not romantic love. Pinkerton's power is simply given to him as a second nature (Browne 248–50). As if looking through the wrong end of the geopolitical telescope, Gallimard instead projects his needy sexual obsession onto Asia, still just as unaware as Pinkerton, but now the current of power has started to run the opposite way. His prediction is palpably absurd given the obdurate resistance of the Vietnamese. But it is worse than absurd, it is pathetically deluded. His erotic pathology will render him a dupe of a grotesque and intimate deception. We cannot help but notice the tremble of excitement with which he delivers his risible speech. As the sarcastic incarnation of latter-day imperialism, the humiliatingly fragile masculinity of Gallimard – played by Jeremy Irons assuming his usual mask of ravaged despoliation – the film enacts its cruel reversal of Pinkerton's stolid presence and all he is said to symbolize politically in the opera.

The political significance of scenes of this type is so obvious that it makes parts of Hwang's text play into drumming agit-prop. Much of the play is coloured by the way Hwang unmasks the Orientalist and sexist projection of a Euro-American *libido dominandi*. The ironies that Hwang harvests he gathers by resituating Gallimard at the moment of Western imperialism's final expenditure. Cronenberg further amplifies this strategy, for there is something already exhausted about Irons's Gallimard even as things begin. That something might be called his masculinity, but should perhaps be left noted as his self-mastery, leaving him too open to the desire of the Other and leading him to the erotomania of male masochism. In this complicating light of inversion, the decadent erotic scenario of *M. Butterfly* is the answering allegory to the opera's metaphor, telling of a twilight attenuation of the Western erotic dream corresponding to Pinkerton's noontime presumption of political and sexual mastery.

The scenario of reversal would be agit-prop in the film also were it not for Cronenberg's starkly formalized direction. Cronenberg initially seems to sharpen Hwang's didacticism, but, by bringing more and more sexual investments into the projection, obsession, and seduction and by bringing them more fully into the film's foreground, the director gives rise to a supplementary mutation that was a minor element of the play. The erotic supplement introduced into Hwang's text is something that cinema does well. This is because films are obliged to decide on precisely how to frame and to assemble shots to articulate a plot. Theatre accumulates narration through tableaux and language, films through angles, perspectives, visual constructs that are necessarily very specific in their significance. Cronenberg exfoliates the implicit perversions of Hwang's text into mico-structural terms of on-screen looks, sound cues, and editing patterns to reveal, in precise terms, the mechanisms of the obsessive compulsive masochism that consumes the film's protagonist. This is Chow's point: that while Hwang wants to pull the Butterfly myth apart and reassemble it in a reprimanded form, Cronenberg has focused this intent at another level, that of the erotic drives funnelled through a constricted set of cinematic locutions.

The play *M. Butterfly* is a post-Brechtian-postmodern piece reliant on busy pastiche and given to occasional bursts of humanistic earnestness and mocking but also opportunistic blasts of exalting opera music. Cronenberg seriously diminishes these excitements. Oddly for a filmmaker, and especially one who has made such hypertrophic spectacles as *Scanners*, *The Fly*, and *Naked Lunch*, Cronenberg eschews spectacle with this film, even when the plot and a generous budget allow him to indulge. Instead, he transmutes Hwang's material another step, away from its polyphonic busyness and towards a singularly monologic cinematicization built to the specifications of a cold stylistic mannerism.[4] There is still much of the play and little looseness with the plot in the film, but there is a certain irresponsibility with its sexual politics foreign to Hwang's ideological solemnity. In his last scene with Song and Gallimard, it is plausible that Hwang wishes these two men could just recognize and embrace one another. Cronenberg never invests much in that unattainable prospect. Instead, his formal articulations *serve* Gallimard's perversity insistently, and therefore more disastrously, than Hwang's dramaturgy. Cronenberg congeals the film around the character and closes his figuration cinematically into an obsessive serialism in the service of erotic solipsism.

After the titles and a short prelude that introduces Gallimard, the first developed scene brings him reluctantly to a performance of excerpts from *Madama Butterfly* at a diplomatic soirée. He starts off bored. Like others of his international cadre, to him the prospect of an evening of operatic excerpts performed by Chinese singers seems a cultural trial a minor embassy official (he is, in fact, an accountant) must endure, though offering a slightly happier prospect, as he mentions, to watching Chinese acrobats. His German colleague, Frau Bader, has to feed him bits of the opera's story as the performance proceeds. Then, with a swiftness toying with comedy, Cronenberg shows Gallimard becoming transfixed. The cinematic choices in this sequence set what will become the film's recurring, indeed rigidly repetitious, formal pattern. Beginning with smooth lateral tracking shots interrupted by close-up cutaways to Bader and Gallimard, Cronenberg then shifts to steady cross-cutting between Gallimard in closer and closer framings and Song Liling, as Butterfly, seen on stage in rigidly symmetrical long-shot compositions. The series is extended over several cuts, until Gallimard leans forward into the fill light of an extreme close-up that illuminates his staring eyes. There is then a sharp ellipsis, negotiated by an abrupt cut and sound bridge. After another gliding track through the post-performance gathering, during which we overhear a woman say, 'But she has no voice,' Gallimard is shown in close-up staring once more at Song. She is offstage now, but framed again in a symmetrical long shot similar in design to the one that previously showed her onstage. The framing in these two closely matched sequences uses cone-like depth-of-field to centre Song fixedly against a light source at the back of the frame. Song moves slowly through an archway and down a staircase towards Gallimard. Then, after a brief cutaway, Gallimard steps into what had been his own point-of-view shot, greets Song, and initiates a conversation with her.

The exchange is carried by a shot-reverse-shot series of close-ups that rhyme with the performance's editing pattern. Gallimard begins by stammering out his adoring response to the opera: 'You made me see the beauty of the story ... her pure sacrifice.' Song sharply reprimands him for this appreciation of Butterfly because she is the masochistic symbol of racist myth, 'one of your favourite fantasies ... the submissive

Oriental woman and the cruel white man.' Song then walks away into the funnel of yet another deep-focus shot, again set up as Gallimard's point of view, but not before tossing off an invitation to visit the Beijing Opera, 'for your education.'

These two sequences invite viewers to speculate, on the basis of pacing and the rhymed patterning of stylistic cues – camera placement, serial close-ups, and the symmetrical design of the long shots – that the opera performance seduces Gallimard and that Song's post-performance excoriation of the opera is further seduction. Gallimard is not abashed by her defamation of the opera's Orientalist fantasy. He laps up the abuse eagerly. Song's sharpness – she is sharp about erotic abasement – is the lure beginning the romance. Offstage and out of costume, Song continues to perform the Oriental female, most importantly by using her speaking voice musically. This Song will do throughout the film. His/her speech sharply contrasts with his/her singing, heard just twice and to no great effect. The overheard comment about that voice is true. Just the opposite is true of her speaking voice, which becomes a main instrument of Gallimard's seduction.

There follow two very brief scenes (covering three weeks) in which Gallimard's growing fascination with the Butterfly image is represented. No one else notices. It is treated like a pornography habit.[5] These scenes, though apparently incidental to the plot, deserve closer inspection. In the first of them, immediately after the encounter with Song, Gallimard is shown in his bedroom with his wife. She remarks of the Chinese that their speaking is musical, but their singing is unbearable. She then performs a bit of 'Un bel dì' and Cronenberg cuts to the couple in bed looking at themselves fixedly in a mirror. The other short scene following shows Gallimard obtaining a record album of *Madama Butterfly* and gazing from above at its kitschy drawn cover (shown in a point-of-view close-up) depicting Cio-Cio-San kneeling before Pinkerton. The severing of music and image, and the comment on the Chinese speaking voice in these two short scenes, indicate by a deft self-reflective gesture the separate channels of Gallimard's seduction. It will involve the opera's tragic music not at all, although both Song and Gallimard's wife in these successive scenes very similarly agree it to be the opera's source of beauty. The mirror shot and the close-up of the album cover pointedly condense the point-of-view constructions from the *Madama Butterfly* performance segment into these intimate, short scenes, so that the pattern of already-obsessed point-of-view editing is continued even in these apparently incidental passages.

Gallimard does visit the Beijing Opera, as invited. The performance features Song. He visits backstage and walks her home, continuing their conversation, and now his seduction is explicitly initiated. Cronenberg ensures that we compare the two large opera performance segments separated by that brief two-scene interval. The Chinese opera itself hardly resembles the *Madama Butterfly* performance at the embassy soirée: Song is not fixed at the centre of the stage this time and Cronenberg cuts to other faces in the audience. A working-class Chinese crowd surrounds the uncomfortably finicky Gallimard. Now Cronenberg displaces the formal articulation of the earlier opera performance segment to the subsequent passage, taking place backstage. Gallimard approaches a translucent crimson curtain that closes off a dressing space and hides Song. Cronenberg keeps Gallimard fixed there and cuts back and forth between close-ups of him, all awkward and uncertain, and his point-of-view stare at the luminous curtain and Song's shadow. These reverse shots are flattened inversions of the cone-like deep-focus shots seen in the earlier segment. They put even greater emphasis on her speaking voice. Then Song suddenly peeks out in close-up to ask for a light for her cigarette, jutting from her mouth, and pointedly returns Gallimard's gaze. For a rather long span of the passage, Song is only a voice and a shadow. In this respect, Song's voice briefly takes something of the phantasmatic characteristics that Michel Chion (*Voix* 125–37) terms acousmatic, which makes it that much more enticing. Her postponed close-up makes this obvious when its occurrence suddenly fixes Gallimard in the doubled action of her intent gaze on her spoken demand for a light. Song has performed her veiled presence and appearance, they did not just happen. There follows a second walk and conversation. Again Song is the critic of Orientalized femininity, and again she makes another invitation, this one more intimate.

The episode does not end abruptly this time. Gallimard has a lyrical interlude in which he encounters a man 'fishing' dragonflies from the river. The man gives Gallimard one, the ambiguous equivalent of a butterfly. He comes to possess in metaphor – the dragonfly – what he so fixedly gazes upon. Gallimard's glazed joy with his new possession in the cab conveying him home is palpable. It is also odd, for a dragonfly is not an ornamental insect like a butterfly but a more ambiguous possession, a predatory insect.

By the close of this second and last of Song's opera-performance sequences, Cronenberg has set a firm pattern of cinematic-formal alternation marked by framing, camera mobility, editing, and sound. This pattern will recur repeatedly in the scenes when Gallimard returns to Song in his/her home. At the end of the Beijing Opera segment Gallimard had arrived at her doorway. Two sequences later, he enters and Song's home becomes the intimate stage of her erotic performances consisting of artful poses, voice, lovemaking. Cronenberg's formal patterning is unyielding throughout these segments and becomes itself the filmic correlative of Gallimard's obsession because he is the constant focalizer of these scenes. There is no other perspective allowed. The film's expression of its plotting is wrapped around Gallimard. What matters is not that Cronenberg has not taken what Hwang has given him – though the adaptation excises a good deal – but that the film mutates the material on another, formal level: the busyness of the play is sheered away. Cronenberg's unhurried camera, steady eye-line matching, recurring shot-reverse-shot elaborations, and decisions as to light, colour, and to burnish the cinematography – all these devices steady the playwright's text and incline towards a certain affectlessness turning on a wheel of luxuriant erotic repetition. The result is to deflate the play's postmodern energies on behalf of a favoured Cronenberg trope: the intersplicing of enervation and obsession.

The resulting narrational pattern, then, has two effects. First, it effectively isolates Song and Gallimard, beginning obviously with the two sequences that took place amid crowds, and now and thereafter closing in completely on their closely closeted intimacy. It is not until much later, when Gallimard has returned to Paris and Song visits him there, that the public world breaks in significantly. Song never ceases to continue her performance, a staging of the feminine that prompts Gallimard repeatedly to call her 'My Butterfly.' There are, in fact, nine of these encounters. They conclude with a final tenth, after a lengthy ellipsis in their relations: a confrontation between the ex-lovers in a French police van, the film's penultimate sequence.

The other effect is that Cronenberg's style undercuts operatic 'ecstasy,' so that while Hwang's play sometimes allows emotional flights, and quotes from the opera to power these, Cronenberg pulls the wings off *M. Butterfly* the better to close in on the erotic obsession that becomes a figuration of male masochism – Gallimard's masochism.

Let's return to the first effect for a moment. The formal patterning closely inscribes a recurring repetition-variation series that shapes the film's rhythm and narrative spine as itself a type of serialism. By this I mean that the spine of the film consists of the nine slow and protracted erotic encounters closely rhymed in framing and cutting. Gallimard's ceremonial returns to Song each begin with another accented gaze, another reprimand, followed by Song delivering another erotic performance for her enraptured prey. It is this serialism of episode and formal articulation that leaves the strong formal impression of *M. Butterfly*. The second effect expressed by Irons's performance, and that the serial quality subtends, is the obsessive sensibility. The film's strongest psychological impression is the erotic pleasure and anguish of Gallimard. The implantation of perversion is dug deep into the film's fabric. In producing these impressions, Cronenberg has effected a displacement of the peculiar kind of ecstasy, or hypostasis of ecstatic suffering, that *Madama Butterfly* is about aesthetically. Hwang is a bit insensitive to the ideological value of opera aesthetics. The combination of erotic exultation and exaggerated dying – in short, the familiar feature of operatic stylization – is not the object of his essentially didactic critique. Hwang regrets that Song and Gallimard cannot finally embrace as gay lovers, but he does not exult in the tragedy that they cannot. Puccini would, and in *Madama Butterfly* does, exult in his heroine's tragedy.

In 'Mounting Butterflies,' **Susan McClary** uncovers the ideological value of opera's musical aesthetics when she shows that Puccini wrote arias whose vocal range and breathing requirements for Butterfly imprint a performative torment on the character extraordinary even for an opera. McClary's point is that in doing this Puccini achieves the musical form of voluptuous sadism. Her intention is political critique like Hwang's. However, McClary contributes a further sense of how the opera's musical coding of feminine transport into cruel ecstasy constitutes a formal-musical correspondent of Orientalist projection. That it is, nonetheless, an enduringly engaging feature of the opera is not to be denied. It is this ecstatic dimension of the opera that Cronenberg drains away from the film *M. Butterfly*, and in doing so Cronenberg mutates a feminine ecstatic transport into the masculine affixation of Gallimard's delicious suffering – a voluptuous masochism.

What is emphatic in the dialogue of the first segment of *M. Butterfly*, and which Cronenberg's direction accepts, is Hwang's presumption, given to Song here, that the erotic source of the pleasing pathos of *Madama Butterfly*, Cio-Cio-San's idealized masochism, should arouse our indignant recognition. If Gallimard seems hopelessly naive about the opera's meaning, and Song has to explain it to him, he will later pay for this innocence by being insanely wilful in his misperception that the Butterfly figure is reincarnate in Song politically or sexually. Ironies proliferate from the salient difference between the indignation we properly should feel and what Gallimard comes to feel – desire, then exultation, then obsession, and finally suicidal despair.

Let's step back for a moment. No one should find it hard to agree that, in Song's first scene with Gallimard, Hwang is rehearsing the corrective interpretive denunciation of the erotic and political significance of the opera. Marina Heung is exemplary in her denunciation of this type when she writes:

> Puccini's popular opera is in many ways a foundational narrative of East/ West relations, having shaped the Western construction of 'the Orient' as a sexualized and sexually compliant, space that is ripe for conquest and rule. Many scholars have analyzed the ways in which race and gender are mutually imbricated within Orientalist discourse and practice, constituting a nexus along which racial and sexual domination operates reciprocally. Central to the Western Orientalist imaginary, the figure of the geisha (whose most well known incarnation is Cio-Cio-San / Madame Butterfly) epitomizes an exoticized and subservient femininity that is leavened with a mix of passive refinement and sexual mystique. As a master-text of Orientalism, *Madama Butterfly* confirms the Asian woman's perpetual sexual availability for the Western male even as her convenient demise delimits such liaisons; in the end, Cio-Cio-San's suicide recapitulates the fate of the expendable Asian whose inevitable death confirms her marginality within the dominant culture and history. (Heung 160)

We should add to this, after McClary, a remark on the opera's eroticized execution of this 'recapitulation' that is pertinent to Gallimard's first testimony to Song about the beauty of the opera's sacrificial story. The particular combination of sex and death woven into opera at every level of its musical and dramatic architecture serves to imprint upon Butterfly such a performative luxury that Puccini's aesthetic coding of what the quotation above addresses is the opera's most seductive feature. Cronenberg mutates this aesthetic seduction when he drains performative and musical ecstasy from the film. The main object of Hwang's *M. Butterfly*'s 'deconstruction' is, like Heung's denunciation, a 'myth' cobbled into an opera from Orientalist codes embedded in the source stories, a play, the ethos of the late nineteenth century, and so on. The film's mutation is faithful to Hwang's themes. These derive from a genealogical project of contemporary criticism of the opera that seeks to strip back its beauty and tragic power – the source of its durable popularity – and looks back to its literary sources and the imperial ideology that they baldly express. Hwang and Cronenberg exceed the opera's critics by one crucial step, however, by expressing a symmetrical perverse eroticism. Cronenberg's adaptation goes yet a step further by fixedly focusing on it. The final mutated grotesquerie consists of driving Gallimard, not Song, to ritual suicide. It is the culmination of the inaugural segments already described: their implications come to be uncoiled, fully extended, over the rest of the film and reach that grisly end.

Moreover, the film *M. Butterfly* is anything but aesthetically compact. When Cronenberg excised much of the play's busyness he replaced it with his cinematic serialism. It serves a painfully and luxuriantly distended inversion of the aesthetic of McClary's operatic sadism into a cinematic representation of masochism.[6] Gallimard will only initially take the position of Pinkerton. When he repeatedly addresses Song as 'My Butterfly,' the meaning of the phrase becomes progressively more ambiguous. Just who is speaking and spoken of? When it is revealed that Song is a man and there is no longer a plausible Butterfly, Gallimard becomes 'My Butterfly' himself. In the scene in the police van, Song disrobes and demands Gallimard's embrace as a man. It is the end of the long series of their encounters and Gallimard responds with the words, 'I am a man who loved a woman created by a man. And anything else ... simply falls short.' The implication is that Rene was also himself created by a man, in some sense by Song, who created him and Butterfly so that Gallimard could create 'My Butterfly' as his own solipsist's spectre of the ideal feminine.

That Song attacks the position of the Butterfly even as she acts out its masquerade off- and onstage and displays herself before Gallimard as the erotic lure that Butterfly has long represented (Chow, 'Dream' 76–7) is crucial to the ironies of *M. Butterfly*. Song's critique *is* seduction. The conjunction occurs in three performative registers – as Butterfly, as Chinese opera heroine, and as the voice behind a screen. One staging is Western, another is Chinese, the third and thereafter recurrent register is specifically cinematic. It is as if Cronenberg were returning to the visual tropes of Josef von Sternberg's *The Blue Angel* (1930) or *Shanghai Express* (1932). The film never ceases to speak of the Oriental feminine, but Gallimard is locked into the obsessive gaze that Cronenberg's découpage has built for him. The critiques become for him so much soothing-stinging reprimand from his demanding mistress. Inextricably, seduction and critique unfurl Song's eroticism as always a stylized performance, an unreal chimera of male desire. While Song never ceases to say so, Gallimard's place before his/her luminous crimson curtain sutures him into obsessive-projective desire and he is deaf to criticism, slave to his inverted vision and to the phantasmatic sound of that voice. Indeed, he hears only that voice and sees only what his enraptured desire projects. The rest of the film will play out the implications of that imaginary position Gallimard occupies before the veil, clutching at the lure, the luminous shadow of Song. Gallimard will travel along the trajectory of his gaze, as he repeatedly performs an astonishing imaginative feat of 'seeing as' guided by Song, whose private sexual performances are no less calibrated than her stage turns (as she has occasion to explain to Madame Chin, her espionage 'control'). Gallimard's seeing the man Song as 'My Butterfly' – misrecognizing the art work Song makes for him – is, then, anything but compact or exulting, but rather a distended, tortured obsessive-repetition. The effect of Cronenberg's filmic serialism is, then, finally to articulate Gallimard's experience formally as the masochist's endless waiting for the blow to fall.

Song's indignant initial cautions to Gallimard begin by signalling to us – and finish by explaining to us – that this Butterfly knows that performativity is a fatal strategy. The fatal rapture the plot unfolds proves to be Gallimard's, not Song's. This fatal performativity is the film's prime and focal mutation; its tightly bound primary focus, however, is Gallimard's enraptured gaze, then despairing solipsism. The logic of the interaction is worked over numerous times, without suspense or much hesitation and, before the film ends, with Gallimard reconstructing 'My Butterfly' in prison before a rapt audience of fellow inmates. The obsession has become the delusional madness concluding in suicide. Lovingly dressing himself, applying grossly overdone make-up as he ritually recites a version of his first, blurted declaration to Song, he finishes by slashing his throat with his make-up mirror, uttering the words: 'I am Rene Gallimard ... also known as Madame Butterfly.'

Other contemporary filmic 'deconstructions' of operas place a different emphasis, on *narrative* rather than performativity. It is, for example, the object of Sally Potter's film *Thriller* (1979). Using back-projection excerpts and soundtrack collage, Potter conflates another Puccini opera, *La bohème*, with Alfred Hitchcock's *Psycho* (1960) and purposely mixes the music scores of each. Bernard Herrmann's *Psycho* score is famous for the mimetic slasher effects of strings that accompany the film's shower murder of Marion Crane. The further effect, amplified by editing in the shower sequence, is to make it seem as if the filmic apparatus itself – rather than the Mother / Norman Bates character – is murdering the heroine. The *Psycho* interruptions assaulting Puccini's arias in *Thriller* are very dissonant. They are also clearly didactic: the 'classic arts' (Puccini) and 'classical cinema' (Hitchcock) are to be regarded as the same – their plots kill their heroines. What differentiates them is merely cosmetic, an aesthetic attitude. Potter makes this argument at Puccini's expense no less than Hitchcock's. In making this argument, *Thriller* incorporates Laura Mulvey's feminist film theory (1975) into the monologues written for Potter's Mimi, whose role here is ruminative and retrospective rather than dramatic. Mimi is looking back on her story from beyond the grave, and mediates it equipped with the thesis that classical narratives murder women. Already dead and existing as *Thriller*'s hypodiegetic exegete and narrator, Mimi investigates her own case and Marion's and deduces that they were murdered by the same patriarchal drive of narrative art. Mulvey argues that classical narrative channels unconscious castration anxiety, invariably prompted by screen images of a woman, or at least those the camera privileges by emphatic framing or accentuated shifts in pacing. Woman as anxious object of the camera's gaze is modulated into pleasure through the ways narrative links up with masculine sadistic drives. Mulvey proposes a range of narrative exigencies to express this sadism. Besides an obvious sadistic result of narrative's psychoanalytic economy such as the bloody murder one finds in thrillers like *Psycho*, there is a symmetrical strategy of 'overvaluation' of the image of women in melodramas and musicals. Cults glorify the screen image of the female stars – movie divas like Garbo or Dietrich. *Thriller* conflates both strategies of classical narrative and finds their joint source in opera. Potter's Mimi is at once overvalued opera diva and murder victim, simultaneously adored and sadistically killed.

Anyone accepting this feminist theory could pursue *Madama Butterfly*'s connection to the movies by investigating the same issues of classical narrative in this opera as well. This is not, however, the way Hwang-Cronenberg's *M. Butterfly* proceeds. *M. Butterfly* twists away a bit from the economy of classical narration and towards the excessive repetitions of serialism as well as towards stylized performativity. However, to grasp the mutation Cronenberg effects, there is some need to track diverse senses of 'classic' that pertain to opera and to *Madama Butterfly*, and to cinema in terms of performativity as well as narrative.

At its better-known intersections with film culture, opera plays a familiar symbolic role of cultural or canonical 'classic.' For modern European art cinema, and particularly for German and Italian directors, opera serves as a symbol of national history. Fassbinder, Kluge, and Syberberg among German directors have consistently used German opera as a cultural symbol of Germany. Italian operas figure similarly in many of Visconti's films, and several of Bertolucci's (Landy 107–50). This notion of 'the classic' or 'classical' in European national cultures exemplified by European filmmakers' allusions to opera cannot be developed here. It is introduced just to suggest the sense of a cultural ideal, one associated with tradition, the past, taste, and high or at least bourgeois art, in order that it be distinguished from the practical notions of 'classical' as a set of formal attributes, among them narrative norms, shared by various genres and media, including the novel, theatre, and narrative films. This practical sense of classical pervades film criticism.

It comes as a bit of a shock to recall that Puccini's *Madama Butterfly* belongs not to some distant past of canonical great classics but to the era of early modernism and the birth of twentieth-century popular culture. Its composition and early performances are contemporary with Paul Cézanne's *Apples, Bottle, and the Back of a Chair* (1902–6), Arnold Schoenberg's *Verklärte Nacht* (1899), Picasso's 'Rose Period' (1904–6), and Freud's *The Interpretation of Dreams* (1900). Its initial career overlaps the first exhibition of the Fauves (1905) and the first phase of film production and exhibition (1896–1906). Moreover, Puccini derived his opera from modern stories, not from folkloric or classical sources. John Luther Long's *Madame Butterfly* adapted the first Butterfly story, by Julien Viaud (writing as Pierre Loti), *Madame Chrysanthème*, in 1898 and, in 1900, David Belasco staged it with great success. Puccini encountered Belasco's version, and remade it into his opera. By 1915, the year Mary Pickford starred in Sidney Olcott's *Madame Butterfly*, the first film adaptation, the opera was already firmly established as the canonical version of the Butterfly story (Browne 230–1).

It was the narrative and performative techniques of Belasco more than Puccini's operatic staging that mattered to ambitious filmmaking in 1915 and that shaped what film critics regard as an emergent 'classical' narrative film form. The adaptation belonged to a period when developing cinematic codes drew from naturalistic theatre. The Pickford-Olcott *Madame Butterfly* did not pretend to be a filmed opera. Browne is thorough in explaining the consequences (233–5), noting that the filmmakers went back to Long's version, but that they seem to have done so with an eye to obtaining useable equivalents to the opera. The characterization of Pickford's protagonist, for example, relied on Puccini's ennobilized Butterfly and not her more feckless prose precursors, if we accept the judgement of Gina Marchetti, who writes, 'Puccini is credited with taking the pathetic story of a simple, ignorant girl, treated as a doll-like object speaking comically mangled English in the short story and the play, and turning it into grand tragedy with Butterfly as the noble defender of her honor brought down by the cruelties of her fate' (80). Marchetti's *Romance and the Yellow Peril* is a critique of the ways Asians are represented across a range of Hollywood films. She seeks to show that modern Western colonialism permeates the literary and theatrical versions of the Butterfly story, the opera, the Pickford-Olcott *Madame Butterfly*, and other related films. Not unlike Potter, Marchetti takes classical narrative as a whole to be a guise for imperialist ideology. So, the Butterfly figure carries 'colonialism' and 'racism' and 'Orientalism' in all its manifestations despite variants in plotting, style, or medium.

The year of the Olcott-Pickford *Butterfly*, 1915, is also the year of D.W. Griffith's *The Birth of a Nation*. The connection between Belasco and Griffith is, for film historians, so strong that it gave rise to the cliché that Griffith was the Belasco of the movies. Pivoted on 1915, the period of *The Birth of a Nation* marks a moment in which American film, which had struggled for recognition as a respectable entertainment, was now succeeding in becoming an equivalent to mainstream realistic theatre (Gunning 31–56, 151–87; May 43–95). A leader in this theatre, Belasco staged his *Madame Butterfly* within the realist mode associated with his name. The prestige of that representational system forms the direct link between Belasco and Griffith rather than the array of specific techniques that did, in fact, join them. Griffith, and not he alone, strove for the better part of a decade to bend film towards theatre's perceived capabilities, and these, in the main, may be boiled down to 'character psychology,' or how to represent the traits, motives, and emotional aura of a stage protagonist. It was this psychological capacity of theatre that gave it its surest respectability, and it was a capacity that ambitious filmmakers of the period were especially bent to achieve, in the absence of the spoken (or sung) word.

The link is relevant to the Olcott-Pickford *Butterfly*. Although it was in many respects typical of its period, the size of the production notwithstanding, rather than a solitary masterpiece, Griffith's *Birth of a Nation*'s extraordinary success marked a quantum leap in the reputation of

American narrative cinema by demonstrating that movies could now performatively and narratively approximate theatre's levels of character psychology and, therefore, undertake the thematic seriousness that theatre represented. While knockabout comedies, Westerns, and chase films still abound in 1915, a star like Pickford could now essay adaptations of *Madama Butterfly* with less fear of reprimand from the cultured than she might have five, even three, years before. More than the rise of 'Hollywood' (which signifies an industrial set-up), the achievement of formal norms in narrative filmmaking practices marked the birth of what critics now regularly refer to as 'classical' narrative cinema.

Part of the shock of matching the late date of Puccini's *Madama Butterfly* in its status as a European classic to such developments as these is that the opera feels as distant from the birth of the mass art of movies as it does from *The Interpretation of Dreams*. Puccini's opera *is* a modern artefact; yet, the high-culture penumbra around it successfully rendered it then and now a timeless legend. This is perhaps why critical analysis of the opera in terms of late-nineteenth-century imperialism seems a more bracing sort of defamation than, say, renewed attack on *The Birth of a Nation*'s racism or excoriation of *Psycho*'s misogyny. Critics unhesitatingly call the opera 'tragic,' even those who defame it. Opera gathers this remarkable exalted atmosphere by *not* conceding anything essential to a theatrical realism like Belasco's. The accomplishment of Griffith and his colleagues was oddly symmetrical: to have absorbed Belasco's theatre into a style of filmmaking soon to supersede Belasco's style of theatre in an emerging popular culture is to have made film the polar opposite of opera, namely, the most modern medium and genre. The capacity of opera utterly to resist realist theatre and then to ignore cinema is a great part of the genius of its culture and the maintenance of its semblance as a classical form, at least within the European ethos. This is a genius for the ideal of classicism in the midst of modernity, and it is a genius, one hastens to declare, that film has never possessed.

'Mutation,' as I have used it as a metaphor in discussing *M. Butterfly*, implies organicism and this can be misleading. Film is only in the rarest of instances able to claim an organic spirit of form. But organicism is an extraordinarily powerful concept attached to ideas of classicism and Romanticism alike. The efforts critics have made in excavating the gestation of *Madama Butterfly* serve to show that the opera was never in the manner of classical art organic but offered just a semblance of organicism. Scholars press ideological critiques by building a textual genealogy to dissolve the semblance and with it the sense of the Butterfly figure and her accompanying musical articulation as classical work. The specific consequences for *Madama Butterfly* are that it becomes, under such critique, a modern construct. Once exposed critically this way, the analysis also exposes the opera as a caricature proclaiming colonialist ideology that is only masquerading behind a classicist aesthetic and its terms of timeless tragedy, its aspect of organic form, as well as the loveliness of its musical organization. The Butterfly figure stands revealed always as a cobbled-together Orientalist stereotype, and these critics show that stereotype to be ideologically overdetermined by a modern code belonging to the imperialist backstage whatever elan its manifestation as opera possesses.

The mutations of Hwang's *M. Butterfly* do not work, then, on any truly organic substance, for there is none inside *Madama Butterfly*. Hwang's play works on the construct, seeing it as an ideological contraption that the play goes about stripping down and rebuilding into another machine to expose the opera's feints and seductions. The result is that Hwang replies to the opera with a post-Brechtian, postmodern contraption of his own. The scholars' criticism of the opera is understandably the same in Song Liling's denunciation to Gallimard in the speeches that Hwang's 'deconstruction' supplies to the character. The play is born of contemporary scholarship and it never ceases to talk of the *modern* Western symbolic projection of Oriental woman.

What is 'deconstructed' is the symbol's classical and legendary reputation. In effect, Butterfly's character seems, under such critical scrutiny, never to be mutating in later revisions – like Hwang's play – from some organic basic original. The truth of Marchetti's denunciation of the precursor stories and the successive films indicates that the opera itself condenses but does not correct or transform its sources. This is a critical position that Hwang has, for example, put to work in his play in the irony of his historical reverse-telescoping.

Now, though a source of particular indignation to the critics who denounce it, such an ideological coding process is not unique to *Madama Butterfly*. It is wholly characteristic of modern cultural artefacts whenever they seek the pretence of a classicism – not the least Hollywood movies. Capitalist modernity requires the appearance of cultural continuity and that continuity is an ideological project. (For that reason, modern popular and middlebrow culture provokes the response of modernism and all its projects of unmasking and parodying and excoriation.) Nevertheless, as some contemporary criticism confirms, with the very vehemence of its denunciations of works like *Madama Butterfly*, the powerful effect of the code is to have arrested the flow of its historical sources in lasting form. The ideological demand for the appearance of cultural continuity has, in fact, been met. *Madama Butterfly* will continue to survive all its critiques and its 'deconstruction.' The proper effect of an appealing semblance of 'organic' works regarded as classics is to remain durably persuasive. Puccini brought off this proper effect by arresting the historical and ideological process generating the Butterfly figure and giving it a persuasive form and classic shape. That matter was settled before the First World War and has endured since; all the recent defamation has not affected the opera's reputation. And so, perverse variants like the film of *M. Butterfly* do, therefore, appear as *late* mutations, and in a curious way Cronenberg seems bent on a perverse kind of homage to the truth that his film cannot damage *Madama Butterfly*.

The critiques of *Madama Butterfly*, like Hwang's and Marchetti's, are largely denunciations of the opera's story material. The forces of analysis could be turned another way towards performance and characterization. Indeed, opera seems to oblige us to do so and, then, we speak differently of 'legends.' In early cinema, the 'legendary' takes on a peculiar but useful parallel meaning. There was a period of filmmaking, between about 1900 and 1910, when the plots of most films were already widely known before the films appeared. Noel Burch speaks of such films as confirmatory rituals 'predicated upon the knowledge of the audience' (97). Period films appeared against a popular-culture background characterized by adaptations, excerpts, and replications across media. The syntax of such films as Porter's *Uncle Tom's Cabin* (1903) was a concatenation of tableaux that ritualized the story and the character as static pictures. Porter's film did not narrate, as later films do, indeed as his *The Great Train Robbery* (also 1903) had begun to do. It was not a lack of technique but a choice conditioned by the legendary stature of the *Uncle Tom's Cabin* text that shaped Porter's film. Such a relation of legendary story materials to films is even better known in the genres of opera and ballet. In these musical forms, too, the narrative arrives before us as already familiar, as legend in the sense of a tale that everyone knows. Such a story is never authored in this film, or opera, or ballet, but only rendered once again. All storytelling in these forms is, or is made to seem, a retelling. The actual age or provenance of the story material hardly matters provided the transformation into film, opera, or ballet succeeds, as Puccini succeeded with *Madama Butterfly*.

Examples from early cinema attest that the legend does not have to touch the narrative form for the material to be effective. A certain primitivism serves as well as sophistication. Operas notoriously narrate weakly, deploy story material using outlandish plot contrivances, and rely on tableau forms of narration (rather like early cinema). Operas have continued to use these primitive forms successfully well past the rise of naturalistic theatre. Why does a legend persuasively endure as classic in operas and not in other media and genres like Griffith's silent films or Belasco's realist theatre? The familiar answer is 'the music,' whose sophistication vastly surpasses operatic narration. The asymmetry between operatic dramatic narration and its musical narration is crucial to opera's cultural position. Now, it is through music that opera imparts its very full character psychology. The centre of its classicism is performance, the singer's voice, which equals and often exceeds the power of the dramatic actor's psychological effect. The fabled silliness of opera plotting hardly matters, for it is performative extravagance that holds its power. Of *Madama Butterfly* Browne writes:

> It is operatic form, a certain combination of drama and symphonic music that lifts the story from potential melodrama to high art. It is precisely the operatic idealization of this suicide, turning suicide into a sacrifice that enables the story to transcend its realistic foundations. The medium for this transvaluation of source materials, including the conduct of Pinkerton, is the opera's intensity of emotion ... It is not discourse, but the order of affect – its intensity, range, and scale – that legitimates operatic form. (245)

In opera primitive narration suits the sense of the legendary better than the sophisticated, and is cultivated without apology and without tending to the realist narrativization that films sought in theatre during the era of Griffith and Pickford. That suitability seals operas' claims to classicism even in the case of so modern a work as *Madama Butterfly*. When cinema arrogated for itself realist theatre devices and the long era of so-called 'classical' cinema began, it traded one cultural sense of classical for another formal and pragmatic one. In a linear and parallel mode of narration, which the cinema rigorously pursued under Griffith's leadership, plotting is filled out horizontally using montage and other devices that could isolate an actor's performance and insert it into an artificial, narrativized space and narrated temporality. The classical cinema is the achievement of that horizontalizing of form, of filling out a story narratively. The parcelling of cinematic space entailed by editing permitted the rise of psychological characterization, notable for its absence in early cinema's tableau staging no less than was articulated plotting. In opera, narrative is extended differently – one might say vertically – retaining the tableau form (well after it was abandoned by theatre) and expanding its representational volume with the singer's *voice*, with all that we consider operatic performativity. Hence, the retention of the tableau as a staging form means something different from the backwardness it did in film plotting after about 1910. The grandeur of opera is performed, which is to say sung, characterizations, which assume a pride of place that completely overshadows the need for linear narrating. Opera's assumption that its stories are already legendary – even ones of so recent a vintage as Butterfly – consisting of already known material, is intensified and enlarged by heightened pathos, and the concomitant dignity of characterization possesses an affective energy that cinema scarcely ever approximates. All this is obvious to those who know opera, but it bears recalling in order to mark a moment *before* the historic deviations of cinema from the tableau staging it briefly shared with opera – let us say, in 1904 – and to help grasp a subsequent parallel between them.

Marchetti's reading of the Olcott-Pickford *Madame Butterfly* peruses a consequence of such a contrast and comparison. First, as mentioned earlier, Marchetti's textual genealogy of *Madame Butterfly* leads her directly to defame the opera and its film versions together because they all 'represent Japan as a fragile, powerless woman, who cannot resist the attractions of the West, but who self-destructs as a consequence' (80). For Marchetti there is an ideological system of representations that always *is* 'Madame Butterfly,' and it is Western colonialist racism that is, in its every manifestation, to be exposed as the genetic code (or ideological blueprint, rather) of the Butterfly myth. But this denunciation is the obverse of the opera's effect: it's always an already-known modern colonialist text because it is an already-known legendary tragedy. She adds, '[T]he preponderance of Butterfly stories fails to provide the reader or viewer with a clear moral focus since they depict the heroine as a fool and the hero as a cad' (81). As we have seen, the principal departure for *M. Butterfly*'s mutations arises from taking advantage of the problem of a fuzzy moral focus, which only points out how remarkably easily positions are flipped: Gallimard becomes the fool, and Song the 'cad' of the encounter. But then Marchetti says something else about the Pickford *Butterfly*:

> [T]he Pickford persona ... brought the character down from its associations with Puccini and grand, operatic tragedy into the world of Pickford's

working-class heroines. If anything, Pickford's Butterfly mediates between these two extremes by emphasizing the sentimental aspects of the character. Neither too grand nor too lowly, the Pickford Butterfly can function as a flexible point of identification for the star's primarily female middle and working-class fans. (83)

In this remark Marchetti suggests that the film enacts a new sort of 'neither-nor' identification, still to be condemned for lack of moral focus, however. The issue for her is the representation of *character*, or rather how character is inhabited by a star persona. Pickford's Butterfly is neither Loti's doll-like fool nor Puccini's exalted tragic heroine. This 'neither-nor' novelty of the film hinges on Pickford's repeatable character, which is also an abstract one – for that is what a movie star was already becoming, a repeatable abstract character. I would like to extend Marchetti's remark slightly by drawing on Miriam Hansen's analysis of the rise of classical film narrative and its effects on characterization. Hansen argues that early American cinema was socially specific in its depictions. In offering recognizable points of identification for viewers, the films communicated that specificity in terms of class, gender, and ethnicity. The figures appearing on screen are not at all nuanced psychologically (tableau imaging precludes it), but are immediately recognizable in terms of class and ethnicity. The films addressed viewers in their concrete social position: the viewer took a stance from his or her class or ethnic or gender position towards the characters. However, one of the costs of the maturing narrativity of American filmmaking was the deracination and denaturalization of screen characters in the manner they set points of identification for viewers. This shifting of cinematic address, for Hansen, distinguishes classical film narrative.

Her example is a transitional work, *Musketeers of Pig Alley* (1912), directed by D.W. Griffith. The film concerns the travails experienced by an unnamed Girl (played by Lillian Gish) and her fiancé in the midst of a minor gang war on the ethnically mixed Lower East Side of New York. *Musketeers* has often been praised for its early street realism and moral tolerance. Critics usually suggest that the director was appealing to a working-class clientele. Hansen, however, argues that 'Griffith projects an audience already removed from the social environment the film purports to represent, to whom he tenders picturesque values' ('Early' 229). The slums become an exotic locale; most of the characters marked by class are ethnically exotic specimens and with respect to the plot so minor as to be regarded as part of the scenery. The exception, Lillian

Gish, the film's star, manifests the distinction between performers possessed of psychological persona and those relegated largely to the *mise-en-scène*. Viewers are invited to identify with the Girl through 'the narrating gaze' (*Babel* 75) and with no one else. The Girl is not, however, *socially* kin with the viewer, for she has no particular social or ethnic identity. The intimacy the viewer shares with her as the fulcrum of the narrative is abstract. Her character psychology is a formal-performative effect. The Girl passes through the socially detailed milieu, but her subjectivity is not *of* that social or ethnic milieu. Hansen concludes that films like *Musketeers of Pig Alley* 'advance a process by which empirical spectators were to be transformed into the meta-spectator constructed by the classical text' ('Early' 229). That is, viewers leave their own social, ethnic, and gender identity and assume an abstract identification with the character, which is likewise abstracted into an order of sentiments and vicissitudes detached from the social setting. The early-cinema figure, a non-psychological but pointedly socio-ethnic character, now becomes a psychologically detailed 'meta-character.' This is the consequence of the meeting of a new mode of performativity and a developing film form that soon constitutes the 'movie star' and the classical narrative together. Its initial and practical purpose was to provide movies with a gentility acceptable to bourgeois taste – the movie star will always implicitly be middle class even when playing a character who is not – and the early American film industry was very conscious of that purpose. The consequent process, of viewer–character co-positioning in American cinema, begins to mature around 1912 and its narrative sophistication comes to entail a tremendous social abstraction. 'By taking class out of the working class and ethnic difference out of the immigrant,' Hansen concludes, 'the universal-language metaphor became a code-word for broadening the mass-cultural base of motion pictures in accordance with middle-class values and sensibilities' (*Babel* 78). In other words, films enter their own peculiar order of classicism, and legends will now be made *inside* the films that depict them – and not drawn from the audience's pre-knowledge. The stars are born who are characters in a much fuller affective and psychological sense, which is also an abstract sense that, once it has become successfully repeatable and famous and popular enough, renders the star a legend and imparts a legendary quality to many (though not all) the characters the star plays.

By 1915, and Pickford's *Madame Butterfly*, the process has already become part of the star system, and the legend of Mary Pickford – 'America's Sweetheart' – explains why the 'neither-nor' feature of this

Butterfly effects a revision of both its literary antecedents and of Puccini all at once. Butterfly becomes Pickford's already-legendary persona *plus* the legend canonized by Puccini. The 1915 film becomes classical like the opera, though by entirely different American filmic ways and means, and in a somewhat different and decidedly popular sense.

Now, we should perhaps apply this claim interpretively. The word that Marchetti, and other critics, use for the opera is 'tragedy.' The context of her argument suggests that by 'tragedy' she means the exalted performance of suffering. But is *Madama Butterfly* a tragedy? I don't believe so, nor does Marchetti when she actually conducts her analyses; nor do other critics, like Heung, who is explicit about calling it 'melodrama.' What is at stake in melodrama is bourgeois sentimentalism: the internalization of a morality without foundation in a character's material reality. *Madama Butterfly* is such a case of misrecognition on the part of its protagonist about her actual situation. The tragic hero is, in contrast, defined by recognition. His/her pathos concerns the impossibility of his/her situation being otherwise and of the hero recognizing that. It is not primarily subjectivity that is at issue in tragedy, but what the protagonist *is*, by fate, or by a collision of ethical imperatives, as is the epigonic heroine of the type, Antigone. Butterfly is not doomed by gods or even by the collision of cultures, as Browne shows us. Instead, the Butterfly legend is typical of a modern melodrama in serving a sentimental spiritual economy whose predominant form is the creation of imaginary subjectivity. In the modern drama of subjectivity, the protagonist becomes the contradiction whose necessity is not ontologically grounded, as it is in tragedy, but is contrived by narrative. This is why the villains of such narratives no longer partake of the nature of *nemesis* or moral evil, but are morally idiotic. They are hypocrites, carriers of false values and pointless cruelties against natural sincerity. Few characters are more obviously a villain of this modern melodramatic kind than Pinkerton is. In the opera, he serves principally to set the terms of the heroine's expectant solitude. While awaiting his return, she achieves the full extent of imaginary subjectivity and in doing so she misrecognizes her actual situation for the realm of sentiment. Butterfly internalizes a Christian-Romantic imaginary in an act of self-creation and this leads to her suffering and downfall. She is already an internal exile from her traditional social position when the opera begins, for she is an orphan, her exile effected by her father's prior suicide. The Western Christian-Romantic values she embraces do not exist in the opera, except in her imagination, which permits her to become a subjectivity. She misrecognizes these values as real and available to her, but does not thereby misrecognize herself. The melodramatic-sentimental code permits her an exalted authenticity that means, despite her real circumstances, that she recognizes herself. This is why a significant portion of the opera is devoted to her religious debate with the Bonze, her uncle and Shinto priest, over the propriety of her Christian marriage. Her misrecognition of that event, which is a fraud, is one of the occasions for her pathos and dignity as a subject to arise. These passages of the opera originate from her being a self-created subject. Sentimentally, *we* recognize that Christian righteousness and Romantic love, by their nature, should be extended to everyone, whereas none of the villains in the opera share that recognition, which is why they are villains.

The opera is in this sense of its expressive form a modern-bourgeois allegorical tale of imaginary subjectivity – and not a timeless classic. Its modernity is one whose inner dynamic of imaginary self-making was Flaubert's favoured analytical subject, as in *Madame Bovary*. Imaginary subjectivity is the controlling Romantic myth subtending the themes of the organic. In the ethics of the bourgeois Victorian era this passes for classicism, and this is the era in which Puccini's opera is rooted. One hardly need add that *Madama Butterfly* is innocent of Flaubert's corrosive ironies about that myth or that the culture of opera tends to ignore the techniques of modern-bourgeois norms that subtend its melodramatics. Quite the opposite, Puccini's *Butterfly* manifests the dignity of the bourgeois subject as if she were a chastely classic-tragic heroine, like Antigone, and she embodies these values, imaginary or not, impossible or not, and the opera vilifies Pinkerton not as the colonialist carrier of these values but as their betrayer. The sadism of the opera's cruel articulations cannot diminish the dignity of the heroine's delusion, but expands and exalts it sentimentally through the performance of her suffering. The question that is inevitably to be raised is whether this conception would be possible were Butterfly not constructed as a Japanese woman whose imagination is itself composed to be innocent of ironies and, in consequence, helplessly sincere in her misrecognition. It is clearly this feature of the opera that especially arouses the indignation of critics who seek to unmask, among other things, the heroine's dignity and glory.

Marchetti makes the important point that the Olcott film, while *denaturing* Butterfly's Japanese-ness performatively (as Hansen's analysis would lead us to expect), builds up the role of Adelaide, Pinkerton's wife, in order to substantiate Christian values to Butterfly's disadvantage. As a Japanese woman, she can never embody these values and be a proper mother. In other words, the film expands upon the opera's second Western figure as a morally authoritative one in the register of maternal femininity. The villain Pinkerton has an authentically virtuous sidekick, the Western and Christian wife and mother, and this shifts the axis of the film's sentimentality. Now, since Butterfly cannot really embody Christian-Romantic values or assume the righteous form of motherhood, the film recasts the racist colonialism of the pre-Puccini sources more openly as the heroine's delusion, which Marchetti calls her 'excess.' In the opera, the same subtheme is operative, but Butterfly's pathos arises from the nobility of her great mistake, for she does indeed embody Christian-Romantic values in the grandeur of her solitude. It is those values failing her, not her failure to embody them, much less her 'excess' in being delusional, that leads her to catastrophe.

All this brings us close to Hansen's reading of the transition to classical cinema, which concerns how a character emerges from a socially abstracted situation to stand in relief against its *mise-en-scène* to become a legendary, because an imaginary, subjectivity. While the cinema does not express this process in a performative register remotely as compelling as the diva's voice, films manage a comparable effect through an array of technical usages the chief of which is the close-up, an especially privileged domain in silent film virtually owned by the first female stars, like Gish and Pickford, and then by the close-up's concluding apotheosis, Garbo. Personality in cinema, too, becomes the recognized site of an interior drama, always created by the classic film text itself in offering the complete and self-contained narrative of that subjectivity's drama.

M. Butterfly seems to puncture this melodramatic classicism by inversion, by moving Gallimard from the powerful Western starting position of erotic predator projecting onto Song a tragic romance. But Cronenberg's adaptation makes it now Gallimard who misrecognizes material reality – that Song is a man, a Maoist spy, a performer of femininity. The 'deconstructive' *M. Butterfly* perverts the lack of moral focus that Marchetti discusses in the opera. Puccini's Butterfly mostly speaks in Pinkerton's absence, and in so doing, constantly speaks of herself. And in any case, an aria is close kin to the soliloquy. The opera is a drama of interiority. So is, in its way, Gallimard's inversion, given his solipsism, an interior drama. However, Song is always there, the lure of the feminine, and not-there, not a real woman; this is a different and perverse version of

Marchetti's 'neither-nor.' When in the opera Pinkerton's absence becomes Butterfly's final loss of him, the vacuity of all she loves and esteems is exposed with disastrous results. The opera is based on a single subjectivity held in suspense between two positions, her imaginary one and the material one. It is for this reason that the meanings the legendary character Butterfly represents are all-important, and why her Japanese-ness vis-à-vis Western-ness is critically at issue. The critical excavation of the political codes behind that suspension that the play *M. Butterfly* articulates leads to corroding the legendary subjectivity of the character to expose its codes of imaginary subjectivity as well. The film wants to unmask the real question of how Butterfly is allowed to be suspended this way. The film's answer takes the obvious form of another question: What happens if Pinkerton-Gallimard is the one torturously suspended? The film elaborates this question through its serial form, which eventually serves to keep Gallimard hanging in masochistic desperation. The short answer, which we have already given, with Chow, is pathology. In Cronenberg's handling of *mise-en-scène*, of point-of-view, of close-ups, and of Song's voice, the ravaged Gallimard is no longer an exalted subjectivity but a pathological solipsist and an obsessive erotomaniac. The longer answer and its political meaning will, in *M. Butterfly*, involve a grotesque erotic mutation of the classic legend, and Gallimard will be the one obsessed, to the point of introjecting the Butterfly persona, a considerable mutation of Cio-Cio-San's self-imagining through Christian and Romantic ideals of love. In returning the opera to its genetic source, namely imperialist racism, this way, the film reverses the erotics of colonialist ideology and thereby batters Puccini's classicism. The disillusioned end of modernity, incarnated in Maoist China and the Vietnam War, does not readily fold into legend.

Some aspects of the mutation have been simple to describe because they involve direct substitutions and reversals: the film's use of a man in the Butterfly role, Puccini's *Madama Butterfly* as intertext and matrix of seduction, returning to the Orient in the era of the Vietnam War. Other aspects are not so easily described. *M. Butterfly* has its *two* characters play out the drama over again as self-conscious performance. It unmasks the older exalted drama as misrecognition, now on the part of the Westerner. Instead of Romanticism and Christianity, Gallimard is possessed by a private erotic cult of *Madama Butterfly* itself that Song has brought down from the opera stage into the sexual encounter, where Song has re-reconstructed Butterfly's sentimental exaltation for Gallimard as a perverse eroticism, built out of the performative codes of Orientalist transvestite femininity. At the espionage trial, Song answers the prosecutor's question of how Gallimard never recognized he was not a woman with 'He was very responsive to my ancient Oriental ways of love all of which I invented myself just for him.' Cronenberg retains much of the romance of the story in mutated form by redistributing the gender-image of the Butterfly figure to a man who is fragile, fascinated, and self-absorbed. Cronenberg thereby perversely unmasks sentimental misrecognition and imaginary subjectivity as an *erotic* problem, degrading melodrama's sentiment into Gallimard's pathology. The dramatic reversal is itself simple: initially the cruel master, Gallimard becomes the masochist, while Song's passivity becomes cool sexual control. But when he discovers that Song is a man and an agent (of the newly masculinized Orient of Maoism), the reversal becomes the catastrophe, for Gallimard convulsively absorbs the Butterfly role into himself and then commits suicide. The gloried solitude of Cio-Cio-San becomes the squalid staged transvestism of Gallimard, whose identity has come to utter ruin.

Now having become the Pinkerton of the tale, Song returns home to China, a point that Cronenberg accents by breaking with his serialism and into the only extended piece of cross-cutting in the film, showing Song on a flight home and Gallimard in prison. A Butterfly-like biography of sorts has been given Song: Song's father has been destroyed before the film has opened, and Song is now contracted to be seducer; the opera's Suzuki becomes the sexless Maoist Comrade Chin. When Song's role is completed, 'he' (now in a suit) may still desire to be Gallimard's lover, but there is nothing left of the Frenchman for Song to love, or of Song's impersonation for Gallimard to love. The prospect of erotic rapprochement has dissolved along with its imaginary 'seeing as.' In the unmasked encounter in a French police van, Song's removal of his man's suit and his offer in love of his naked 'me' are the final trauma to be inflicted on the broken Gallimard.

The scene is the inverted equivalent of Pinkerton's catastrophic return in act 2 of the opera, which entails the revelation of Butterfly's material, which to say, actual situation. I do not accept the view of the film that Song is powerfully affected by the affair with Gallimard. Hwang does. Despite the scene in the police van when Song declares that he is the same person ('It was always me'), the shots of him on the plane represent him as the new Pinkerton, perhaps regretful but unbroken. Cronenberg shoots the van scene flatly and Lone performs it coolly. But a persuasive solution to the problem in Hwang's script with respect to this scene eludes the director. Hwang's didactic intention here is humanistic and sentimental, but it is really too late for Song's unmasking to save Gallimard. Hwang has Song make an appeal for human recognition of the Chinese man behind the Orientalist feminine image. Gallimard's failure to recognize Song in his real person – as a homosexual man – means, to Hwang, the moral failure of the West, still, to recognize the common humanity of the Other. As Chow remarks generally, 'For Hwang, the significance of the fantasy is that of a content that needs to be changed; it needs to be changed because, by using people as objects and things, fantasy dehumanizes them' ('Dream' 66). In contrast, Cronenberg has invested so much in Gallimard's erotic pathology, a mutation on imaginary subjectivity, that he has left the character no capacity for recognition.[7] Further humanistic critique of this kind, by the end of the film, is beside the point. Cronenberg treats the passage, as does Irons's performance, as the trauma that breaks him – breaks his imaginative construct – and this goes against Hwang's intentions. It is the recurring pattern of Cronenberg's films that there is never a natural or authentic humanity behind the deformative projection; desire and fantasy in Cronenberg truly transform and there is no going back to some original self. This is why Gallimard's misrecognition is not made pathetic as a moral falling short, but is rendered grotesque, a subject burst open by mutation for critical scrutiny. The film's dialogue, which keeps talking about the myth of the 'Oriental woman' long after the first sequences discussed above, fills the textual volume of *M. Butterfly* with ideological criticism in place of a heroine's arias. Criticism of the kind discussed at some length here, in effect, fills the film's semantic space. The film's world is, in consequence, an enervated world having no vigour and no spiritual generosity to donate to imagination and the misrecognitions that a bourgeois melodramatic imaginary subjectivity requires. They become delusions and fodder for mania, the grotesque version of performativity, and these *M. Butterfly* delights in making its raison d'être. We are in the end game of bourgeois subjectivity, though not yet outside it.

Notes

1 The play is not another adaptation of the Butterfly tale, but uses its narrative material and its stereotypes to shape story material that Hwang drew upon from a real news item concerning the peculiar case of a French diplomat, Bernard Bouriscot, who was convicted of espionage for turning over sensitive doc-

uments to a Chinese spy. The spy was a man with whom Bouriscot had been having an affair for twenty years in the belief that his lover was a woman. He was a transvestite performer with the Beijing Opera. See Beard 338–9 and Hwang (1989) 95–6.

2 Hwang's play makes its critique of the opera as if the Butterfly figure were a unique construction of the West. However, examples of the passive, indeed sacrificial, woman destroyed by political machinations abound in Asian drama. Critically reflective recent Asian films that develop this figure in interesting ways include the Japanese director Ichikawa's *An Actor's Revenge* and the Chinese director Chen's *Farewell My Concubine*. Both films place transvestite opera performers at their centres, and both deploy available transvestite Butterfly-like codes in this Asian performance tradition. These are aesthetic codes for the actors who deploy them, here the protagonists, but they are also erotic codes to those male patrons who, in both films, consume the performances and then seek to possess the performers sexually. The disjuncture between these types of codes is put to great dramatic use in these films. Although they are such committed transvestites as to be ambiguous in their masculinity, the actor-heroes display stubborn strength, while the films' arrogant consumers of spectacle, erotic fantasy, even presumptively of the bodies of the actor-heroes, prove to be fatally weak men.

3 Unlike Chow, Beard takes the view that the play resists Cronenberg and the film is an oddity – and hence a failure – among the director's adaptations, which include works by William Burroughs, Stephen King, and J.G. Ballard. Although Beard is an adamant and unreconstructed auteurist in writing *The Artist as Monster*, and accordingly presses the case for a thematically unified Cronenberg, his view that *M. Butterfly* is an anomolous Cronenberg film was shared by most film critics, who simply take the play and the film director as a bad match.

4 Icy precision is Cronenberg's other métier, as can be seen in even such baroque horror pieces of his as *Dead Ringers* or *Videodrome*, where formal precision reins grotesque spectacle and channels it precisely. Later, in fact in the films starting with *M. Butterfly*, Cronenberg has become more and more an intimate formalist. The trend climaxes in his recent *Spider*.

5 Indeed, not unlike Max Renn's solipsistic relationship with 'Videodrome' in the film of that name, which in fact is preceded by him staring at a set of stills from a Japanese porno film of an Asian woman in traditional costume being taken sexually from behind.

6 I am drawing here loosely on Gilles Deleuze's (1971) account of masochism and on Gaylyn Studlar's (1988) application of it to film analysis.

7 See Chow ('Dream') further, 87–8, in which she explains the scene in Lacanian terms and recuperates 'this tragic moment' from Hwang's didactic humanism: 'Song, by the very gesture of understanding with which he tries to regain Gallimard's love, has destroyed that lure forever ... Song's naked body [is] ... the traumatic Real that tears apart the dream of "Butterfly," forcing Gallimard to wake up in the abyss of his own self.'

White Nagasaki / White Japan and a Post-Atomic Butterfly: Joshua Logan's *Sayonara* (1957)

BRIAN McILROY

Day after day
behind the butterfly of death's wings
corpses increase, laid like eggs one on another.
      Horiba Kiyoko, 'The Sky' (Vance-Watkins and Mariko 4)

V-Constant Vertigo
Still I dread
the white Nagasaki.
      Terai Sumie, 'White Nagaski: A Haiku Sequence' (Ibid. 13)

The initial success of romantic tearjerkers reflected their collective capacity to stroke the emotional sensibilities of suburban housewives, but recent analysts suggest that the 50s melodramas are actually among the most socially self-conscious and covertly 'anti-American' films ever produced by the Hollywood studios.
      Schatz, *Hollywood Genres* 224–5

HANA-OGI: My father was killed by American bomb dropped on my country. You have been my enemy. I have hated Americans. I have thought they were savages. There's been nothing but vengeance in my heart.
MAJOR GRUVER: Miss Ogi, there were an awful lot of Americans killed, too, and I think we be best to forget about that.
      Logan, *Sayonara*

Nagasaki. In Europe and North America, the word conjures up a very specific resonance. The historically minded might be aware that the city was a Treaty Port in the late nineteenth century, a prescribed geographical area for Europeans and Americans to meet and interact with the Japanese (Hoare). Others may be aware that it was the strongest outpost, albeit of a generally weak effort, of Christian influence in Japan (Hein and Selden 91; Marx 82). Still others might be conscious that it was the setting of Puccini's popular *Madama Butterfly* (1904). Most of all, of course, we 'know' Nagasaki as the unwilling recipient of 'Fat Man,' the plutonium atomic bomb dropped by the Americans in August 1945. That bomb is estimated to have caused 70,000 people to lose their lives. As the Japanese women poets above suggest, predominantly white America sent a deadly whiteness to Nagasaki, and perhaps it remains the ultimate nadir in relationships between East and West. The fates of Hiroshima and Nagasaki in 1945 undeniably represent the return of American imperialist power in the region, and I suggest here that the reception of *Madama Butterfly* and other similar narratives are now inextricably bound up with Western notions of – and anxieties with – that 'terrible success.'

What gives the opera its particular poignancy post-1945 is the audience's ability to empathize with Butterfly, a victim figure who represents a fragile Japan. Vaporized people leave no strong trace, and it is thought that most of the Nagasaki victims were women. The opera also works its magic because of the shame and regret of Pinkerton and Sharpless, Americans who fail to act in a way that will save Butterfly. One might see an element of this continued defensiveness in the way the Enola Gay exhibit at the Smithsonian in 1994/5 had to downplay the effect of the bomb to cater to prevailing American sentiments. In some respects, the Madame Butterfly narrative is a call for American foreign policy to be allied to a compatible and compassionate domestic policy, the need for which is revealed by the desiccating effects of racial prejudice. 'We are all Americans now' seems to be the implied message and desired outcome. Butterfly tries to be American but is denied full rights, spurring the critic to wonder if the continued Western attraction to the opera is at least in part due to the innate flattery of a Japanese woman forsaking her heritage to be 'one of us.'

The traditional view sees Butterfly as a woman who has sacrificed all, foolishly as it turns out, for interracial love, yet she retains her dignity by committing suicide. The audience understands that contact with the irresponsible Americans means death for the Japanese, both literally and figuratively, since Butterfly returns to ancient Japanese customs after a flirtation with Christian American culture; it is, however, a return to another violent patriarchal order. Her father committed suicide after military failure; she commits suicide after supposedly committing a domestic version of that failure. So, in Japanese terms, one could argue that the Madame Butterfly narrative in *Madama Butterfly* actually reconfirms Japanese fears concerning their ties to the United States, namely, the loss of traditional ways of life, or the loss of the true essence of Japaneseness, and establishes instead what might be called the 'politics of defeat.'

Humanist scholars, including the feminist musicologist Susan McClary, have always asked difficult questions concerning the troubled relationship between art and society. For example, many have queried how we can continue to enjoy the same literature loved by Nazi guards who spent their mornings gassing people and then their afternoons reading canonical works. Similarly, though the question is not as dramatically cast, how can we endorse and endure the many Madame Butterfly narratives, given their origin in sexist, racist, and imperialist notions of the East? One answer lies in conceptualizing textual exegesis within cultural studies as a tool to tell us more about the society and culture that created the artworks rather than those societies they seek to depict. This working backwards to the presumed point of origin helps us shape and explain the circulation of archetypes and stereotypes. My suggested turn in analysis is both structural (implying a renewed interest in dramatic form – particularly of the melodrama) and ideological – suggesting that these versions of the Madame Butterfly narrative need to be read politically in order to grasp their total effects. In addition, I am interested in this essay to look at the medium of film, and its contribution, through the example of Joshua Logan's *Sayonara* (1957), to show how the Madame Butterfly narrative was modulated to suit the mid-1950s. Gina Marchetti has discussed this film at length, with specific reference to issues of gender and race, and what I offer here is more schematic, entertaining the notion that the film can usefully be approached, beyond traditional narrative dynamics, to examine issues concerning sources, performance, and technology.

Rather offhandedly, Robert Irwin in reviewing a book on Orientalist cinema argues that instead of writing about the 'Other' in Hollywood representations of the East, one might as well write about the 'Same,' that is, how the films reflect the attitudes of suburban Los Angeles. Irwin has a good point here worthy of development in the context of a case study. How do American movies 'use' the East? What problems within American culture do they explore? What anxieties do they try to disguise? What progressive social models do they suggest, if any? An analysis of the cultural text of *Sayonara* presents some surprising answers to these questions. Yet it is important to grasp the historical context to situate correctly *Sayonara*'s desire to be radical, for this particular narrative that seeks approval for interracial relationships is – by today's standards – somewhat tame.

The 1950s in the United States is regarded as a time of conformity, consumerism, and – emanating from the Cold War – fear of communism. The decade began with the Korean War (1950–3), which found the Americans fighting North Koreans and Chinese soldiers before a peace deal was struck and a demilitarized zone established. That zone or DMZ still exists, monitored today by more than a million troops. The Korean War is an important American experience (though often forgotten since it had no winner) because it revealed in the many military setbacks (Seoul was captured and retaken) that communism in the East was a power to be reckoned with, and that it could very well progress from Korea to Japan and neighbouring countries. In the inconclusive Korean War we see the seeds of American involvement in Vietnam. Korea also saw the demise of the 'American Emperor' (as the Japanese saw General Douglas MacArthur), who was dismissed by Truman for deliberately antagonizing the Chinese at a time when the American president was looking to strike an accord. To many Japanese, MacArthur had lost face, and so, too, had America.

The threat of worldwide thermonuclear war was exacerbated by the Russians' ability to build their own bomb, and their apparent technological advances in space with Sputnik 1 and 2. The dominance the Americans felt after the Second World War began to come under question, leading in large part to the paranoia of the hearings instigated by Senator Joseph McCarthy, which sought initially to discover communists working for the federal government, though moving outwards to include even Hollywood directors and screenwriters. What is significant here is the 1950s anxiety concerning difference, which although ostensibly focused on ideology, also touched on matters of race. Nineteen fifty-five was the year Rosa Parks, a black woman, refused to sit in the 'black section' of a bus, an act that, in turn, inspired the Montgomery boycott that brought the leadership of Martin Luther King Jr to national prominence. As Brian Henderson observes (445), in that same year of 1955, twenty-nine states still had statutes forbidding blacks and whites to marry, and they stayed in force until 1967.

On a more social and cultural level, the 1950s, as David Halberstam's review of the decade magnificently presents, threw up rebel or transgressive figures that the 1960s would incorporate into the mainstream. Marlon Brando, James Dean, and Marilyn Monroe in film; Elvis Presley, Chuck Berry, and Bill Haley in music; Allen Ginsberg, Jack Kerouac, and William Burroughs in literature; and even Lucille Ball on television, interrogated in their work a very conservative society. In an era when Alfred Kinsey's *Sexual Behavior in the Human Female* (1953), an extremely hefty academic tome, rose up the best-seller lists, and when the dark sexual secrets of Grace Metalious's *Peyton Place* (1956) were a major sensation, one can only surmise that official repression of the libido had become a major issue to resolve and explore. More generally, the role of women in the workforce was actively discouraged through advertising (and narrative films), which promoted instead life in the newly built suburbs with a nuclear family set-up as the ideal goal for the post-war woman.

This combination of masculine dominance, white prejudice, and libido is evident in the life and work of James Michener. A popular but serious writer, who won the Pulitzer Prize for fiction for his *Tales of the South Pacific* (1947), Michener embodies many of the contradictions of American society of the post-war era. He hated communism; he served in the military; he believed (in the early 1950s) that interracial marriages could not work in the long term, and he advised those who sought his counsel against them. Yet Michener was a well-travelled and enlightened figure for the period, heavily involved in the Asia Institute and the Fund for Asia. In fact Michener (an orphan himself) and his second wife adopted a Japanese American boy, Mark, but when the marriage broke up, the boy left with the mother, and a few years later the child was returned to the orphanage. Very soon after the novel *Sayonara* was published in 1954 (a novel dedicated to Mark), Michener met and married his third wife, Mari Yoriko Subusawa, a second-generation Japanese American who had been interned during the Second World War on the West Coast, along with 110,000 other Americans of Japanese ancestry (Hayes 126). This marriage was to last, and it is hard not to speculate on the influence of this change of heart in Michener being replayed in the change of ending from the novel (racial separation) to the film version (interracial union).

Apart from the ending and the addition of one key character, both novel and film trace the same narrative. In 1951/2, at the height of the Korean War, a fighter pilot, Major Lloyd Gruver, is sent to Tokyo for rest and relaxation. There he meets his presumed wife-to-be, Eileen, the daughter of his commanding officer, General Webster. Gruver is asked to intercede to dissuade one of his own unit, Joe Kelly, from marrying a Japanese woman, Katsumi, but finds himself serving as best man. While he considers furthering his relationship with Eileen, Gruver is captivated by a Japanese dancer and singer, Hana-ogi, with whom he falls in love and whom he seeks to marry, against the express restrictions of the military code of the time. Joe Kelly is ordered home, and since this means that he could not bring his Japanese wife back to the States (a law was eventually passed in 1953 to allow American GIs to do just this), he and his wife commit suicide rather than end their relationship. Gruver is persuaded not to pursue marriage with Hana-ogi, and they both return to their respective careers. What Michener succeeds in conveying is Gruver's gradual appreciation of Japan, its people, and its art. By stopping short of endorsing an interracial marriage, however, Michener undermines the potentially transgressive quality of his work. That the novel was tremendously successful speaks to its ability to encapsulate American thinking about Japan in the mid-1950s. Japan was still an exotic and feminine other, much as in previous Madame Butterfly narratives, but the novel shows the men as equally committed to interracial relationships as the women. These men are no ordinary Pinkertons.

If there is one facet about *Madama Butterfly* critics agree on, it is that it is a melodrama. What melodrama means, however, shifts depending on what medium is discussed. Certain common characteristics are, nonetheless, possible to discern. These include the focus on emotion and sentiment, on relationships between men and women, on sudden violent death, on agonized abrupt departures, and on stark and immediate choices. What gives many, though not all, melodramas their visual and visceral power is the combination of realistic setting, decor, and costumes juxtaposed with almost hysterical emotions and feelings expressed by the main characters, who are surrounded by 'excessive' evocative sounds or music.

To understand the film version of *Sayonara*, it is useful to bear in mind the form of film melodrama that typified the 1950s. Television at this time was only beginning to take over as the main entertainment vehicle, and had not achieved the stranglehold on melodramatic form that one could argue it has today, with that medium's endless number of 'soaps.' As the movie audience fell away, and theatres closed, studios went into decline. One of the results of this downturn was an effort by the studios to seek out blockbuster material, and to capture images that television could not compete with. Logan's *Sayonara* offered an adaptation of a best-selling novel from a renowned writer, along with possibly Hollywood's leading male actor, Marlon Brando. Furthermore, Logan was excited that he would be the first Western filmmaker to film inside the famous Kabuki Theatre in Tokyo and be able to use authentic Nô plays and players, and Bunraku puppeteers, as well as the all-women Takarazuka opera company. (None of this occurred, however, due to a stand-off between Logan's producer and the Japanese entertainment company that controlled these enterprises, and Logan was reduced to rounding up any Japanese performers he could find in Kyoto and creating his own theatrical spaces.) Decamping to Japan for many months added expectation to the finished product, and since the film was nominated for ten Oscars and won four, in addition to being a box-office success, Logan clearly had backed an American topic of interest.

Moreover, the film is shot in Technicolor and Technirama, colour and widescreen processes that provided the director and cinematographer with a chromatic array of possibilities in establishing an exotic East. In this choice of technology, Logan follows in an honourable tradition, since the first Technicolor film in American film history is reputed to be Chester Franklin's *Toll of the Sea* (1922), also a version of *Madama Butterfly*, starring Anna May Wong (Cook 255). As John Belton suggests, widescreen processes, such as Technirama, emphasized 'spectacular excess' and enhanced the presence of the actors, leading the audience into a more participatory mode of spectatorship (192–5). In its theatrical widescreen Technirama version, *Sayonara* approximates contemporary operatic spectacle, something that cannot be grasped in its video version. Technicolor and widescreen films also declared the excitement of new technology, leading critics such as Ed Buscombe (86–7) to argue that these films are symptomatic of late bourgeois capitalism, since the latter is distinguished by its emphasis on innovation and the promise of immediate profits. These film technologies dovetail neatly with a narrative and a generic form seeking to break traditional values.

Film scholars have been attracted to melodrama for a variety of reasons. As Christine Gledhill (5–39) outlines, feminists found these 'tearjerkers' to be a site for debate of women's issues; Marxists found them interesting for revealing the basic contradictions of human beings' emotional needs in the midst of an unremitting bourgeois capitalist system; psychoanalytic critics saw the influence of Freud in the many Oedipal triangles worked out in these films. More recently, post-structuralist and postcolonialist–inclined critics have been attracted to the way in which melodrama punctures the classic cinematic realist text (with its naturalistic acting and emphasis on action and understatement), and privileges instead unrestrained emotional outpourings and the domestic sphere. These critics see melodramas as a form of critical irony.

Whereas a theatre or opera production can be recast and remounted endlessly, a film production provides a perfected performance, since remakes are few and far between. This characteristic quality of film puts extra emphasis on its stars, and here Marlon Brando is a fascinating Pinkerton for the 1950s. We must thank Truman Capote for giving us an insight into Brando's ideas at the time of the shooting of *Sayonara* in Japan. Capote's profile of Brando, published originally in the *New Yorker*, heaped a degree of ridicule on the famous actor, but also captured 1950s Orientalist attitudes, and those that were manifestly under reinvestigation. Imagine the scene Capote found: Brando in a hotel that offered Western and Japanese rooms (Brando chose the latter), attended to by a stream of hotel workers enraptured by 'American star quality.' He seems a more obvious Pinkerton outside the film than in it. Capote was to complicate this vision, and by extension the American involvement in Japan's 'reconstruction,' by ending his article with reference to a sixty-foot-high poster of Marlon Brando's face in downtown Kyoto promoting the comedic film *The Teahouse of the August Moon* (Daniel Mann, 1956), in which Brando plays a wily Okinawan interpreter, who somehow undermines the U.S. Army's rehabilitation program for the island. Brando as 'Yellow face' is a strange and wonderful rebellious forerunner to his part in *Sayonara*.

Brando reveals in discussion with Capote his belief that only the search for love keeps him motivated (Brando as Butterfly?), and he promotes strongly his desire in his professional work to break through the normal expectations of contemporary society to find different kinds of alliances. Capote notes that Brando is reading Colin Wilson's *The Outsider* and various works on Eastern religions. In short, he has come to Japan prepared to immerse himself in the culture, while simultaneously aware that he is on the outside looking in. His reading of Wilson's book is consistent with most of his 1950s screen characters – an angry disabled veteran in *The Men* (1950), an explosive personality in *A Streetcar Named Desire* (1951), a Mexican revolutionary in *Viva Zapata* (1952), a leather-clad, motorcycle-obsessed juvenile delinquent in *The Wild One* (1954), and, of course, his Academy Award–winning performance as a hardened longshoreman in *On the Waterfront* (1954). These are all forceful personalities bridling at the restrictions of their parents' generation.

Brando saw in *Sayonara* an opportunity to discuss interracial marriage and also racial prejudice. It was his decision to play Major Gruver as a bigoted Southern U.S. military brat, who is at first very comfortable in espousing racial separation. Given his later sympathies with the ideals of the Black Panthers, one imagines that Brando saw links between this prejudice against the Japanese and that directed towards American blacks back in the United States. The star did work on the screenplay, although little of his efforts actually ended up onscreen. One critical decision he did influence is the change of the novel's ending to a march to the marriage bureau. The 'sayonara' or 'good-bye' of the novel to interracial love and marriage is replaced in the film by a 'good-bye' to stifling careers and bourgeois norms.

Though the film attempts to even the gender power relationships, the production still gives the Americans most of the cards to play. Hana-ogi, the lead dancer/singer of the Mitsubayashi opera company, who often plays and dresses as a man, and who harbours personal grudges against the Americans because of the war, is nevertheless quickly able to forgive the past (an American dream wish, since the United States needed Japan onside during the Cold War); she looks forward to becoming a mother and has an expectation of part-time teaching. For his part, Gruver, we assume, will give up his military career, or at the very least any chance of a meteoric rise within it. Somehow, despite the film's good intentions, we think the American core values of individualism and choice are shown to be paramount. Logan avoids the subject of whether or not the couple will live in Japan or America.

Two steps forward, one step backwards would also be one way to grasp the addition of the character Nakamura, the Kabuki actor. Director Logan thought that Japanese men needed to be tastefully represented, and he suggests that a relationship between the jilted Eileen and Nakamura is developing by the film's close. From a narrative perspective, it is interesting that the Yamadori figure in the opera is given shape here as one who does not desire a Butterfly such as Hana-ogi or Katsumi but Eileen, who represents the stolid Kate character of the opera. The effect of Nakamura's voicing of erotic desires, however, draws attention to a casting problem. For whatever reason, Logan chose the Mexican actor Ricardo Montalban to play the Japanese actor. One wonders if this decision had more to do with Hollywood's growing general sensitivity to minority casting for Hispanics than with any intentional slight on Japanese American male actors who could have played the role. After all, Miiko Tara, who plays Hana-ogi, was discovered by a Los Angeles talent scout. The casting of Montalban led to consternation in the Japanese press, worried – as it turns out unduly – that the Americans would make fun of one of their traditional arts.

One of the most interesting features of *Sayonara* is how the subplot of Kelly and Katsumi shadows more directly the opera *Madama Butterfly*. Katsumi is compliant, even willing to undergo facial surgery to remove the natural Asian shape of her eyes in favour of a Caucasian one (similar perhaps to Butterfly's willingness to explore Christianity to make herself more desirable to Pinkerton). Kelly and Katsumi commit a double suicide (together they are 'Butterfly' and the racist American military policy-makers represent the uncaring and impotent 'Pinkerton' and 'Sharpless'). Their radical decision is nonetheless undermined by the fact that the restrictions that caused this despair would soon be lifted; that Kelly has no family or ties back home and appears not to consider a life as a civilian in Japan; that the suicide of pregnant Katsumi defers discussion of interracial marriages and the children that result (indeed sends a negative message about them). Logan is aware of this latter problem since he chooses to include in Gruver's and Hana-ogi's final melodramatic conversation a discussion of future children. At Hana-ogi's raising of the issue, Gruver can only state the obvious that their children will be half white and half yellow, for he cannot promise to overcome American or Japanese disapproval. In this way, the film is an exercise in wishful thinking and a plea for racial tolerance generally. Such tolerance is also of political value, as General Webster makes clear that Japanese nationalism does exist, and could be reignited if America proves to be an unworthy 'master.' This threat is rendered visually by the scene in which Japanese men beat up Gruver and his friend Mike while other Japanese are seen carrying anti-American signs.

Another key aspect of the film in relation to Brando and the Madame Butterfly narrative is that of performance. Brando's Method acting provides an unusual set of skills to transform the initially bigoted 'Pinkerton' into a love-besotted, enlightened figure. Method acting is stereotypically understood as Stanislavskian in origin, emphasizing intense research of a role, always drawing on the actor's own emotional subjective experiences, and leading to a gritty performance best used for realistic drama. Symptoms of this approach would often manifest themselves in fist-clenching, mumbling, and awkward silences and gestures, where the body often replaces spoken language as the purveyor of meaning. At first glance, it seems odd to have a Method actor in the midst of a melodrama more suited to grand gestures and histrionics; as

Raymond Carney (326–7) has noted, however, Method acting and traditional melodramatic acting are not oppositions; rather, the Method is just a toned-down version of melodramatic acting that still struggles to speak the unspeakable and convey the ineffable.

We do not have to look far into the film *Sayonara* to see what Peter Brooks terms the 'melodramatic utterance' (41), where desire and the inner self rebel against repression and expected social roles. Major Gruver, ace pilot, returns from having shot down two enemy aircraft, but no joy is expressed in what he has done. He sits in his cockpit almost comatose, exhausted, pensive. Later, he reveals to his friend Mike, almost in a daydream kind of manner, his anxieties about following in his father's military footsteps. And when confronted by Hana-ogi's confession of hatred for Americans, his face scrunches up, his eyebrows knit, and he appears deeply pained as if he has suddenly moved into another realm altogether. When he discovers the suicide of Kelly and Katsumi, instead of a violent explosion of rage (a more natural realistic reaction), he hunkers down quietly, groaning, withdrawn, stroking his forehead slowly, again lost in an inner world of deep emotion.

Behind this Method performance the visual landscape gushes with reds, purples, and dark and light blues whenever the two leads develop their relationship and have to deal with highly charged emotions. This colour scheme is all the more noticeable when we incorporate the costume makeovers Hana-ogi undergoes. She initially wears a white suit, hinting at her androgynous nature, then traditional Japanese dress as the relationship with Gruver is established, and yet she also appears in a wide range of costumes when she is at work on the stage. At some moments she looks as if she is starring in an Oriental version of a Marilyn Monroe musical like *Gentlemen Prefer Blondes* (Howard Hawks, 1953). As such costume changes suggest, she is – like Japan itself – both old and new, in constant flux, a prize for the Americans to capture and control.

If we are to believe the professional manuals published in 1957 (Buscombe 90), colour cinematography was viewed as unrealistic, best suited for musicals and fantasy. In most dramatic films, colour was to be subordinate to the narrative; however, exceptions were made for the female star, who could be 'beautified' almost at the expense of the plot, and for those films in which luxury or spectacle was attempted. For the latter, in which I would place *Sayonara*, the use of colour approximates the role of music in opera, a tonal *mise-en-scène* that modulates over time and space. Perhaps the best example in the film is the love scene in which Hana-ogi and Gruver are shot in close-up, lit only by the range of colours of the fireworks exploding around them. Naturally, the film's non-diegetic music, and the diegetic music and songs connected to the stage performances, suggest an emotional line of development; but my point here is that in the luxuriance of colour, supplemented by Method acting, we come to appreciate the essence of melodrama – scenes and sequences that bear down on us with crushing intensity, and that portend major changes and upheavals, violating established norms. In a more general and speculative manner, there exists a correlation between American technology and Japan that stretches from military hardware, such as atomic bombs, to cultural properties, such as the introduction of Technicolor and widescreen, and the sheer dominance of Hollywood film in Japan from the occupation to the present. American bombs have been replaced by a cascade of American images.

Looking at the film *Sayonara* in concert with the Michener source allows us to see the social break within the 1950s. While ten thousand GIs married Asian women during the Korean War, they did so silently, as this act was officially disavowed. But by 1956/7 the yearning that was evident in the 1954 novel could be articulated more forcefully as a respected minority opinion, just as being supportive of black civil rights was slowly but surely turning, in the white population, from a minority view to that held by the majority. While it may seem unduly procrustean to say so, the concentration on racial difference in the film can only serve to comment on internal American politics and the race laws of the time. Arguably, the acceptance of Asian American yellow was easier for American whites than the acceptance of American blacks. We do have films lauding the Japanese in the 1950s, but we have to wait to the 1960s for black characters in American films to begin to take on serious and controversial roles, as in Stanley Kramer's *Guess Who's Coming to Dinner* (1967).

Perhaps it is no accident that the film that beat out *Sayonara* for major Oscars in 1957 was David Lean's *The Bridge on the River Kwai*. This film also examines how East meets West, but in wartime, and serves mainly to emphasize respect for racial difference and – this is where it differs significantly from *Sayonara* – respect for racial separation. Lean's film starred Alec Guinness as a British officer who strangely takes charge of the building of a bridge for the Japanese commander of a POW camp in order to prove the superiority of Western values over Eastern ones. Lean is astute enough to illustrate how both British and Japanese commanders do not imagine a non-traditional future and subsequently die because of their failure to dream. In the final analysis, however, the *realist*

The Bridge on the River Kwai spoke to the past; by contrast, the *melodramatic Sayonara*, with its variation of the Madame Butterfly narrative, spoke (for 1957) to an imagined liberal future.

This essay has argued that it is important to analyse projections or representations of the 'Other' *not* in order to sit in judgment of an intolerant or naive past, but to open up discussion of the varied tensions apparent at a historical moment. The Madame Butterfly narrative, the still fresh experience of 1945's cataclysmic events, the American need for Japanese support, and the necessity to acknowledge and accommodate rebellious American youth all came together with the suggestive Michener text, Brando's distinctive strain of Method acting (along with his personal politics), and the new technologies of Technicolor and Technirama to declare that the old ideologies based on racial and national prejudice urgently needed rethinking.

Playing Butterfly with David Henry Hwang and Robert Lepage

SHERRILL GRACE

I have a vision. Of the Orient.

Hwang, *M. Butterfly* (1988) 92

Il nous faut un miroir et pour moi ... c'était l'Orient.

Lepage, quoted in Charest, *Robert Lepage* 42

From Pierre Loti, David Belasco, and Giacomo Puccini to David Henry Hwang, David Cronenberg, Ken Russell, Alain Boublil and Claude-Michel Schönberg, and Robert Lepage, male artists have worshipped the idea of Butterfly. Why? Why are all these men playing (with) Butterfly? If Rene Gallimard in Hwang's *M. Butterfly* can be believed, it is because Butterfly is the 'Perfect Woman' (4), and such a woman can only be created, believed in, and, ultimately, *played* by a man. But this perfect woman is, of course, a fantasy. Moreover, in most of her twentieth-century incarnations she ends up dead: the perfect woman, it seems, is a dead woman. End of story. And yet, as we know, and as all the other chapters in this book make clear, Butterfly cannot be put to rest. We – Western artists, critics, and audiences (male and female) – keep resuscitating her, reincarnating her, reinventing her, playing and replaying her. Why? What does the story or the *figure* of Butterfly mean? Above all, why is it Puccini's opera that is so frequently replayed?

In what follows, I explore some answers to these questions by examining two contemporary North American plays in which Puccini's opera, in particular, and what I call the Butterfly narrative, in general, operate in design-governing ways – David Henry Hwang's *M. Butterfly* and *The Seven Streams of the River Ota* by Robert Lepage and Ex Machina.[1] This search for answers will facilitate a close, comparative look at two major works for theatre, and the comparison will shed some light on why Butterfly matters and on what possibilities lie hidden in the kimono of her story. Beyond these particular questions lies a larger one that intrigues me: when *opera* is played within a stage play, a type of intertextuality results that differs, I suspect, from the more common play-within-a-play structure or trope, and the reverse strategy of play-within-opera does not achieve comparable results. There is something special, for both author and audience, about the incorporation of an opera or parts of an opera within a play.[2]

My approach to Hwang, Lepage, and these two Butterfly texts is by way of comparative textual study informed by key concepts from the work of Homi K. Bhabha on cultural narrative and Sidonie Smith on autobiography. Although the playwrights' use of Puccini's opera provides my starting point, there are other reasons (including both men's active interest in opera)[3] for my choice of authors and texts. For anyone coming to the work of Hwang for the first time through *M. Butterfly*, the 'Afterword' puts baldly what the play itself creates – Hwang's personal sense of speaking from an ironically privileged position on the margins of American society. Unlike Caucasian men, Hwang can claim to know how Asian women behave (94). More to the point, he knows 'Butterfly [the opera and the narrative] only as a cultural stereotype,' in which an Asian woman, or man, plays 'the submissive Oriental number' (95). He claims that it is his insider-knowledge, as an Asian-American man existing *outside/*on the margins of the 'sexist and racist clichés' of the *Madama Butterfly* story of 'archetypal East-West romance' (95), that enables him to recognize and replay that narrative through the actual contemporary news report of Bernard Bouriscot and a Chinese actress-cum-spy. In doing so he hopes to expose, critique, even sabotage many of those clichés from the dominant culture.[4] At the end of the play, through the figure of Rene Gallimard, Hwang presents the complex infrastructure of Western ideology and imperialist practice, which he attempts to turn destructively inward on itself. Whether or not he succeeds, or the degree to which his ending works as sabotage, is a complex question that only a performance can resolve (see **Rachel Ditor and Jan Selman** on this point).

Despite his soaring international reputation, as a *Québécois* playwright Robert Lepage might be seen as occupying a position on the margins of *Canadian* society. Certainly, he is aware of this position and exploits its potential in much of his work. This position, at once different from yet strikingly similar to that of Hwang vis-à-vis the United States, enables Lepage to observe what francophone Canadians often describe as an Anglo-Saxon hegemony within the Canadian nation state, while also understanding, from the inside, as it were, the price and power of being constructed as the Other by that state.[5] The price, similar to that of Asian othering in the United States, is the stereotyping and second-class status resulting from what Edward Said calls 'Orientalism,' which is exacerbated for Hwang and Lepage by its *practice* within one's own country. The power is the power of vision, of seeing things differently. It is what Bhabha calls the 'power of supplementarity.'[6] Someone coming to Lepage for the first time through *The Seven Streams of the River Ota* will, in fact, have difficulty locating *Lepage* at all because, as author/creator/originator, he has deliberately disappeared into the ensemble work (a methodology of supplementarity) of the theatre company Ex Machina. For Lepage's claims to know things, one must turn to his other works, such as *The Dragons Trilogy* (1986), his complex autobiographical play *the far side of the moon* (2000), and to Rémy Charest's *Robert Lepage: Quelques zones de liberté*. For example, in *The Dragons Trilogy*, a six-hour, three-part collaborative exploration of multiculturalism set in three Canadian Chinatowns, Lepage creates what Natalie Rewa summarizes as 'a *performance* of cultures in the theatre' (159, emphasis added) rather than cultural conflict, racism, and misunderstanding. He does this, notably in part 3 (set in Vancouver), by replaying the Butterfly narrrative without Puccini's music, which he will not include until *Seven Streams*.[7]

Although I do not wish, for a moment, to oversimplify the extremely complex and multifaceted margin-centre dynamic of Quebec–Canada relations or of ethnic and race relations within the United States, I do want to suggest that both Lepage and Hwang occupy analogous positions and use those positions to deconstruct (Hwang 95) and decentre (Lepage, quoted in Hunt, 115) aspects of the dominant Western discourse of identity (national, racial, ethnic, sexual, and linguistic), which they find encoded in the Butterfly narrative. By empowering themselves through their individual hybridity and their art, they invite us to share in their 'metonymic interruption' (Bhabha 306) of Western (and North American) cultural/national narratives and to see cultural difference, not as an excuse for othering, but as an opportunity to create new 'strategies of identification' (Bhabha 313). That they approach Puccini and the Butterfly narrative so differently and, as a result, create such profoundly different plays, demonstrates several things: the provocative elasticity of the Butterfly narrative, its extraordinarily dense cultural significance on all levels (political, national, racial, sexual, personal, and so on), and the power of its plot and, above all, of Puccini's music. When replayed within a stage play, or, at least, within these two plays, *Madama Butterfly* represents the 'power of supplementarity' of which Bhabha speaks. As I hope to show, that power is greater in Lepage's play than in Hwang's because *M. Butterfly* cannot entirely escape its Broadway trappings and, perhaps inevitably, risks becoming trapped in the sentimental clichés it invokes (see **Kate McInturff** on this risk).

The fundamental difference in the use of that power is present, in snapshot, in my two prefacing quotations, and because it informs the discussion that follows, it is worth a comment now. The brief passage from Hwang's play is, in fact, spoken by Gallimard at the end of the play as he puts on Butterfly's ceremonial kimono (in Puccini and Lepage it will be a wedding kimono), moments before he kills himself to the blaring accompaniment of the 'Love Duet' from *Madama Butterfly*. Lepage's is spoken in the playwright's own voice in conversation with Charest and in response to Charest's comment that *The Dragons Trilogy* would never have been written as it was if Lepage had travelled in China. Lepage's reply turns Charest's comment inside out because he insists that, for him, especially in *Seven Streams*, the 'Orient' is his way of better understanding the West ('Ma fascination pour l'Orient m'aide beaucoup à comprendre l'Occident,' quoted in Charest, 42). The 'Orient' is his mirror on himself, on *us*; it is his way of understanding the self by contemplating the opposite or Other ('son contraire,' Charest 43). '*I* have a vision,' insists Hwang's Gallimard; it is mine, and to preserve *my* 'Orient' untainted, unchanged I will die. 'We all need mirrors,' Lepage explains; we need them to see ourselves, and my mirror is the 'Orient' of the River Ota, which will show you, not Japan, but yourselves (Charest 42; see also Hunt 116). The vision and the mirror both invoke *Madama Butterfly*, but where Hwang narrows and fixes the 'vision' to show that it excludes all but the self (Gallimard's 'I,' reflected in his mirror), Lepage's mirror-text reduplicates, reflects, and includes a continuum of selves-in-others.

M. Butterfly is a three-act memory play. It opens and closes in a Paris prison cell where, speaking in a dramatic and historical 'present,' Rene Gallimard has 'played out the events of my life night after night, always searching for a new ending to my story, one where I leave this cell and return forever to my Butterfly's arms' (91). Over the course of the three acts, Gallimard retells and performs his autobiography through a series of highly theatrical (staged) flashbacks.[8] The image he creates of himself is of a man so absorbed in his affair with a beautiful Chinese opera singer that he fails to see her as a male spy and not the seductive, compliant Butterfly he wants her to be. At the same time as this confessional self-performer comes across as a blind fool, with unquestioned racist and sexist assumptions, he also emerges, both in the text and even more so in performance, as pitiable, an object of his own and his presumably Western audience's sympathy – a man who has loved not wisely but too well.

Act 3, on which I want to concentrate, begins in a Paris courthouse in 1986 (the actual year of Bouriscot's trial), but we already know that things will not end quite as Gallimard would like. Song has repeatedly demonstrated his capacity to step out of his assigned role in Gallimard's memory play/autobiography (see 47, 63). Then, by the end of act 2, the challenge to Gallimard's fantasy is clear. When Song steps forward to address us and insists on speaking *his* mind, Gallimard objects ... in vain:

GALLIMARD: You have to do what I say! I'm conjuring you up in *my* mind!
SONG: Rene, I've never done what you've said. Why should it be any different in your mind? Now split – the story moves on, and I must change. (78)

'Change' and a story that 'moves on,' however, are precisely what Gallimard finds insupportable. Although China could not force him to face himself, a Paris court, where he is tried for espionage and where Song is revealed – *changed* from an 'Oriental' woman in a kimono to an Asian man in an Armani suit – can and does.

Covering the years between 1986 until Gallimard ends his story, act 3 reaches its climax in scene 2 when Song forces Gallimard to look at his naked body and acknowledge that Song Liling is 'a man' (88). The key irony and failed peripeteia of this play begins and ends here, *not* in 3, 3, because it is here *in memory* that Gallimard replays his choice of fantasy over reality, of loathing over love, of a 'universal' over an 'embodied' subject (Smith 5), of self over – and to the exclusion of – the Other. As the man Gallimard remembers him to be, Song appears to have offered Gallimard a chance for truth and life: 'I'm your Butterfly. Under the robes, beneath everything, it was always me. Now, open your eyes and admit it – you adore me' (89). But Gallimard, of course, does not want *that* truth. Instead, he rejects Song and the embodied subjectivity he represents. He rejects him night after night in his memory play until the final night, when he re-enters the dramatic present to embrace his Butterfly in himself.

In my reading of 3, 3, Rene's desired ending is atavistic because he chooses to withdraw further and further into his own mind, his 'vision of the Orient,' until he becomes Butterfly, 'a woman created by a man,' by which standard anything else 'simply falls short' (90). Trapped within the prison of his Western mind and fantasy, caught in the replay of his own memory, Gallimard can only 'look in the mirror and see nothing but ... a woman' – the Butterfly of self (92). The love that warps his judgment, blinds his eyes, and rearranges his face is narcissistic. It is profoundly ironic that the Cartesian *cogito* without which Gallimard cannot imagine life betrays him: he *thinks* he is Butterfly, therefore he *is* Butterfly ... and must kill himself. The revenge Hwang takes on Gallimard, and through him on Western concepts of the subject and on the binaries of gender and race, is further ironic because, in playing the role of Butterfly to the death, Gallimard reveals the misogynist fantasy of the man who would choose a woman created by a man and played by a man over a real woman (Helga or Renee, for example) or, for that matter, a real man (Song). Gallimard's suicide *as Butterfly* exposes the solipsism, violence, and danger implicit in the West's vision of the 'Orient.' But it is by no means only Gallimard's final act that plays out these implications. From the beginning, Gallimard has constructed his life in terms of Puccini's opera. That he mistook himself through most of it (opera/life) to be Pinkerton underscores the self-deluding danger of the opera and of the Butterfly narrative.

M. Butterfly opens and closes with the 'Love Duet' from the end of act 1 of *Madama Butterfly*, but this is not the only music from the opera or, indeed, the only opera music we will hear. The first music we hear is the 'percussive clatter of Chinese music' from traditional Peking Opera (1) and here, as at later points in the play, the Chinese music will be replaced or drowned out by the Puccini (see 20, 84, and 87). The more deeply Gallimard sinks into Puccini's music, especially the 'Love Duet,' and identifies his life story with the Butterfly narrative, the more completely is he unable to *hear* anything else, even though he tells us he regularly attended Song Liling's Peking Opera performances.

Hwang uses the first six scenes of act 1 to retell the Butterfly narrative and give Gallimard time to play key passages and arias on his prison tape recorder. The choice of music emphasized by this replaying is significant. Gallimard's plot summary touches upon many of the key ideas and events *he* finds important: Butterfly as 'a feminine ideal' of the girl who wants 'to be treated bad' (6); Pinkerton as a cad and 'wimp' (5); the package deal purchase of house and 'wife'; Butterfly's wedding kimona, her rejection of everything for Pinkerton, her inevitable abandonment, loss of child, and suicide. The snippets of music replayed range from Pinkerton's roving Yankee duet with Sharpless (7) to Cio-Cio-San's 'Un bel dì' (25) and the 'Death Scene' (which is the 'loudest thing' in the play, 84). As each piece is played back for us, Gallimard recreates scenes from his life, including the years and events from before his 1960 meeting with Song Liling, as if to stress the degree to which the Butterfly narrative underscores everything he was and is. By far the most important music from the opera, however, is the 'Love Duet.' It opens and closes the memory play and frames Gallimard's victory (as he thinks of it) over Song in act 2 (34–41), when he forces 'her' to say 'she' is his Butterfly. Although the repetition of the 'Love Duet' in the final scene, as Gallimard kills himself, may at first glance seem an odd choice over Puccini's death-scene music, in the larger context of the play, which is, after all, the memory play of a man obsessed with his fantasies and personal life, it is the perfect choice. It is not actual or staged death that has fascinated him, but love, the romantic, heterosexual love of an adoring, compliant Asian woman for a powerful Western man, the love in short of Puccini's 'Love Duet.'

As the final scene of Act 1 makes clear, it is not his love for Song that Gallimard celebrates by repeating the words of the duet but his power over her and her compliance in the role of *his* Butterfly. The irony of this scene, however, is that the words he *and Song* repeat are *not* Cio-Cio-San's but Pinkerton's: 'Vieni, vieni' (41). Even here, Gallimard's self-indulgent vision of the Orient deafens and blinds him to who is really saying what. In act 2, Song will again play Pinkerton to Gallimard's Cio-Cio-San, when he softly sings Pinkerton's roving Yankee lines from act 1 of *Madama Butterfly*, and Gallimard will almost recognize his inner Butterfly as he crawls towards Song with 'Pinkerton ... vanished from my heart' (60). Then, in act 3, when Song offers Gallimard his last chance to choose reality over fantasy and to 'become something more. More like ... a woman' (90), Gallimard will refuse both his own and Song's reality. He may kill himself dressed up as Butterfly rather than Pinkerton, but when he does so it is to maintain masculine control over the the story, to retain ultimate power over life and the subject in his own hands. Gallimard is still, and only, a man.

As its title suggests, the number seven has symbolic, topographic/metaphoric, and structural significance in *The Seven Streams of the River Ota* (see Charest 111–12 and Lepage 139), but for the moment I want to concentrate on its seven-part structure. As we move through these parts we are also crossing fifty-four years of twentieth-century history, from 1943 to 1997, two continents, and five countries. The play, with its ensemble creation and production and more than two dozen characters, is epic in scope and requires approximately seven hours' playing time. Structure, therefore, is more than usually important for controlling and shaping the play.

Part 1 is set in Hiroshima, 1945–6, in the Japanese house that will provide the unifying set for the play. Nozomi, a *hibakusha* (survivor of the bomb), her face scarred by the blast, rediscovers herself and a modicum of happiness through her relationship with Luke, an American soldier whose post-war military assignment is to photograph the 'physical damages ... caused by the bomb' (3). Nozomi's mother-in-law has removed all mirrors from the house, but Nozomi persuades Luke to photograph her, thus enabling her to see her face and him to understand something of the psychological, emotional damage caused by the bomb. They have a brief affair, he returns to the United States and his American wife, and Nozomi bears their child, Jeffrey Yamashita, who will stay with his mother and provide a crucial link forward to subsequent parts of the play: in fact, the actual account of Nozomi's death and Luke's return to visit his son are played in pantomime through part 2 (26, 31).

Although Lepage has, as yet, made no mention of Butterfly or Puccini, the subtext here is clear. Luke is a Pinkerton figure, Nozomi plays Cio-Cio-San, the mother-in-law has Suzuki's role, and Jeffrey is little Sorrow. And the story, as Lepage replays it, is almost the same, but not quite. Most importantly, the child stays with his mother and in his mother country. When Luke returns, as he must, to the United States, he is a changed man. Nozomi dies, but her death is *not* staged as a dramatic suicide for honour or love. Precisely why she dies is unclear, but it seems more closely related to the aftermath of the war and the bomb than to Luke's absence.[9] When she dies she is wearing a white kimono, with a white cloth covering her disfigured face, and her mother-in-law replaces Luke's photograph of Nozomi with her pre-war wedding photograph. The stage instructions do not specify that her kimono is *the* kimono, but the link is clear and the white wedding kimono with gold cranes is firmly established as a key semiotic sign and metaphor in the play.

Parts 2 and 3 move away from Japan while keeping it before us in the person of Jeffrey Yamashita. Part 2 takes place in 1965 in a New York rooming house, where Jeffrey finds his American half-brother and dying father. Underlying this encounter of the brothers, but never openly stated, is their relationship, through Luke, and the replaying, through film and photography (see note 8), of the events leading up to Jeffrey's birth and Nozomi's death. The theatrical effect of the photography balances the psychological and ethnic levels of the plot because in the person of Jeffrey Japan is brought to America (a New York rooming house) so that America can be incorporated by him and returned to Japan. Part 3 moves even further afield, geographically and chronologically, to 1985 in Amsterdam. Jeffrey Yamashita and his wife Hanako arrive to be with Jeffrey's half-brother, who has come to Amsterdam for a medically assisted suicide because he is dying of AIDS. Once again, images and memories of the war in Japan are presented (largely through photographs), and a crucial link is established between Europe and the Pacific during the Second World War. Significantly, Japan has not been allowed to slip from our mind's eye, and in the next part we return to Japan, bringing Europe with us.

Part 4 is the central, pivotal part of *The Seven Streams of the River Ota*. In ways far too numerous to enumerate here, all aspects of the play flow through this structural mid-section. Part 4 is called 'The Mirror,' and it is both structured as a mirror, with two sub-parts, and uses mirrors and mirroring techniques throughout. The two, paralleled settings are Hiroshima in 1986 and the concentration camp at Terezin in 1943. The latter is contained within the former; Europe is brought to Japan, as it were, in the person of Jana Capek, a Terezin survivor who has come to Hiroshima to visit Jeffrey Yamashita's sister-in-law Ada (the Dutch woman who married his half-brother), who is the surviving daughter of the Jewish opera singer whom we are about to meet. When Jana opens the doors of the wardrobe in the Hiroshima house, she finds herself facing two mirrors, which '*turn transparent so we can see behind them*' (45). Jana's experiences in the camp (her memories, if you will) then emerge from these mirrors, although the *staging* of these scenes with live actors, not photographs or film, stresses embodied subjectivity. Jana is only a child during these mirror scenes (2 to 13), and as she opens more and more mirrored doors we meet the older woman who will introduce her to opera. That Puccini's opera should appear only in Lepage's fourth, central, mirror act is, I think, crucial to the significance of the opera and to the way Lepage uses the opera to inform and supplement the larger meaning of the play.

Sarah Weber, a Jewish-German opera singer, always speaking to the

Czech child in German, will introduce her to costumes (a yellow kimono), make-up, and Puccini's *Madama Butterfly*.[10] In this opera-within-the-mirror-within-the-play, Sarah will retell the Butterfly narrative in answer to Jana's questions: 'Was ist butterfly?' 'Und was macht der Mann?' 'Und was tut die Frau dann?' 'Ist das Kind jüdisch?' (50–1). Sarah weeps as she retells the story, dons her Butterfly wig, make-up, and kimono, and prepares to hang herself. Part 4 draws to its close with the '*first measures of the finale of* Madama Butterfly' (56) and Sarah singing the specifically designated words of Cio-Cio-San's farewell to her child:

> O a me sceso dal trono dell'alto Paradiso, guarda ben fiso, *fiso di tua madre la facia che te'n resti una tracia*, guarda ben! Amore, addio! Addio piccolo amor! Va. Gioca ... gioca. (57, emphasis added)

> Oh, you who have come down to me from high heaven, look well, well on your mother's face, that you may keep a faint memory of it, look well! My love, farewell! Farewell, my little love! Go and play ... play.

After this strategic emphasis upon remembering the mother's face, and with the final 'gioca,' the stage instructions tell us that '*the music swells*' until its '*climactic point,* [when Sarah/Butterfly] *stabs herself.*' That part of the stage used to perform the opera is blacked-out, but part 4 ends with '*the lights switch[ed] so that the audience can see its own reflection in the downstage mirrors*' (57).

I will return to Lepage's playing of *Madama Butterfly* after summarizing the last three parts of the play, which mirror, in many ways, the first three on the other side of part 4. Part 5, set in Osaka, introduces a Québécois couple, a Québécois actress, and a play-within-a-play (a Feydeau bedroom farce). The key element, for my purpose, is the introduction of another affair that will produce another son, Pierre Maltais, who will play a key role in part 7. Part 6 returns us to Hiroshima, now in 1995, and provides many structural, thematic, and visual links with earlier parts of the play. Jana is now living in Japan, where the estranged wife from the Québécois couple in part 5 is interviewing her and preparing a documentary for the fiftieth anniversary of the bombing of Hiroshima. This return to Hiroshima, together with the replaying of events from the Second World War in Europe and Japan, provides the structural bridge across the River Ota into the final part of the play.

In many ways, part 7, set in Hiroshima in 1997, mirrors part 1, but this is a mirroring with difference and certainly not a repetition. Not only are we back in the same house in the same city, but the white wedding kimono with the gold cranes hangs prominently displayed on a wall. As the scene opens a young Caucasian man, Pierre Maltais, enters to meet the older Japanese woman who owns the house, Hanako Yamashita (Jeffrey's widow). Pierre has come to Japan to study Japanese dance, and he will rent a room from Hanako. When her son, David, arrives, however, tension builds between the young men until, in a 'dream' sequence we see the scene of Luke and Nozomi making love from part 1 slowly replaced with Pierre and David in silhouette behind the screens (134). Once more East and West embrace in this Hiroshima house, except that this time it is a gay embrace. When David leaves, however, Pierre turns to the woman.

On one level, the woman Pierre turns to is Hanako; in the final moments of scene 12 he enters her bedroom and closes the door behind him. However, scene 12 is largely devoted to Pierre's discovery of the woman within himself and of a woman's story.[11] He tells Hanako that he is working out the choreography for the story of a woman who survived the bombing of Hiroshima – a *hibakusha*. To help him understand this role/person, Hanako makes him up, and dresses him in Nozomi's wedding kimono. As he turns to put his arms into the kimono, other key characters from the play appear and disappear in its folds: Pierre becomes Sarah, who becomes Nozomi, who becomes Pierre once more. Hanako, who is holding the kimono, is similarly replaced by Jana (opposite Sarah), then by Luke (opposite Nozomi), who disappears into Hanako. Once fully attired, Pierre '*performs a butoh dance in which a woman moves gracefully, then experiences a moment of terror and pain*' (147). His *hibakusha* dance performed, Pierre collapses to the tatamis; he has played his role, but despite the parallels with Cio-Cio-San, he does *not*, finally, do a Butterfly. Instead, he plays his woman as a survivor. And to emphasize this difference, Lepage does not call for a single note or word from *Madama Butterfly*. The music we hear throughout part 7 is Japanese.

In his conversations with Rémy Charest, Lepage comments extensively on *The Seven Streams of the River Ota*, but nowhere is he asked about Puccini's influence. Instead, commenting on opera in general, he describes the power of theatre as at its height when it is musical because the lines must be delivered non-naturalistically (Charest 148). He goes on to assert that 'à l'opéra, le sous-texte, c'est la musique. L'intention se trouve là' ('in opera, music is the subtext where meaning resides,' ibid.). In

Seven Streams, Puccini's *Madama Butterfly* is the *sous-texte* in which much of the play's meaning lies, not because Lepage replicates Puccini but because he re-accentuates and replays both the Butterfly narrative and a crucial aria from the opera. As my summary of this complex play indicates, the Butterfly narrative informs the diegesis, frames the action, and drives the plot, notably in its three most strategic parts – one, four, and seven. The basic elements of the Butterfly narrative are all there in part 1, with the significant differences already noted, and they are thoroughly re-visioned when replayed in part 7. Moreover, by the time we reach part 7 we have already passed through the mirror of Part 4 and experienced the embodied sound of the *sous-texte*. Within the context of this narrative, both parts privilege three specific elements borrowed directly from Puccini – the kimono, the child, and the mother's face. What is not similarly privileged is Pinkerton, and through him exploitation and death. The opera, as replayed here, is not used narrowly to account for the 'Orient' or for one woman's suffering and tragedy. The only point at which *Madama Butterfly* is named and described is in part 4, and the only music from the opera to be sung – by a German Jew, not a Japanese Geisha – is that of the mother's farewell to her child as she begs: 'guardo ben fiso, fiso di tua madre la facia che te'n resti una tracia' (57).

And, indeed, the traces persist, *because* of the *sous-texte*, across the play in the repetitions, mirrorings, multi-media effects, photographs, plays – and opera-within-the-play, in the verbal and visual echoes, and above all in the complex biological/psychological/sexual/cultural links established among the characters: Sorrow becomes Jeffrey becomes David becomes Pierre; Cio-Cio-San becomes Nozomi becomes Sarah becomes Hanako; Pinkerton becomes Luke becomes Pierre, and so on, in a potentially endless exfoliation of continuing, yet related, differences. Will Pierre and Hanako create another child? Possibly. And would that child make new connections and perform further changes to the narrative? Very likely. The only closure achieved by *Seven Streams* is, in fact, an anti-closure, an opening out, a celebration of survival and new possibilities, all of which converge and flow on through Hiroshima. It is Hanako who tells Pierre (and us) why: 'C'est la rivière. Ce que j'aime de cette maison, c'est qu'elle est située juste à l'endroit où la rivière Ota se divise en sept parties' ('It's the river. What I love about this house is that it's located right where the river Ota divides into seven streams,' 139).

It is difficult to imagine two stage works more theatrically different than *M. Butterfly* and *The Seven Streams of the River Ota*, and yet both plays use the opera and the Butterfly narrative, and both present critiques of Western hegemonies, Orientalist discourse, and the consequences of racist and sexist stereoptyping. Each play foregrounds the playing of roles, and each flaunts the theatrical power of the stage, most notably in their reliance on the play-within-a-play process. Each play foregrounds key tropes (and props) such as mirrors, make-up, and kimonos, each explores the politics of gender and crosses boundaries of sexual identity, and each constructs a vision of the 'Orient.' Where they differ in their use of the opera is in *how* they play Butterfly and *where* they perform her story.

While remembering major events from the last fifty-four years of world history, *The Seven Streams of the River Ota* is not a memory play, but an embodied history, with an epic array of interconnected characters. *M. Butterfly*, however, re-presents memory play as an *auto*biography, where personal history plays out in the mind of one obsessed man. Whereas *Seven Streams* is heterogeneous, polyphonic, open-ended, flowing with the river of time, *M. Butterfly* is homogeneous, monologic, static, and closed. Where Hwang gives us, in Gallimard, a man trapped by the literal Butterfly narrative box he creates in his mind, Lepage performs an escape from this box by refusing to take it literally. *Seven Streams* turns the tragic into the comedic, a death wish into a celebration of life; *M. Butterfly* shows us a man who rejects the comic, life-affirming possibilities of his story and kills himself instead in an attempt to give his life tragic importance, an importance undermined by Song's last words: 'Butterfly? Butterfly?' (93) and reduced to sentimentality by his life's histrionics. That Song's question can be asked at all after the spectacle of Gallimard's desperate grasp at agency is the ultimate irony.

But what of Gallimard's agency (something much debated by **Rachel Ditor and Jan Selman**)? What does his fanatical clinging to faith in the Western mind, to what Sidonie Smith calls the concept of the 'universal subject,' amount to? And does the 'power of supplementarity' that I earlier claimed for the operatic within a play operate here? To answer the second question first, I would say – self-delusion. Because Hwang constructs this drama as Gallimard's memory play, he has deliberately hoist this foreign devil on the petard of Western rationality, and he has, through Gallimard's appeal to our sympathy, disallowed supplementarity (at least in his play with the opera), unless, of course, Bhabha's supplementarity can be located in Song, who plays Butterfly as a gay part and can step into or out of the role at will. But *M. Butterfly* is not Song's story.[12] Hwang's Gallimard is an ironic mirror because he reflects a warning (that depends on the audience's distance from the character if it is to be grasped) to the West about the self-delusionary, self-destructive narrative of the superior, universal masculine subject that renders the body (all body, but especially the female body) superfluous by silencing and excluding it: '[T]he universal subject consolidates sovereignty through exclusionary practices' (Smith 157). That Gallimard should then see himself as 'nothing but ... a woman' (92) is, within the mutually reinforcing narratives of Butterfly and the universal subject, entirely fitting. As Smith explains, '[T]he realms of the universal subject and the socially abject mutually constitute one another' (10). Poor Gallimard has no other way out than to kill himself; to *be* a woman is a fate worse than death. Whether or not Hwang, the playwright, has escaped the petards of pity and sentiment hovering over Gallimard's end can only be decided, I think, in performance.

Lepage's project in *The Seven Streams of the River Ota* is, like Hwang's, to expose and explode the sterile, deadly binary on which the Butterfly narrative rests. He does this, however, with unequivocal success, by harnessing the full 'power of supplementarity.' The multiple parts of the play, its complex mirroring yet open-ended structure, and its ensemble creation and performance all constitute a form and methodology of supplementarity. No single character dominates the play; no isolate mind contains the action. Instead, the play spills over, exceeds its bounds, in a multimedia, multilingual performance of multicultural encounter and cross-cultural embrace. Here the transvesting operates back and forth across boundaries, most powerfully perhaps, but by no means only, in Pierre's butoh dance. *Seven Streams* takes the centripetal drive of the universal subject and redirects by embodying it in not one but many bodies to create a centrifugal force. By releasing (while controlling) the 'power of supplementarity,' the play celebrates sexuality, fecundity, and continuity, and affirms life (see Lepage, quoted in Charest, 104–5).

In their very different uses of the opera, these plays suggest much about what happens when opera is played within a play, and their use of *Madama Butterfly* focuses and clarifies this. Consistent with the dramatization of a self-destructive universal subjectivity in the one and the life-affirming embodied subjectivities of the other, is the way the opera is played in each and the choice of music in each case. In *M. Butterfly* we hear Puccini on a tape recorder, that is, as disembodied voice technologically transmitted. In *Seven Streams* Sarah *sings* Cio-Cio-San's death-scene aria. At first, all we hear is a soprano's off-stage voice, but when the mirror doors open she appears in the wedding kimono slowly moving upstage and singing (this may be lip-synced in production for practical vocal reasons, but the representation of embodiment is nonetheless clear). Dialogue, words already embodied by actors in a live theatre production, is thus expanded with the full force of the operatic voice; the constraint of spoken words is shattered by the singing of one of opera's greatest arias.

Here, above all, is Bhabha's 'power of supplementarity' in the voice of a German-Jewish opera singer performing Puccini's *Madama Butterfly* within the mirrored memories of a Czech concentration-camp survivor who is visiting a house in Hiroshima – that other place of cataclysm – that rests on the spot where the River Ota divides into seven streams. What is bitterly ironic fable in *M. Butterfly* is a celebration of life in *Seven Streams* because, instead of the hopelessly romantic, misguided 'Love Duet' stressed by Hwang's Gallimard, Lepage's characters focus on the mother's face and on the child, both of whom link the opera, in its most tragic moment, with the flow of life beyond the stage – in Europe, North America, and Japan. When Hwang plays Butterfly we may enjoy his revenge on the Western universal subject or may remain trapped by our identification with Gallimard's spectacular confession. When Lepage plays Butterfly we are invited to dream of 'un bel dì,' when the Other('s) voice supplements and enriches our own subjectivities, and to imagine a world beyond the binaries of East and West.

Notes

1 In this discussion I use published texts because they provide valuable information in stage instructions, notably concerning the music. For my earlier discussion of Lepage see Grace 2001.
2 A number of operas come to mind in which a play is staged, such as *The Tales of Hoffmann, Ariadne auf Naxos*, and *I Pagliacci*, and there are certainly plays *about* opera or opera singers such as Terence McNally's *The Lisbon Traviata* and *Master Class*, Michel Tremblay's *Impromptu à Outremont*, and Simon Fortin's *A Country in Her Throat*, among others. One of the few plays I know of, beyond the two I am examining here, in which an opera is staged, is Louis Nowra's *Cosi*, which provides another set of comparisons that are beyond the scope of this discussion.
3 Lepage has considerable experience with opera, the most notable being his staging of the Canadian Opera Company and the Brooklyn Academy of Music's 1992 co-production of *Bluebeard's Castle* and *Erwartung*, which won

the Edinburgh International Critic's Award in 1993. Hwang has collaborated with American composer Philip Glass and has written the libretto for the Canadian composer Alexina Louie's new opera *The Scarlet Princess*.
4 For similar and conflicting views on this point, see Kondo, Lye, and K. Ma.
5 It is important to note that, speaking from within the Quebec 'nation,' Lepage is sharply critical of Quebec xenophobia, internal hegemony, and exclusionary practices (see Charest 55–60).
6 Bhabha describes supplementarity as an interruptive 'renegotiation [not negation] of ... traditions through which we turn our contemporaneity into the signs of history' (306).
7 Rewa is the only critic, thus far, to identify Puccini's importance to Lepage, and she is writing of *The Dragons Trilogy* four years before *Seven Streams* was first produced (155–9). James Frieze and Jennifer Harvie both comment on the Butterfly elements in *Seven Streams*, but I disagree with Harvie, who reads this use of Butterfly material as an example of 'typically Orientalist ... recidivist exoticism' (123).
8 That his story can be seen as autobiographical is important in several ways, not least for Hwang's adroit setting up and sabotaging (or more precisely setting up for self-sabotage) of the traditional Western concept of the rational subject (the masculine 'I') in Gallimard; for discussion of this Western subject, see Smith 2–18, 157.
9 The stage instructions for Nozomi's death, staged as a pantomime viewed by her son '*through the camera*,' calls for her to lie down with '*her hands over her face*,' which her mother-in-law then covers '*with a small white cloth*' (26). After viewing this memory scene, Jeffrey tells his half-brother that his father left them when he was 'quite young' and that his 'mother died ten years ago' (27). This is the only information we will get, but the implication is that Nozomi dies, not when Luke leaves but some years later when her son is about ten. In any case, Jeffrey only visits the United States; he returns to Hiroshima to marry a Japanese woman and live there.
10 Lepage uses English, German, French, Italian, and Japanese in the dialogue to create a multilingual play that enhances the polyphonic strategies of the text in performance. The published text carries translations.
11 Lepage's views on the feminine and on Japan as feminine are problematic but beyond the scope of this discussion; see Charest 19–20.
12 At least, it is not in the sense of memory play. However, insofar as Gallimard can be seen as acting out Song's proposition from act 1, when he asks Gallimard to imagine a beautiful Westerner killing herself for a 'short Japanese businessman' (17), then it just might be Song's version of the Butterfly story after all.

PART FOUR

Contexts

Madama Butterfly and the Absence of Empire

RICHARD CAVELL

for William Weaver,
with fond memories of the Urbino Summer School, 1980

Prelude: In Four Modulations

One: in 1984, Malcolm McLaren cut an album called *Fans* in which Cio-Cio-San appears as a digitized voice-over in a post-punk parody of the famous aria in Puccini's opera. McLaren was, in many ways, the great impresario of punk rock in his capacity as manager of the notorious band The Sex Pistols, whose 1977 single 'God Save the Queen' sent up what Greil Marcus calls, in *Lipstick Traces*, 'England's dream of its glorious past, as represented by the Queen, ... the nation's basic tourist attraction, linchpin of an economy based on nothing, save England's collective amputee's itch for Empire' (11). In the 1980s, McLaren reinvented himself as a musician in his own right, declaring with his album *Duck Rock* that the record had become the ultimate musical instrument, sign of the postmodernist collapse of master narratives into fragments and montage. 'Back in Nagasaki,' says the voice-over on *Fans*, 'I got married to Cio-Cio-San. That was her name in those days. And I was her man.'

Two: in 'Flirting with the Foreign: Interracial Sex in Japan's "International Age,"' Karen Kelsky has written that

> [s]ince the late 1980s, a small population of young Japanese women has become the subject of intense controversy within Japan and abroad for its

allegedly aggressive sexual pursuit of white, black, Balinese and other non-Japanese (or *gaijin*) males. The activities of these women – labelled 'yellow cabs' (*iero kyabu*) in a racist, sexist slur coined by their foreign male conquests and appropriated by the Japanese mass media – have inspired best-selling novels, television documentaries, films, and, in the early 1990s, a heated debate in the major popular magazines ... These women are interesting not only for the controversy that they have engendered in Japan, but also because they defy standard Western Orientalist understandings of the Asian-Western sexual encounter, typically based on the *Madame Butterfly* trope of Western male power over and victimization of the Oriental women. (173)

Kelsky argues that

the goals and behaviour of the so-called yellow cabs are in fact of considerable theoretical significance for a Western audience, for they constitute not only a coherent, although indirect, critique of Japanese patriarchy, but also an instance of the increasingly shifting and contested grounds of encounter between Japan and the West, and finally, the emerging local/global continuum along which both people and theories must now be tracked ... In the age of *M. Butterfly*, things are no longer so simple. (174–5)

Three: from a poem called 'Your Cio-Cio San,' by Martin F. Manalansan IV, an Asian–North American poet:

you gasp as you grab
my biceps, never knew
that people like me
grew muscles not just sallow
yellow skin.

you try to grapple me, hold me down,
pin my fate to the mattress.
but i pull loose.

standing above you, my body juts
into the darkness,
i pull you up to me,
hairy legs enveloping my waist, man-child
to mother, we cling,

climbing some mountains,
scaling some heights.

i raise you up from the chilly sheets,
a boy, squealing with delight
at being up so high, in the thin winter air.
you moan and shout.
biting my lips,
i try hard not to laugh at your
strangeness, amazed at how
someone so laconic
could become so verbose,

your mouth agape, seemingly dis-oriented.
your body curls up.
an ivory landscape, quivering.

you lay
spooned against my groin.
fetus-shaped, fragile and pale.
i let you sleep.

i am your new geisha boy, you say,
but wait till morning, when my mask is in order
and i crack the whip for real.

Four: a painting (oil on plywood) by Canadian artist Derek Root. It represents a vastly expanded page of Ovid's *Ars Amatoria*, superimposed on which is the photography-based painting of a Japanese woman, traditionally arrayed and adorned. The painting is titled 'Mikado'; it is for sale at a store named 'Liberty.' One block away there is another store, this one selling Japanese and Chinese antiques. It is called 'The Orientalist.'

The Butterfly Plague

As for the butterflies, they continue to breed. They suffered losses, but which of us doesn't? Theirs are by the millions; ours are by ones ...
   They have certain habits and a certain history.
   We know that history repeats itself.

> We also know that it does not.
>
> Timothy Findley, *The Butterfly Plague*

Why Butterfly? What remains so enduring about that novel by Loti, that story by Long, that play by Belasco, that opera by Giacosa/Illica/Puccini? Why is it that Butterfly appears again and again across a vast spectrum of cultural production? As the linguistic hybridity of the title *Madama Butterfly* indicates, it is first of all the borderlines that these works explore that have such a profound attraction within contemporary cultural production; they speak to the concerns of cultures increasingly uncertain of their self-representations within an increasingly mediatized and globalized technoscape, as David Henry Hwang and David Cronenberg have variously shown. With the collapse of the grand narratives of the West and the concomitant collapse of an 'Orient' constructed as the Other of that 'West,' new configurations are sought, to which the hybridity of the Butterfly mythos seems to speak most powerfully. It may also be that the interdisciplinary ethos which welcomes a narrative that has been taken up by a number of different media is itself a sign of the displacement of narrative as a mode of configuring not only social and cultural emplotments, but disciplinary knowledge itself (as Janet Murray has suggested). This displacement is configured in a variety of ways in the opera, from its refusal of narrative coherence and the related displacement of the aria (as Jeremy Tambling suggests), to the role of spying in Hwang and Cronenberg, where narrative (including the narrative of gender) is withheld, to the role that Puccini's music plays in postmodern works, where it is reduced to the ultimate of musical clichés (as McLaren demonstrates so tellingly).

It is a similar, and related, narrative, that of colonization, that Anne McClintock seeks to complicate in the opening pages of *Imperial Leather*, where she writes that 'imperialism is not something that happened elsewhere – a disagreeable fact of history external to Western identity. Rather, imperialism and the invention of race were fundamental aspects of Western, industrial modernity' (5). McClintock's statement expands the notion of colonization to include the colonizer, as in the master/slave paradigm that Manalansan plays on in his poem, and it is this powerful bi-valence that characterizes McClintock's readings throughout her book.

McClintock is thus opposed to the naive construal of postcolonialist critique along a linear axis that takes one from colonization through postcoloniality to a state of blissful hybridity, the sort of model proposed by Francis Fukuyama in 'The End of History,' where the end of history neatly coincides with the fall of the Berlin Wall and the opening of a McDonald's in Red Square. The 'figure of linear development' (10) that this axis implies, writes McClintock, contains 'an unbidden, if disavowed, commitment to linear time and the idea of development' (10), which was the very model of imperialism. 'Metaphorically poised on the border between old and new, end and beginning, the term [postcolonial] heralds the end of a world era but by invoking the very same trope of linear progress which animated that era' (10).

Whereas a naive postcolonialist theory such as that developed in *The Empire Writes Back* posits a discontinuity *between* the colonial and the postcolonial, McClintock argues for the importance of observing the discontinuities *within* these historical moments. For example, she writes that

> since the 1940s, the U.S. imperialism-without-colonies has taken a number of distinct forms (military, political, economic and cultural), some concealed, some half-concealed. The power of U.S. finance capital and huge multinational corporations to command the flows of capital, research, consumer goods and media information around the world can exert a coercive power as great as any colonial gunboat. It is precisely the greater subtlety, innovation and variety of these forms of imperialism that make the historical rupture implied by the term postcolonial especially unwarranted. (13)

To put it another way: postcolonial theory, as currently construed, seeks to write a coherent narrative for a set of phenomena that resists narratives of this sort precisely through their discontinuity – what McClintock calls their 'greater subtlety, innovation and variety.'

McClintock's theoretical model is complicated enough to treat the postcolonial and the imperial as overlapping, and this is especially so in terms of the argument that she makes throughout *Imperial Leather* that 'gender [is] a constitutive dynamic of imperial and anti-imperial power' (14). David Henry Hwang explores this intersection in *M. Butterfly*, his play of 1988, which he calls 'a deconstructivist *Madama Butterfly*' (86).[1] This deconstruction of *Madama Butterfly* was suggested to Hwang by the opera itself, as he writes in the afterword to his play:

> I felt convinced that the libretto would include yet another lotus blossom pining away for a cruel Caucasian man, and dying for her love. Such a story has become too much of a cliché not to be included in the archetypal East-West romance that started it all. Sure enough, when I purchased the

record, I discovered it contained a wealth of sexist and racist clichés, reaffirming my faith in Western culture. (86)

However, neither the opera nor the play can be so neatly determined. Marjorie Garber argues in *Vested Interests*, for example, that, as a play of category crisis, *M. Butterfly* cannot be subjected to interpretive closure in the way that Hwang proposes for the opera:

> Man/woman or male/female, is the most obvious and central of the border crossings in *M. Butterfly*, but the fact that the border is crossed twice, once when Song Liling becomes a 'woman,' and the second time when Rene Gallimard does so, indicates the play's preoccupation with the transvestite as a figure not only for the conundrum of gender and erotic style, but also for other kinds of border-crossing, like *acting* and *spying*, both of which are appropriations of alternative and socially constructed subject positions for cultural and political ends. (239)

Yet gender is not *wholly* a conundrum for Hwang: he knows what a man is – as Song declares, '[B]eing an Oriental, I could never be completely a man.' Robert K. Martin has perceptively noted that this statement 'illustrates the equation between the Western and the masculine, but it leaves the term "man" undeconstructed' (103), thus falling back on a binary of gender, and erasing the possibility of alternative sexualities. Martin goes on to point out that the problematics of this binary emerge in the play's last scene:

> As Gallimard puts on the makeup, wig, and kimono, the audience is expected to participate in a ritual renunciation of masculine power, in the abject humiliation of man as woman, the powerful becoming the powerless. The scene works dramatically, but what does it suggest intellectually? What place does it leave for drag or for gender instability? In a play about the 'feminine' as the colonised other, the ultimate humiliation is indeed to become feminine ... Even more than in the opera, the play's conclusion focuses on the Western male and his suffering. (104)

A comparison with David Cronenberg's version of this scene, in his movie version of *M. Butterfly*, is informative. The scene is highly staged, with the prisoners forming the audience, the scene being played out similarly to the theatre version. What is striking, however, is the absence of affect among the audience; while they applaud Gallimard's performance at the end – which includes his suicide – they remain unmoved, as if a reversal had taken place between the real and the performed. This sets up a question about the role of fantasy in Orientalist constructions, a question addressed by Rey Chow in an essay on Cronenberg's film called 'The Dream of the Butterfly.' Like Martin, Chow critiques Hwang for buying into the very Orientalist stereotypes he seeks to deconstruct; specifically, she focuses on the role of fantasy in Hwang's play. As she puts it,

> if the most important thing about fantasy is not the simple domination of an other, but ... the variable positionality of the subject, whose reality consists in a constant shifting between modes of dominance and submission, what could be said about the relations between East and West, woman and man, that is perhaps alternative to the relations they are assumed, in antiorientalist discourse, to have? (63)

The film portrays this problematic, according to Chow, by proposing that the attraction between Song and Gallimard is mutual, that this is not the one-sided love of a Western male for a woman who represents the feminized East. The irreducibility of that love, as represented in the film, is that it is neither purely Orientalist nor purely homoerotic (ibid. 70). This notion of fragmentation, of the end of the grand narratives of desire, and of their *Ruling Passions*, as Christopher Lane has recently put it, is brilliantly embodied in the cassette tape of *Madama Butterfly* that Gallimard places in the player in his last, dramatic scene in the prison. Chow remarks that the opera, like Gallimard's Orientalist props, has become a portable object, unmoored from its local habitat, and this unmooring applies to the protagonists as well. Each had supplied for the other the illusion of a fixed identity. As Chow puts it, 'The "Butterfly" that was Song ... shielded Gallimard from the "Butterfly" that is himself' (81).

Yet Chow also admits that this reading does not exhaust the visuality of this last scene in the film; she focuses on the use of a mirror shard as Gallimard's instrument of suicide, 'a mirror ... that has lost its reflective function,' thus problematizing the possibility of ever confirming an identity. In these terms, it is not Gallimard, the stable identity, who performs Butterfly, but Butterfly, the fantasy, that performs Gallimard in a startling rendition of Wilde's apothegm that 'all men kill the thing they love' ('Ballad' 839). But what of the audience of prisoners who witness this scene – why do they receive it so emotionlessly? I would suggest that in this all-male world, this world without private identities, this scopophilic regime, they have seen it all before. Here in the prison, more powerfully than anywhere else, the Other is revealed as *appallingly* the Same.

Madama Butterfly and the Absence of Empire

Social and political institutions are invested [by the Empire] ... not with authority – for none is truly original – but with the sign of authority ... In other words, what [is] revere[d] as authority is always the sign of authority. Though nothing now remains of the original founding authority of the fathers except the place of its absence ... this very vacancy at the heart of the world is itself almost sacred.
Lionel Gossman, The Empire Unpossess'd

A debate similar to the one that McClintock discerns within postcolonialist critique has grown up around the 'reading' of opera in the last few years. This debate has oscillated between a position that sees opera as Wagnerian *Gesamtkunstwerk*, on the one hand, and another that sees opera as a more discontinuous and differential art form. Nietzsche's invitation at the end of *The Birth of Tragedy* (written under the profound influence of the doyen of Bayreuth), that we come with him to worship at the altars of both the Dionysian and the Apollonian gods, has been taken up by contemporary, post-structuralist theory not as an incitement to unanimity but as an inducement to embrace the discontinuity and displacement of the inevitable incommensurability of Apollonian text with Dionysian music.[2]

That opera can function – and function well – in the absence of the unity towards which the *Gesamtkunstwerk* would appear to gesture is illustrated by works such as Stein and Thomson's *Four Saints in Three Acts* or, paradigmatically (because of its formal concerns), Schoenberg's *Moses und Aron*,[3] where the radical *dis*continuity between speaking and singing, *Sprechgesang* and *melos*, becomes the highly dramatic motive force of the opera.

Like *Moses und Aron*, Puccini's *Madama Butterfly* is a conversion narrative – indeed, it is two conversion narratives, Cio-Cio-San's and Pinkerton's – and this similarity provides a port of entry into the formal and what might be called the topological concerns of the Giacosa/Illica/Puccini collaboration. Those concerns go back to the foundations of the form, which, for Slavoj Žižek, involve 'a kind of symbolic exchange between the human subject and his divine Master: when the subject, the human mortal, by way of his offer of self-sacrifice, surmounts his finitude and attains the divine heights, the Master responds with the sublime gesture of grace, the ultimate proof of *his* humanity' (178). Yet Žižek goes on to argue that 'this act of grace is at the same time branded by the irreducible mark of a forced empty gesture – the Master ultimately makes a virtue out of necessity, he promotes as a free act what he is in any case compelled to do' (178). This drama of Master and subject is enacted foundationally in Monteverdi's version of the Orpheus story, where Orfeo is consoled by the Divinity for the fateful backward glance, which however will allow Orfeo to re-inscribe, though on a sublimated level, his love for Euridice. If it comes as a surprise to us to be asked to consider *Madama Butterfly* as a displacement of the Orpheus plot, it is because Puccini et al. have displaced the *place* of that plot in such a way as to invite a reading in terms of a historical presence that their work consistently evades.

In this context it is important to note that there is a rather long tradition of what might be called the 'Spaghetti Eastern' within the sphere of cultural production in Italy that is generally associated with opera. As the works of Metastasio and those plays collected in Ghérardi's *Le théâtre italien* demonstrate, the obsession with the so-called Orient antedates *Butterfly* by a number of centuries. Metastasio's *Opere*, long one of the principal founts for opera libretti (Italian and otherwise), contains, along with its dramas on the imperial theme, plays with the title *Le Cinesi* (4: 241–55) and *L'eroe cinese* (7: 101–43). In Ghérardi's collection of *commedia dell'arte* scenarios (*scenari* that were employed by Leoncavallo, Strauss, Busoni, Puccini, Schoenberg, Picasso, and Severini [Tambling 114]) we find a long work with the title *Les Chinois* (4: 163–209). These Orientalist obsessions were fed by the history of religious imperialism as practised by the Roman church (Sansom 50); they place the conversion dramas at the heart of Puccini's *Butterfly* into their appropriate context, and we recall here that Pinkerton's avowal of the joys of plunder is referred to by Sharpless as 'un facile vangelo' (Puccini 188) – an easygoing or even facile gospel.

In the latter half of the nineteenth century, its imperial ambitions secularized, Italy sought to participate fully in the colonial riches of which it saw its European neighbours partaking. According to Jeremy Tambling's recent, deeply theorized study *Opera and the Culture of Fascism*, the imperial theme in *Butterfly* – congruently with the tropes of abjection, undoing, fetishization, and displacement that critics have increasingly noted to be endemic within opera – is represented through articulations of absence, and primarily absence as a troping of empire, and it is to this sense of absence that I want to turn my attention.

We are drawn to the Italian theme in *Butterfly* by its title, 'Madama' having a particular Italian resonance even within contemporary parlance. To this day, Palazzo Madama is the seat (since 1871) of the Italian Senate in Rome; the palace itself was built in the late 1500s for one of the Medici's wives, Margaret of Austria (1522–86), who was known as 'Madama' (Raffaelli 172, 378, 449). The epithet thus has associations with a past inevitably seen from the vantage of 1900 as redolent of lost glories. The double frame of reference here – outward to a sociopolitical 'other' and inward to a glorious past that itself is, also, now 'other' – is related directly to the displacements within the form of opera; as Adorno remarked with specific reference to *Butterfly*, 'It is precisely because opera, as a bourgeois vacation spot, allowed itself so little involvement in the social conflicts of the nineteenth century, that it was able to mirror so crassly the developing tendencies of bourgeois society itself' (36).[4]

Tambling argues that *Madama Butterfly*'s concern with these nationalist others belongs within an imperialistic and fascistic tradition that includes Meyerbeer's *L'Africaine* of 1865 (76), whose theme is very similar to that of *Butterfly*; Mascagni and Illica's 'Japanese' opera *Iris* (1898); and its immediate predecessor, *Cristoforo Colómbo* (1892), which Illica had produced in collaboration with Franchetti (136), and whose title nakedly identifies the colonialist enterprise in the service of which these operas were produced. While Italy's African campaigns would not get revved up until the mid-1930s, they had their roots, as Tambling asserts, 'in 1880s colonialism: fascism was not just a parenthesis in Italian history' (80). These colonialist and fascistic enterprises were motivated by a profound national doubt occasioned by forces such as mass emigration and internal economic chaos. 'And the question this prompted,' writes Tambling, was

> *Where was Italy's centre?* Or even, *Where was Italy?* Could it be identified in any complete sense with the peninsula which had been unified in 1870? ... Could it make sense to be a successor to Verdi, the musician of the nation, when, clearly, that nation which his music had encouraged into being was in process of being proved to be elsewhere, displaced, decentred? (128)

Italy had already been humiliated at Adowa, Africa, in 1895, where more Italians died than in all the campaigns of the Risorgimento (79), and the imperialist anxieties provoked by that incident are evident, though at a degree of displacement, in *Madama Butterfly*, as they would be some forty years after Adowa when Mussolini invaded Ethiopia. The opera thus represents Japan, Tambling goes on to argue, 'as a weak feminine little country inhabited by a people content to wait for "one fine day," sitting out the night in non-retaliatory sweetness. It could be argued that the West needed to represent Japan to itself in such a feminine, miniature, non-aggressive way, and, above all, as so economically backward, because of its fears that the reality was very much different' (139). As indeed the reality was: Butterfly opened in Milan on 17 February 1904, a week after the beginning of the Russo-Japanese war, which was the climax of Japanese expansion within the Pacific. At the same time, Japan had recently been humiliated by the United States over Hawaii, and was forced to concede its power over the Philippines (Tambling 138). Hence, the representation of Japan as weak *and* the identification with the imperially successful Americans that we find in *Madama Butterfly* have a specific historical context.

The representation of Japan and the United States in the opera thus masks and mirrors certain anxieties the Italians had about Italy itself. In the United States, for example, a singer such as Caruso could earn vastly more by singing at the Met than he ever could at La Scala (Tambling 128), with all that that implied for a nation that identified itself politically with the production of opera (as, paradigmatically, in the case of Verdi, who came to embody aspirations for Vittorio Emmanuele, Re d'Italia); and it was in the United States that Puccini would locate *La Fanciulla del West*, the opera he wrote after *Butterfly*, where a number of these anxieties are dramatized. In *Butterfly*, Pinkerton, as the representative of the United States, is identified with this topological displacement, singing, in his first aria (which, as Tambling notes [142], is incomplete):

Dovunque al mondo lo Yankee vagabondo
si gode e traffica
sprezzando rischi. (Puccini 186)

Everywhere in the world the Yankee vagabond enjoys himself and trades, scorning risks.[5]

This spatial hegemony has already been countered, however, by the opening scene, in which Goro demonstrates the mutability of spatial conformities in the house that Pinkerton has just purchased:

PINKERTON: E soffitto ... e pareti ...
GORO: Vanno e vengono a prova
    a norma che vi giova
    nello stesso locale
    alternar nuovi aspetti ai consueti. (182)

P: And the ceiling ... and the walls ...
G: They come and go at will in order to help you, in the same room, replace familiar arrangements with new ones.

This mutable space contrasts powerfully with the totalized space of the imperialist Yankee.[6] Yet part of the interest of *Butterfly* lies in the fact that both Pinkerton and Cio-Cio-San will have to show themselves to be likewise mutable, Cio-Cio-San converting to Pinkerton's strange gods – 'I bow to Mr. Pinkerton's God' (202), says Cio-Cio-San, who, at the beginning of act 2, will refer to this as her 'American house' [220]) – and Pinkerton undergoing a conversion experience at the very end, when he realizes that Cio-Cio-San truly loved him. On another level, of course, the ending of the opera re-inscribes Cio-Cio-San within conventions of Romantic love that are themselves problematical, especially as they serve to concretize essentialist notions of gender and harken to an imperial past.

The incompletion of Pinkerton's opening aria, its continual interruption, betrays mixed motives, Tambling argues, as does Pinkerton's vacillation between first and third persons, all of this betraying 'a death drive which is a motive force behind his imperialism, ... especially his sexual imperialism' (143). 'Such pursuit,' Tambling continues,

> makes [Pinkerton] a melancholic, both in the sense that he has a nostalgia for what is past and gone, hence the death wish, and also in a sentimentality about home, which is registered in the use of the kitsch material of the "Star Spangled Banner." The musical text performs a critique of imperialism as kitsch-inspired, exoticism as an empty dream. In this attitude, the individual Yankee is of no importance; but Sharpless and Pinkerton clink glasses at "America for ever." The nation **is** important; and because it is important, the nation spreads itself round the globe. Hence we have the remarkable intrusion into Italian opera of American words and phrases and American music. Further, Pinkerton's commitment to marry a real American wife later on ('una vera sposa Americana') and his and Sharpless's plan at the end, in which Madama Butterfly co-operates, effectively, for the child to become an American, will be handed over to the American

patriarchy, which must be preserved. These are moves which belong to nationalism and imperialism alike. (143)

The fact that Pinkerton looks forward to 'vere nozze' and 'una vera sposa americana' (190) is powerfully suggestive of the imperialist tendency to conceive of the colonized as unreal, as an absence; here the house that Goro shows to Pinkerton becomes symbolic of the European perception of a lack of substance within the colonized: 'È una casa a soffietto' (182), says Pinkerton of the house – a house that a breath could blow down, a house of cards. Yet this is also the house of the colonizer, the house that Pinkerton and Cio-Cio-San so ambiguously share. In addition to converting to Pinkerton's strange gods, Cio-Cio-San is eager to adopt his ways, kissing his hand at one point and replying to his puzzlement, 'They told me that over there, among well-bred people, this is the mark of greatest respect' (209).

The beginning of the second act of the opera heightens our sense that Cio-Cio-San desires to believe the myth of Pinkerton, gone now for some three years. (It is thus highly ironic that Butterfly, when telling Pinkerton that she is from a once-prosperous family, adds that 'non c'è vagabondo che a sentirlo non sia / di gran prosapia' [194; 'there isn't a vagabond who, to hear him, isn't of great lineage'], using the very word Pinkerton used to describe 'lo Yankee vagabondo.') Despite Suzuki's protestations that '[n]obody's ever heard of a foreign husband who has come back to his nest,' Cio-Cio-San insists that Pinkerton will return 'colle rose / alla stagion serena / quando fa la nidiata il pettirosso' (218; 'with the roses in the sweet season when the robin makes his pretty little nest'). Here it is Cio-Cio-San who insists on performing herself within a coherent narrative of desire, which is as resplendent musically as it is clichéd textually. This disembodiment of the operatic as grand narrative through the use of cliché, figuratively conveyed in *Orfeo* by the decapitation of Orpheus and in the opera by Butterfly's disembowelment, is ultimately the site of the opera's testimony against itself and its grand designs:[7]

> Un bel dì vedremo
> levarsi un fil di fumo sull'estremo
> confin del mare.
> E poi la nave appare.
> Poi la nave bianca
> entra nel porto, romba il suo saluto.
> Vedi? È venuto! (218)

> One lovely day we'll see a thread of smoke rise at the farthest edge of the sea. And then the ship appears. Then the white ship enters the port, thunders its greeting. You see? He's come!

This is grand narrative as desire, and desire as fetish, however; like Euridice, Cio-Cio-San will be (re)taken by death before Orfeo/Pinkerton can reclaim her (in a brilliant allusion to the imperialism of artistic representations), and all that will be left is the music – disembodied song. The scene between Cio-Cio-San and Suzuki is followed by one between Sharpless and Cio-Cio-San that duplicates the opening one between Pinkerton and Sharpless (suggesting the basis for the homosocial triangle that Hwang and Cronenberg explore). In this case it is Sharpless who is unable to complete his narrative about Pinkerton's unfaithfulness, and Butterfly who now claims to abide by the laws of the United States. This reversal will be completed at the end of the opera, when Pinkerton suddenly realizes Cio-Cio-San's love for him – his notion of a 'real' wife and a 'real' culture thus irrevocably unmoored – and Cio-Cio-San reverts to the traditions of her father (at the very moment, historically, when the samurai had finally been routed), neatly summarized in the sword that is also the phallus, her *essentialist* act of suicide leaving us with no position, within the opera, to judge the events we have just seen: *neither* the 'West' *nor* the 'East,' in the terms that she has been forced to experience them, is 'real.'

The opera's repeated changes in position are congruent with the topology articulated by Goro at its beginning, and, in a final irony, Cio-Cio-San will find not a man waiting for her, but a woman, Kate Pinkerton. Here we see the ultimate articulation of the shifting positionalities of colonized subjectivity that critics such as Anne McClintock and Rey Chow have written about. The fact that such positions are articulated within an opera traditionally identified as univocally within an imperialist discourse (as by Hwang, for example) should serve to remind us of the ambiguities of the colonialist enterprise, which has meaning precisely to the degree that it is founded on what is not there.

Notes

1 Gallimard figures a classic example of what I call 'cultural transvestism'; see Cavell.
2 Levin summarizes this controversy.

3 Lacoue-Labarthe states, in his reading of Adorno's 'Sakrales Fragment: Über Schönberg's *Moses und Aron*,' that that opera derives its power from the fact that Schoenberg 'does not order his work according to a dramaturgy of the Wagnerian type' (49).
4 In my view, the mirroring to which Adorno refers is not as neutral an activity as he would imply.
5 The translations are Weaver's (1981), and appear on the facing page of the libretto.
6 In Jean-Pierre Ponnelle's video version of the opera, it is America itself that is shown as a papier-mâché fantasy, during the dawn sequence that precedes the end of the opera.
7 See, in this context, Said's discussion of *Aida* in *Culture and Imperialism*.

The Taming of the Oriental Shrew:
The Two Asias in Puccini's *Madama Butterfly* and *Turandot*

MARIA NG

Often, when Westerners mistake me for a Japanese, my response is one of annoyance – why do Westerners assume that all Asians are the same: small, inscrutable rice-eaters? In our post-essentialist age, concepts of difference should ideally be part of any cross-cultural interaction. Indeed, Cultural Studies valorizes the 'reconception of notions of identity' (Appiah and Gates 1) and encourages a non-homogeneous approach towards representing other cultures. However, differentiation of ethnic identities is not a late-twentieth-century concept, nor is it a guarantee against prejudice. Different Asian nations have always been subjected to different types of prejudice, which the West has developed in response to historical and social contacts. These differentiations have been established for self-serving purposes, quite unlike the idealistic aim of cultural criticism, which believes that the articulation of difference can empower traditionally marginalized or silenced communities. Instead of contributing to breaking down the walls of stereotypes built around nations and ethnicities, these embedded differentiations only serve to reinforce stereotypical identities and multiply the repertoire of biased rhetoric. In its examination of two Puccini operas with East Asian themes, this essay illustrates that within the general binary of the West (mis)representing the East, one can detect embedded differentiations between the Asian nations and cultures. A comparison of Puccini's versions of Japan in *Madama Butterfly* (1904) and of China in *Turandot* (1924) will show that, although both operas fall under the category of Orientalist fantasy, each also reflects a historically specific awareness of the difference between Japanese and Chinese cultures.

The European perception of China underwent considerable changes from the eighteenth to the nineteenth century. Tracing the reversal of

Western responses to Asian cultures, the historian Michael Adas reminds the reader that 'no culture or civilization has been as lavishly praised or as widely acclaimed as a model to be emulated as was Qing China in the first half of the eighteenth century' (79). But with the advance of industrialization and the 'ascendancy of science' in Europe, Chinese achievements came under increasing criticism and the 'Chinese attachment to ancient customs and teachings and hostility toward innovation' was thought to be key impediments to its joining the European nations in equal rank (85). In a series of lectures on the 'Philosophy of History' delivered in the 1820s and 1830s, and later published, Hegel confirms this change of European attitude towards China in the industrial age. He admires China's governmental organization, but deplores its overall lack of progress. In his critical analysis of the oldest Oriental empire, Hegel concedes that the Chinese 'have as a general characteristic, a remarkable skill in imitation.' But they are, 'on the other hand, too proud to learn anything from Europeans, although they must often recognize their superiority' (137–8). Hegel also singles out the Chinese use of corporal punishment as an indication that in China 'the feeling of honor has not yet developed itself' (128). In *The Philosophy of History*, China is presented as ancient and cruel. This popular concept of a distant land of unspeakable decadent customs is echoed in Thomas De Quincey's *Confessions of an English Opium Eater*: '[I]f I were compelled to forego England, and to live in China, and among Chinese manners and modes of life and scenery, I should go mad' (108). De Quincey's fear of and repugnance against China were based, like those of many other Europeans, not on any direct observation and first-hand experience, but on the general perception that China was antiquated, unscientific, and degenerated. This view is best summed up by the memorable line in Tennyson's 'Locksley Hall' (1842), where the poet claims: 'Better fifty years of Europe than a cycle of Cathay.'[1]

China's imperial policies regarding foreigners and foreign cultures reinforced this image of a non-progressive country. At the root of Chinese attitude towards the West was 'the assumption that China was the "central" kingdom and that other countries were, by definition, peripheral, removed from the cultural center of the universe. The Chinese, therefore, showed little interest in precise information or detailed study of foreign countries' (Spence 119). Like China, Japan also resisted European advances and demands for trade before the nineteenth century. But unlike the Qing dynasty, Japan adopted a more pragmatic policy regarding the problem of encroaching Western modernization. By the mid-nineteenth century, Japan decided that the best way to counter European and American aggression would be to learn more about them, especially in areas such as industry and military production. In 1860 an envoy of 77 Japanese was sent to the United States, and in 1862 another mission was sent to Europe, touring many European countries, including Italy (Beasley 56–88). These contacts resulted in Japan adopting Western technology and in Western countries sending technicians and personnel to Japan, to put into practice industrial reforms such as 'plans for cotton-spinning and sugar refining ... By June 1867 the cotton mill had been completed and was beginning operations under its British technicians' (ibid. 113). Other missions followed after the Meiji Restoration of 1868–9. During a Japanese delegation's visit to London in 1872, Lord Granville, the Foreign Secretary, was told that the Japanese mission intended to 'study [English] institutions, and observe all that constitutes English civilization, so as to adopt on their return to Japan whatever they may think suitable to their own country' (165).

Apart from such diplomatic forays into Europe, Japan was also well represented in international expositions. In 1862, a selection of Japanese objects was displayed at the Fourth International Exposition in London (Beasley 81–2). The first substantial Japanese exhibition was at the *Exposition universelle* in 1867. As an index of the popularity of *Japonisme* in Europe, which began in the second half of the nineteenth century, a private association was formed after the exposition in 1867 by a few French artists, which met monthly at Sèvres to dine in 'an atmosphere entirely attuned to the interests of these lovers of Japan' (Dufwa 42). During these meetings, dinner service and membership cards were designed with Japanese motifs, and '[e]verything, including the watercolour decorating a sonnet transcribed by the host ... was inspired by Japanese style and taste' (ibid. 41–2). Japanese influence in prints, paintings, furniture designs, and music[2] became more and more discernible as the century drew to its close.

One of the artists swept away by *Japonisme* was the German poet and travel writer Max Dauthendey. Born in 1867 in Würzburg, Germany, Dauthendey came under the influence of the Art Nouveau movement.[3] He recalls in his autobiography the various Asian art collections he saw in Paris, where he was living in the 1890s. In a passage reminiscent of the fetishization of the fragile butterfly in Puccini's *Madama Butterfly*, Dauthendey describes his vision of two Japanese women in Park Montsouris, Paris. Half-hidden by a laburnum bush (*Goldregenstrauch*), Dauthendey watched as these two visitors sat on a park bench in their traditional costume:

> Diese vornehmen Damen aus der hohen japanischen Aristokratie waren nicht auffälliger in ihrer Kleidung und in ihrem Gebaren als die Amseln oder die Tauben, die im Rasen ab und zu flogen. Eine zufriedene vornehme Einheit trennte bei ihnen nicht Körper und Kleidung voreinander. Ihre schlafrockartigen Kimonos waren für die Körper schlichte Behälter, wie das Federkleid es für die Vögel, wie das Fell es für die Tiere ist.
>
> These refined ladies from the Japanese higher aristocracy were no more striking in their dress and their demeanour than the blackbirds or the doves which flew to and fro above the lawn. Their bodies and clothes were not separate but joined in a union of elegance and contentment. Their kimonos, which resembled nightgowns, covered their bodies much as *feathers smoothly cover the birds, or fur covers the animals*. (*Acht* 674–5, my translation; emphasis added)

Dauthendey found out that these Japanese women, who were accompanying their husbands on some diplomatic mission, had formed the habit of visiting the park in the early hours, when there was little traffic. In Dauthendey's narrative, the Japanese women are compared to little fragile animals. He also notices, from behind the bush, every physical detail on the women: their chignon, their legs, the draperiness of their kimonos. Like Pinkerton and Sharpless's connoisseurs' exchange regarding Cio-Cio-San's pretty delicacy in *Madama Butterfly*, Dauthendey's appreciation of the Japanese women emphasizes the predatory nature of Orientalist objectification.

While Western art movements were incorporating Japanese elements into print, music, and writing, the governments were becoming increasingly aware of the successive and successful military reforms Japan was undertaking. These reforms resulted in Japan's defeat of China in the Sino-Japanese War in 1894, a triumph followed by Japan's victory in the Russo-Japanese War of 1904 (the year of *Madama Butterfly*) and 1905. Japan's military victories shocked the Western world. Never before in modern history had a major European nation been beaten by a non-European power. After all, the House of Romanov was related to various European royal families. Japan's ability to compete in military and industrial areas 'shattered the illusion that industrialization was a uniquely Western process' (Adas 357). As Japanese historian Seiji

Hishida boasted in 1905, 'Japan's healthy assimilation of western civilization' had gained it admittance 'into the comity of nations on an equal footing' with Western states (255). In comparison, China 'was not only excluded from the rank of the Asiatic great powers, but became the "sick man" of the East' (256).

When Puccini began researching Japanese culture and writing *Madama Butterfly*, European countries had developed an ambivalent international relationship with Japan. Even Finland, which had considerably less contact with Japan than major European powers like Italy, was aware of the Japanese ability to absorb and adapt to elements of Western civilization (Fält, 'Image' 98–9). Artistically, Japan was emulated. But politically, Japan was only grudgingly accepted as part of the imperial community (Greenhalgh 74–5). After all, the Japanese were still Asians, and thus Western anxiety towards and equivocal acceptance of Japan is echoed in Puccini's opera in the figure of Cio-Cio-San. Being Madama Butterfly is only one of Cio-Cio-San's many identities. To her own people and her maid, she remains Japanese. To Pinkerton and to Sharpless, she is a fragile plaything, a butterfly. To Pinkerton's American wife, she is a nameless and disposable inconvenience. Only to herself is she Mrs Pinkerton. She is at once an indigenous Japanese, an exoticized Oriental object, and a Japanese who is willing to succumb to the strength and demands of another culture. This portrait of a Japanese character seems to coincide with the Western view of the new Asian power. Japan was attractive and desirable for its aesthetic qualities; but it must also be contained. Although it could not be ignored, it must not be fully integrated into the Western community. This guarded enthusiasm for a new partnership can also be seen when Pinkerton bargains with Goro, the marriage broker, in the first act: despite his eagerness to consummate the 'marriage,' the American is mindful of maintaining his superiority and advantages during the negotiation.

Western influence and male sexual power are the pervasive themes in the opera. Cio-Cio-San loves Pinkerton and, by default, loves his culture. Although she lives in an uneasy compromise between Japanese tradition and a hybrid version of American culture, she looks forward to a full integration into Pinkerton's life. In her case, male sexual domination is more potent than loyalty to one's traditional culture. Thus, Cio-Cio-San's domestic situation reinforces the emphasis critics of imperialism and its legacy place on gender relationships. As Anne McClintock insists in *Imperial Leather*: '[I]mperialism cannot be fully understood without a theory of gender power. Gender power was not the superficial patina of empire, an ephemeral gloss ... Rather, gender dynamics were ... fundamental to the securing and maintenance of the imperial enterprise' (6–7). As a Japanese hoping to become part of an American household, Cio-Cio-San acquaints herself with Christianity, with foreign words, and, pathetically, with ornithology and entomology. The first act of *Madama Butterfly* is the travesty of a Japanese domestic scene, since Pinkerton bargains in bad faith and signs the marriage contract fully intending to renege on it. He indulges in the formality only because he is certain that, as a Westerner, he is not under the obligation of Japanese rules and customs.

Apart from its representation of a racialized and commercialized gender relationship between a Japanese and a Westerner, the opera is also a condensed example of European exoticization of the Far East, specifically Japan. Cio-Cio-San is consistently described as little or doll-like, very much in line with the general images travellers employ when describing things Japanese. For instance, the Victorian traveller Isabella Bird makes this observation regarding the Japanese in *Unbeaten Tracks in Japan*: '[T]he clogs add three inches to their height, but even with them few of the men attained 5 feet 7 inches, and few of the women 5 feet 2 inches' (16). Japan also became so universally associated with popular symbols such as cherry blossoms, chrysanthemums, kimonos, geishas, and tea ceremony that the culture became only too easily 'representable.' Bird's response to the Japanese people is to 'feel as if I had seen them all before, so like are they to their pictures on trays, fans, and teapots' (16). A Chinese-Canadian writer, under the Japanese pseudonym of Onoto Watanna, wrote a novel called *A Japanese Nightingale* in 1904, the same year when *Madama Butterfly* was first produced. The plot, embellished by images of little dancing girls, cherry blossoms, and teahouses, revolves around the marriage of a geisha and an American. That this particular writer, Winifred Eaton, should use not her own ethnic heritage, but appropriate an Asian culture that was considered more Western, is an indication of the popularity of Japanese over Chinese culture. Carrying this preference for Japan over China to an extreme, Winifred Eaton denied her Chinese ethnicity in her autobiography, and in an obituary for her sister claimed descent from a noble Japanese family (White-Parks 50).

In spite of the West's fascination with *Japonisme*, however, Japan was not truly accepted as an equal partner.[4] As an indication of Western ambivalence towards Japan, anthropological and phrenological calculations for the Japan-British Exhibition in 1910 had to be tailored to somehow include the Japanese as honorary Westerners (Greenhalgh 96–7). The Europeans and Americans mistrusted not only Japan's military power, but also its ability to become a serious trade competitor. A good example of this guarded attitude can be seen in John and Alice Dewey's *Letters From Japan and China*, a record of their travels in 1919. Initially, Dewey and his wife reacted to Japanese culture and custom with lavish praise. Describing a kindergarten they visited, the Deweys write: '[T]he rooms where the little children were are like gardens of flowers ... The work was all interesting' (28). The Deweys enjoyed the types of food and the attentive service they received as honoured guests. Predictably, cherry blossoms play a predominant part in their description. The diminutiveness of Japanese objects is also remarked upon: 'little shop,' 'little peach or plum,' and 'tiny orange trees' are only some examples. But as the Deweys themselves eventually admit: 'The Japanese impressions are gradually sinking into perspective with distance, and it is easy to see that the same qualities that make them admirable are also the ones that irritate you' (156–7). Writing during their Chinese journey, the Deweys began to voice serious criticism of Japan, thus showing that the charm of Japanese tea ceremonies and geishas was wearing off and a more hostile view of Japan was surfacing : '[T]he United States ... ought to be as positive and aggressive in calling Japan to account for every aggressive move she makes, as Japan is in doing them ... It is sickening that we allow Japan to keep us on the defensive' (178–9).

In *Madama Butterfly*, the charm of Cio-Cio-San also wears off when Pinkerton returns to the States. True to his words in act 1, he abandons his Japanese mistress and temporary household. Although Pinkerton remains offstage for most of act 2, he is represented by Sharpless the consul and 'Abra'm Lincoln,' his ship. Individual male sexual power is conflated with symbols of American imperial power, enacting a blending of private drama and world politics. As the Deweys warn in their analysis of the Far Eastern situation and Japan's military dominance, a firm grip must be kept on the Japanese nation, however much one might enjoy the many seductions it can offer a visitor. In both opera and travel narrative, Japan and the Japanese are portrayed as endearing and manipulable, but neither trustworthy nor acceptable as equal partners.

Western fascination with China was grounded in different motivations. After British victories against China in the so-called Opium War (1839–42), the West realized that China was not invincible. As Western nation after nation signed treaties for territorial concessions, the West began to establish pockets of settlements on the coast of China (Spence 156–64). Yet the Chinese language, the Chinese people, and the vast Chinese interior remained closed to the world. The Qing dynasty, the last representative of over two thousand years of Chinese imperial power, intended this door to remain as firmly closed as possible to the 'barbarians.' One can say that Western struggle for concessions from China, in terms of treaty rights and territorial gains, was staged as if various hostile but fascinated suitors were trying to overcome the reluctance of an ailing yet powerful authority. As long as the imperial system was in place, Western nations were careful to observe the outward signs of formal respect. But they were also fully aware that China was weakening, which encouraged some Western nations to push for excessive demands and to underestimate Chinese resistance. The nineteenth century witnessed a series of negotiations and renegotiations of treaty rights, including Britain's demand for 'access for the British to the entire interior of China' (Spence 179). But imperial China, 'sick' though it was, remained impervious to the West until the fall of the Qing dynasty in late 1911.

The West, wary of Japanese hegemony in the Far East, also saw a revitalized and modernized China under the control of Western powers as a possible safeguard against the smaller, but militarily stronger Japan. Again, John and Alice Dewey's letters are a clear index of these concerns: 'An American official here [Shanghai] says there is no hope for China except through the protection of the great powers ... Without that she is the prey of Japan. Japanese are buying the best bits of land' (173). In the Deweys' assessment, the Western powers were by no means united in their policies. Germany was friendly to Japan, and Great Britain signed a secret pact with Japan while ignoring its military action in Manchuria, the northern region of China (167–8). To prevent one particular nation from dominating China, China itself, the Deweys believed, must act and modernize. In contrast to the favourable impressions of Japanese schools they formed during their Japanese tour, the Deweys found the Chinese educational system lacking and the Chinese people lethargic. The Deweys' observation of a Chinese temple is representative of the West's overall impatience regarding China's antiquity: 'We also visited a Confucian Temple, big and used twice each year. It is like all temples in that it is covered with the dust of many years' accumulation. If you were to be dropped in any Chinese temple you would think you had landed in a deserted and forgotten ruin out of reach of man' (189). Accumulated dust of many years, a deserted land, and a forgotten ruin – these impressions of China contrast starkly with the sunny pictures of a youthful Japan.

In Puccini's *Turandot*, China is also staged as a land that looks to the past. Although the princess is in good health, the emperor is ailing, and his part, sung in a falsetto tenor, emphasizes this impression. The chorus in the opera – the people of China – clamours for blood whenever a suitor fails to solve the riddles set by Turandot. The blood thirst in the opera reminds one of the cruel nature of the Chinese reported in Hegel's *The Philosophy of History* or in nineteenth-century travel narratives. 'Blood' is also one of the three answers to Turandot's riddles. The executioner, though silent, is a menacing presence on stage, and the Chinese people's lusty enjoyment of the spectacle of bloody decapitation is felt through most of the opera. Turandot and her sick emperor form the two ends of the spectrum of Western attitudes towards China: hope in the form of a conquerable woman and degeneration in the figure of a tottering old man. But 'hope,' another answer to one of the riddles, is not realizable until 'Turandot,' the third answer, is won. And she is won by a man who can melt her icy reserve, penetrate her defensive armour of pride, and make her succumb completely.

Although the two 'Asias' in Puccini's operas are quite distinct, they share the trope of the exoticized and feminized Oriental object. In *Madama Butterfly*, the charm of Japan is represented by the figure of Cio-Cio-San; in *Turandot*, the past and future of China are depicted in the emasculate emperor and the virginal princess. Superficially, this pattern fulfils one aspect of Edward Said's analysis of nineteenth-century Orientalism, namely, that the Orient was routinely feminized as silent and compliant (*Orientalism* 5–6). Yet for most of the opera Turandot can hardly be described as a compliant figure. Rather, Puccini's Chinese princess bears some resemblance to the historical empress dowager Cixi, who wielded total power over China and was implacably hostile to the West during the last decades of the Qing dynasty (Spence 217–18, 234–6). Portraits of Cixi usually show an old woman of imperial bearing sitting in state, her figure draped in a heavily embroidered robe and her extremely long fingernails curving like talons over the armrests of her throne. Unlike the figure of Queen Victoria, who symbolized both power and motherhood, Cixi symbolized only power, which the West wished to control.

The linkage between the two operas is established more clearly in the pattern of domination: the West over the East. The strategies of domination, however, differ, and this difference reflects Europe's growing anxiety regarding the Far East. Japan, once a willing apprentice of the West, was emerging as a military power, and China, once an imperial enigma, must be taken in hand and used as a bulwark against Japanese encroachment.

Although the two Asian nations in Puccini's operas are obviously dissimilar when juxtaposed against each other, the composer's conceptual frameworks remain rooted in nineteenth-century Western attitudes towards the East.[5] Japanese culture in *Madama Butterfly* is aestheticized in its parts – as cherry blossoms, as geisha girls – and in its central character – as a captured butterfly. The opera is a condensed example of *Japonisme*. In contrast, the grandeur of 'Pekin,' the recalcitrant figure at the centre of the opera, and the image of death and mystery in *Turandot* reinforce the over-determined prejudice the West had formed (and still sometimes maintains) of China. This country had obstinately resisted modernization and Westernization. When Westerners were finally granted glimpses of this 'mysterious' country, they were appalled at and overcome by the differences between the Chinese and their own cultures. When *Turandot* was written, two decades after *Madama Butterfly*, Japan was the dominant power in the Far East, established in Taiwan, in Korea, and in the northern part of China. The West finally awoke to the very real threat of a strong Japan and the need to address the question of power in East Asia. The portrait of China in *Turandot*, as weak but not without hope if foreign alliances are accepted, can be read as an artistic response to this historical situation.

Notes

1 I thank Jonathan Wisenthal for pointing out this reference. Tennyson's 'Locksley Hall' also contains lines such as 'But I count the gray barbarian lower than the Christian child' and 'Mated with a squalid savage – what to me were sun or clime? / I the heir of all the ages, in the foremost files of time.' Like Macaulay's dismissive remark on Asian learning in his 1835 'Minute on Education,' Tennyson's Orientalist lines provide succinct examples of nineteenth-century European attitude towards Asia.
2 For Japanese influence on Western music, see **Susan McClary**.
3 For detail on the influence of Art Nouveau on Dauthendey, see Ng, *Three Exotic Views*. Dauthendey visited the Far East eventually, and on the basis of his Thomas Cook packaged tour wrote a collection of 'Japanese' short stories,

published as *Die Acht Gesichter am Biwasee*. These stories established his reputation as a writer of exotic literature.
4 The term 'West' is used here to denote both European nations and the United States.
5 For Puccini's research method in preparation for his compositions see Carner, *Puccini*.

Iron Butterfly: Cio-Cio-San and Japanese Imperialism

JOSHUA S. MOSTOW

In his essay-introduction to the English National Opera Guide of *Madama Butterfly*, entitled 'Images of the Orient,' Jean-Pierre Lehmann writes:

> It is in fact ironical that the first performance of *Madam Butterfly* at La Scala, on February 17, 1904, occurred exactly nine days after the opening salvoes of the Russo-Japanese war. A year later Japan won a military victory over Russia which astounded – and indeed alarmed – the West. Between the images conjured up in *Madam Butterfly* and the realities of the naval battle of the Tsushima straits – where the Japanese under Admiral Togo annihilated the Russian fleet – there is an awesome gap. (Lehmann 13)

Perception of such 'irony' would seem to be part and parcel of an enlightened self-flagellation on the part of educated white Europeans or North Americans in reaction to 'Orientalism' and its pernicious fantasies, punctuated by a refrain of 'Wrong, terribly wrong – we got it all wrong.'[1] Here I would like to perform the perhaps equally predictable response, by briefly exploring Japanese participation in the creation of the fantasy that informs *Madama Butterfly*. I am contesting, in other words, the claim by **Jonathan Wisenthal** in the introduction to this volume that 'this narrative of "the Orient" is entirely a cultural construct of white, Western nations.' Nothing could be farther from the truth. Like the Meiji-period production of 'traditional' crafts for export such as porcelain, cloisonné, and ivory carving, the Japanese appropriated the stereotypes imposed on them by Europe and America and put them to their own purposes, both domestic and international. In what follows, I would like to sketch a reception of *Madama Butterfly* in the context of Japanese, as well as American and European, imperialisms.

The first thing we might point out in regards to Lehmann's statement is that there were those in Europe, and especially England, who were far from being either surprised or alarmed by the Japanese victory over the Russians. In fact, it was precisely the desire for just such an outcome that had given birth to the Anglo-Japanese Alliance of 1902. It was with English armaments that the Japanese defeated the Russians, and there were many in England who saw the Eastern Sea, Korea, and Manchuria as Japan's natural sphere of influence. In the words of one:

> [T]he Japanese are Tartars; their kinsfolk in the West are the Huns and Turks; in the East the islanders of the Liukiu [Ryūkyū], the peninsulars of Korea, the nomads of Mongolia, and the farmers of Manchuria. In none of these lands and islands has the Chinaman or the Slav any birthright of presence; among men who dwell outside their borders the Japanese can show the justest title to predominance. (Dickins xxv)

Next we might consider the kind of erotic exchange that had taken place between Japan and the European and American powers by 1904. Chief among such exchanges must rank the 'Deer Cry Pavilion,' or Rokumeikan. Designed by the British architect Josiah Conder, it was opened by the Japanese Ministry of Foreign Affairs in 1883. The name of the pavilion comes from one of the songs of welcome from the oldest book of Chinese poetry, the *Book of Songs* (*Shi jing*). Although the collection was originally compiled around the fifth century BC, we can glean from this poem what some of the aims of the Japanese designers of the building and its program were:

> *Yu, yu,* cry the deer;
> they eat the *hao* of the fields.
> I have a fine guest;
> his reputation is brilliant;
> he does not regard people in a slighting way.
> The noblemen take him for a pattern, they imitate him.
> I have good wine;
> my fine guest feasts and amuses himself.
>
> *Yu, yu,* cry the deer;
> they eat the *k'in* of the fields.
> I have a fine guest;
> we play the *si,* we play the *k'in.*

we play the *si*, we play the *k'in*;
together we rejoice and are steeped in pleasure.
I have good wine;
With it I feast and rejoice the heart of my fine guest.[2]

The Rokumeikan was designed as a space for social interaction between the Japanese government and foreign visitors. As the poem suggests, it was a space where the Japanese hoped to prove that they could master new forms of social interaction, such as costume balls, soirées, and charity bazaars. One such event, of particular interest to us here, was the second annual ball in honour of Emperor Meiji's birthday, held in November 1885. It was described in the *Japan Weekly Mail* as follows:

> On the 3rd His Excellency the Minister of Foreign Affairs and Countess Inouye entertained nearly all the principal residents of Tokyo and Yokohama at the Rokumeikan ... to commemorate the birthday of His Majesty the Emperor ... The Rokumeikan is so excellently planned that even a monster entertainment like that of last evening presents no difficulties. Its capabilities have now been repeatedly tested, and we imagine that the hospitable people of Tokyo must often congratulate themselves on possessing a handsome and stable building so admirably adapted for the accommodation, distribution, and easy circulation of large assemblages of guests. In the dancing last evening the Japanese ladies took a large share. Indeed, it has now become difficult to distinguish them from their sisters of the West, so thoroughly have they adopted European costumes, and so perfectly versed are they in the usages of Western Society.

According to Julia Meech-Pekarik: 'The same ball was attended by a French naval officer, Lieutenant L.M. Julien Viaud, better known by his pen name, Pierre Loti. During the summer of 1885, when the French warship *Triomphante*, on which he was an officer, was laid up in Nagasaki harbor, he set up housekeeping on shore with a Japanese girl, who became the subject of his *Madame Chrysanthème*, an instant best seller when it was published in Paris in 1887.' Meech-Pekarik quotes from Loti's description of the ball, contained in his collection of essays, *Japoneries d'automne*, published in 1889:

> At the top of the staircase, four persons – the hosts – smilingly await their guests at the entrance to the drawing rooms. I pay little attention to a gentleman in white tie, decorated with many medals, who is no doubt the min-

ister; instead I immediately turned my curious eyes upon the three women standing beside him, especially the first, who must be the 'countess.' I stop in surprise in front of a person with a distinguished and refined face, wearing shoulder-length gloves, impeccably coiffed in suitable manner; her age indeterminate, obscured by white rice powder; a long satin train of very pale lilac color, very discreet, decorated with garlands of little forest flowers, of deliciously varied nuance; her bodice forming a slim sheath and covered with a stiff embroidery studded with pearls: in short, an attire that would do very well in Paris and is really worn very smartly by this astonishing parvenue. So, I take her seriously and offer a polite greeting. She, in turn, is equally polite and above all courteous, and she offers me her hand in American fashion with a self-confidence that quite devastates me. (Meech-Pekarik 147–9)

Clearly, we are very far away from the inept passing and pidgin English of 'Mrs B.F. Pinkerton.' Equally clearly, the Rokumeikan was living up to its design as a place where the guests of the Japanese – even those who *did* 'regard people in a slighting way' – could 'feast and amuse themselves.'

Norman Bryson has suggested that in the Rokumeikan, women served to neutralize the antagonisms between Japanese men and their foreign male guests:

In place of an outright clash between two antagonists poised for a fight, each side now reconfigures round the third (and excluded) term, woman. It is not that love conquers all – that the spectacle of so many Countess Inoues or bare white shoulders simply makes the men lay down their arms, like Mars conquered by Venus. Rather, the interaction that the presence of women as quasi-available sexual objects permits is such that each side starts to assimilate the other through the milieu of sexuality, localized in the bodies of their attendant females ... The women of Rokumeikan ... were the great equalizers of the show. By virtue of their attendance and their efforts, they took a situation of potentially extreme antagonism and converted it to one of male fraternity: men of different nations, as men, could close ranks around the women of Rokumeikan. (Bryson 97–8)

This ability to 'share' the women as objects of sexual fantasy was made possible by the efforts Japanese women had made to master European fashion and modes of social intercourse, and in so doing they become the legal tender of the modern sexual Symbolic. This is one important context to bear in mind when we consider the construction of Cio-Cio-San.

Japanese attempts to control the images of themselves that circulated in the imaginations of Europeans were not limited to domestic productions. In 1900, the 'Imperial Japanese Theatre Company,' led by Kawakami Otojirō and his wife, actress Sadayakko, travelled across the United States and Europe. Kawakami is often considered the founder of modern Japanese theatre, and his wife the first modern actress.[3] As Arthur Groos writes: 'Adjusting their performances to suit their audiences, the troupe employed a combination of improvisational skill and entrepreneurial genius that generated enthusiastic public response, leading to another, expanded, European tour the following year.' In late April 1902, Giacomo Puccini attended the Milan performances of the troupe, then nearing the end of its second European tour. According to Groos, Puccini not only borrowed musical material from the Kawakami performance, but also re-conceptualized some of the action of his opera.

> After the performance, the composer immediately wrote the entrance of Cio-Cio-San in Act I, using [the Japanese melody] 'Echigo jishi,' which Sadayakko had played in *Kesa Gozen* four days before (a recently re-discovered 1900 recording of Sadayakko allows for comparison with Puccini's adaptation). Puccini also acquired *Nippon Zoku-kyoku Shū*, or *A Collection of Japanese Popular Music* from which he took four of some ten Japanese melodies, three note for note and in the same key. (Groos in Association for Asian Studies 1997, 146–7)

Sadayakko was trained as a geisha, but most of the troupe's repertoire was composed of adaptations from kabuki, a theatre that had banned women from the stage for over two hundred years. Sadayakko's performances, then, were a kind of double cross-dressing: a female actress playing a part usually performed by a male actor in female guise. Kabuki moreover delights in sudden reversals, changes, and revelations, and in many of its long plays the same character would be played by different actors in different scenes. Psychological unity of character, in other words, is not at a high premium.

Modern Japanese theatre (called *shimpa*, or 'new school') at the time had a decidedly militaristic and patriotic bent. This was because Kawakami's first commercial successes in Japan came during the Sino-Japanese War of 1894–5, when his troupe staged realistic portrayals of recent naval battles, complete 'with electrical machinery and a liberal use of fireworks' (Keene 157). Moreover, a common plot in what would become 'conventional shimpa' was 'an out-of-the-ordinary woman sacrificing herself for the man she loves' (Mark LeFanu 57).

The Kawakamis' Milan repertoire consisted of four plays: *The Geisha and the Knight* (*La geisha e il cavaliere*), *Kesa Gozen*, *Kosan*, and *Zingoro* (Groos, 'Cio-Cio-San' 49). The last of these was Kawakami's adaptation of the Pygmalion and Galatea story. The first purported to be an original script by Kawakami, but was in fact an adaptation of two kabuki plays: the 1823 *Ukiyo-Zuka Hikiyo no Inazuma* by Tsuruya Nanboku and a kabuki adaptation of the famous *Dōjōji* story (Shionoya 50). The lead female character of this latter work dies at the end of the play. *Kosan* was subtitled in Paris '*la Dame au Camélia* du Japon,' in which a courtesan agrees to leave her lover, having been asked to do so by his father, and then dies (ibid.). *Kesa*, finally, is described as follows by Shionoya Kei:

> C'est un passage tragique du *Genpei Seisui-Ki* (*Grandeur et décadence des Genji et des Heikè*), récit historique du 13e siècle dans lequel un *samouraï* tombe amoureux de la femme de son meilleur ami, appelée Késa. Bien qu'elle soit fidèle à son mari, elle est bouleversée lorsque ce *samouraï* lui déclare son amour. Elle accepte finalement de s'enfuir avec lui, la main dans la main, à condition qu'il tue son mari, et elle lui indique la chambre où il dort. La nuit tombée, le *samouraï* s'y introduit furtivement et le décapite. Mais sous le clair de lune, il découvre qu'elle s'est substituée à lui pour lui rester fidèle, et que c'est elle qu'il vient de tuer. (Shionoya 19)

> It is a tragic passage from the *Genpei Seisui-ki* (*Glory and Decline of the Genji and the Heike*), a historical narrative of the thirteenth century in which a samurai falls in love with the wife of his best friend, called Kesa. Although she is faithful to her husband, she is distressed when this samurai declares his love to her. Finally she agrees to flee with him, hand in hand, on the condition that he kill her husband, and she tells him which room he sleeps in. Night falls, the samurai stealthily enters and cuts off his head. But under the light of the moon, he discovers that she has substituted herself for her husband in order to remain faithful to him, and that it is she that the samurai has ended up killing.

In other words, no matter which night one went to a performance of the Kawakamis, one was bound to see a heroine die, usually through self-sacrifice.

Such self-immolation was a significant part of the popular Japanese theatre, according to one Meiji-period visitor: 'I suppose one drama in ten contains a case of hara-kiri, or "happy dispatch"' (Edwards 78). Yet this same author (writing in the closing years of the nineteenth century) criticized Cho-Cho-San's suicide in Belasco's play as unrealistic:

> But most of all I doubt the verisimilitude of the alleged motive for self-destruction. Sometimes Madame Chrysanthème counts her money and feels rather relieved when her foreign lover sails away; sometimes she regrets him with genuine sorrow, and might conceivably put an end to her life if confronted with the alternative of an odious match. But what she would not do is what Madame Butterfly does – namely, consider that she had suffered a dishonour expiable only by death. The Western sentiment of honour is out of place in such a connection, for she had been party with open eyes to a legal, extra-marital contract, sanctioned by usage and arranged by her relations. The infidelity of her partner might wound her heart; it could not strike her conscience. (65)

In fact, what European and American visitors were witnessing at the end of the nineteenth century was what has been called the 'samurai-ization' of the Japanese populace (Ueno 'Genesis' and 'Position'). The early modern Tokugawa period (1600–1868) had been predicated on a strict division of society into four social classes (*shi-nō-kō-shō*): the warriors (samurai, or *bushi*), farmers, artisans, and merchants, with the last seen as essentially a parasitic and non-productive class. Despite such a ranking, the entire period saw a gradual impoverishment of the warrior class and the rising economic might of the merchants. Nonetheless, strict separation between the warrior class and all others was enforced by sumptuary laws and other controls. Only samurai were allowed to wear the double swords that were the badge of their class, and only samurai were allowed to commit *seppuku*, or *hara-kiri*. Indeed, even for samurai, *seppuku* was in principle a privilege granted by one's lord, although it could also be performed as an act of protest.

The samurai class had started to come to political prominence as early as the eleventh century, and the practice of self-disembowelment seems to have arisen on the battlefields: a high-ranking warrior, fearing capture by the enemy, would commit suicide, leaving his lieutenant to cut off his head and keep it from the possession of the enemy.

In a Buddhist society, the duty of a wife in such circumstances was to retire from secular life and spend the remainder of her days praying for the repose of her husband's soul. Women did not commit *seppuku*, which was an exclusively male practice. During the brutal Warring States period (*Sengoku jidai*, 1482–1558) and Momoyama period (1573–1600), as the country was being reunified through a series of battles, high-ranking samurai women were indeed executed in horrifying numbers, and some, such as Hosokawa Gracia, committed suicide rather than be taken as hostages or prisoners. But these practices almost completely disappeared under the peace of the victorious Tokugawa regime from 1615 onwards. In fact, by the early nineteenth century, even in such reactionary domains as Mito, the military training of women was largely defunct. As Yamakawa Kikue wrote of her own family under the rule of the conservative *daimyō* (domain lord) Tokugawa Nariaki (1800–60) in the 1830s:

> In Enju's [her ancestor's] house, in accordance with the common custom among bushi families, there was a rack over the lintel of the sitting room on which was placed the master's spear and, below it, the wife's *naginata* [a pike-like weapon with a curved blade at the end that was the traditional weapon of samurai women]. In fact, however, girls, marrying at fourteen or fifteen, did not have time to study anything thoroughly, and were given little more than token training in something as remote from the needs of daily life as the *naginata*. (Yamakawa 19–20)

Samurai women carried short knives (*kaiken*) with which they were supposed to protect themselves and their honour, by death if necessary. Yet even this practice was honoured more in its breach in the first half of the nineteenth century:

> By the end of the Tokugawa period women had almost completely abandoned study of the martial arts; so unusual was it for a woman to be able to wield the *naginata* that one who could became a topic of conversation ... Some girls carried a small woman's dagger and some did not. Chise received one as a reward for not showing any fear when Enju took her and her brother to see a tiger some traveling entertainers had brought to Mito ... However, no one told Chise under what circumstances she should use the dagger or explained how, should it be necessary, to stab herself in the throat ... It was not given envisioning a specific exigency in which it would be necessary to use it on oneself or on someone else. The age of Warring States was long past and people did not imagine that women might actually have to defend themselves from danger. (ibid. 29)

For male samurai during this period, 'protest *seppuku*' became very rare indeed, and s*eppuku* itself had become little more than a form of execution. As Eiko Ikegami writes:

> Around the mid-Tokugawa period, as *seppuku* became more securely institutionalized as the punishment of choice for the samurai class, its actual procedure became in practice not so much suicide as a form of decapitation. The *kaishaku* of the Tokugawa period was an executioner who stood behind the accused man and cut off his head with a sword ... [T]he custom of allowing the *seppuku* to proceed to the point of actual self-stabbing gradually faded away in the peaceful Tokugawa society. Usually, the moment that the accused man began to extend his hand toward the sword, the *kaishaku* beheaded him ... In fact, the ceremonial object might not even be a dummy weapon; sometimes the symbolic item presented on the wooden tray was just a fan. In these cases, the *seppuku* was called *ōgibara*, from the words *ōgi* (fan) and *hara* (belly). (Ikegami 255)

Yet, as Ikegami also notes, in the tumultuous period before the Meiji Restoration, when various factions were advocating 'expel the barbarians; revere the emperor' (*sonnō jōi*), there was a sudden re-emergence of 'real' *seppuku*:

> It is important to emphasize here that during this period of upheaval, many samurai felt the Western threat to their country's security as a blow to their personal pride and independence. Their renewed sense of honor pushed them in the direction of political activism at this point – toward many ideological experiments and radical social movements that eventually brought about the collapse of the Tokugawa government. It is perhaps no coincidence that a revival of 'real' *seppuku* – and not *fan seppuku* – appeared at the end of the Tokugawa period, especially among radical political activists. (321–2)

After the Restoration of 1867, imperial 'loyalists' such as Nariaki were turned into national heroes. With the establishment of a conscript army, the elimination of the *bushi* class, and the amalgamation of warriors, peasants, and merchants into the new class of 'commoners' (*heimin*), the Meiji government encouraged the adoption of the samurai values of discipline, frugality, honour, and, above all, self-sacrifice among the newly minted citizenry. In other words, what had been samurai values, limited by class to no more than 10 per cent of the population, were now turned into 'Japanese' values and averred as 'traditional.' Reinforcing this new ideology, there seems to have been a startling number of honour-motivated suicides in the early works of Japan's modern theatre. The eminent Japan scholar W.G. Aston, for instance, writes of the 1897 *Maki no Kachi*, with its 'several murders and two *hara-kiri* by women' (quoted in Edwards, 85).

Nor were such scenes limited to the theatre; they also took place in real life, and for revealing reasons. Edwards cites some recent examples from his day:

> The assassins or would-be assassins of Viscount Mori in 1887, of Count Okuma in 1889, of the Czarevitch in 1891, of Li Hung Chang in 1895, were prepared to pay with their own lives for what they deemed dishonourable concessions to foreigners. The young girl, Yuko Hatakeyama, who cut her throat in expiation of the outrage offered to the Czarevitch; the young wife of Lieutenant Asada, who, learning of his death on the battlefield, slew herself before his portrait, that she might follow him; the forty soldiers, who took their own lives because the Government gave up Liaotung at the bidding of Russia, France, and Germany – all these were as widely praised and honoured by their fellow-countrymen as Kumagaya or Nakamitsu [famous characters in plays]. (80–1)[4]

It is hardly surprising, then, that foreign residents of Japan at this time should believe self-immolation by women to be a 'traditional' virtue. Lafcadio Hearn, in his *Japan: An Interpretation* of 1904, wrote of 'The Religion of Loyalty':

> In the early ages it appears to have been the custom for the wives of officials condemned to death to kill themselves; – the ancient chronicles are full of examples ... However, it was certainly also common enough for a bereaved wife to perform suicide, not through despair, but through the wish to follow her husband into the other world, and there to wait upon him as in life. Instances of female suicide, representing the old ideal of duty to a dead husband, have occurred in recent times. [Hearn goes on to recount the case of Lt. Asada's wife] ... Besides the duty of suicide for the sake of preserving honour, there was also, for the samurai woman, the duty of suicide as a moral protest ... Among samurai women – taught to consider their husbands as their lords, in the feudal meaning of the term – it was held a moral obligation to perform *jigai* [lit., 'self-harm,' but taken by Hearn to mean the female equivalent of *seppuku*], by way of protest against disgraceful behaviour upon the part of a husband who would not listen to

advice or reproof. The ideal of wifely duty which impelled such sacrifice still survives; and more than one recent example might be cited of a generous life thus laid down in rebuke of some moral wrong. Perhaps the most touching instance occurred in 1892, at the time of the district elections in Nagano prefecture. A rich voter named Ishijima, after having publicly pledged himself to aid in the election of a certain candidate, transferred his support to the rival candidate. On learning of this breach of promise, the wife of Ishijima, robed herself in white, and performed *jigai* after the old samurai manner. The grave of this brave woman is still decorated with flowers by the people of the district; and incense is burned before her tomb. (Hearn 317–18)

Hearn's tone is obviously far from condemnatory. In fact, Japan and her new patriotism were serving as a model for nationalistic renewal in Europe and America.

Here I would like to draw on the research of John de Gruchy, who has examined the role of the Japan Society of London, founded in 1892, in both the aesthetic and political alliances between England and Japan at this time. The profound connection between art and polity as seen at the time is made abundantly clear in the Society's *Transactions*:

Samuel Middleton Fox read a paper before the Society in 1905 entitled, 'Some Lessons from Japan,' in which he spelled out the usefulness and importance of Japanese art to the national program. According to Fox, unlike European art that has striven 'to embody beauty,' Japanese art has 'sought chiefly to please ... While our art is dignified and solemn with its message of edification, theirs is bubbling over with the joy of life' (70). This joy of life is instantly translated into joy of work, and consequently 'at Kobe we find the ships are coaled by strings of happy, healthy, laughing girls' even though, he acknowledged, 'men, women, and children work in the manufactures from twelve to sixteen hours a day at wages from a penny to two shillings' (61). 'In "John Bull's Other Island," one of Mr. Bernard Shaw's characters gives his idea of heaven as of a commonwealth "where work is play and play is life." Life in Japan comes near to that,' Middleton declared, adding that in Japan the dreams of Morris and Ruskin were realized (68). As for Japanese women, 'their women are probably happier than ours,' as they are 'trained (even more than boys are trained) to the bliss of self-abnegation ... [T]he ambition of every woman ... is to be the wife of a great man and the mother of illustrious sons' (75). (de Gruchy, 'Institutionalization' 28–9)

Japan's victory in the Russo-Japanese War was seen by the British as the victory of an ally. More importantly, Japanese bushido and patriotism were seen as providing lessons to the British for a renewed and rejuvenated imperialism (Holmes and Ion). In the words of Alfred Stead, England had to learn from Japan, who 'teaches the world the lesson' of

> self-sacrifice for the good of the State ... This sentiment has been fostered by every ethical conviction of the race, especially by Bushido and Ancestor worship ... As Bushido holds that the interests of the family and its members are one and the same, so should it be with the entire nation. There should be no interests separately for the subjects or the rulers, all should work for the whole, and merge his or her personal interests in those of the whole nation. Thus has Bushido made of the Japanese the most patriotic race in the world (185; 192). (de Gruchy, ibid. 27)

Stead is best known as a proponent of 'efficiency,' of which patriotism and Japan were particular examples (*Great Japan*, 1906). It is difficult not to see a connection between Stead's 'efficiency' and what Puccini and other Italian observers called the 'efficacy' of both Sadayakko's performances and the attenuated version of Puccini's revision of *Madama Butterfly* after its unsuccessful first performance. Groos suggests that the 'drastic reduction' of the plots and actions in the Kawakami productions presented in Europe gave the impression of greater violence.

> Above all, the reduction gave an impression of kabuki theater as leading ineluctably to the inevitable resolution in death, especially by ritual suicide. Milanese reviews of 26–27 April alluded to the 'extraordinary efficacy' or 'terrible efficacy' of the action (*Il secolo, La Lombardia*). Sadayakko's death scene in *La geisha e cavaliere* was singled out in particular as proceeding 'with such simplicity of means and with such terrible efficacy as to make a shudder run down the spines of the audience' (*La perseveranza*). (Groos, 'Cio-Cio-San' 53)

'It is probably no coincidence,' writes Groos,

> that Puccini's justification to Giulio Ricordi of this far-reaching reduction [eliminating the American consulate scene] ... uses the identical language as reviews of Sadayakko to argue for a more concise, effective, and terrible denouement. 'The Consulate was a serious mistake. The drama should

race towards the end without interruptions, tightly knit, efficacious, terrible! Doing the opera in three acts was heading for certain disaster. Don't worry about a version in two acts. The first will last a good hour, the second more than an hour, perhaps an hour and a half. But what efficacy!' (ibid.)

Groos argues that the 'efficacy' of the revised versions of the Kawakami performances in effect 'Orientalized' Sadayakko, making her performances correspond to Western stereotypes of the Japanese as primitive, savage, and childlike. We can see, then, the same effect on the construction of Cio-Cio-San. Yet these same features would, especially in England, become part of a new discourse that valorized such 'efficacious' self-sacrifice.

Cio-Cio-San represents the extreme of self-sacrifice. She is a kind of Lucretia of modern imperialism, the tragic artefact of a traditional Japan sacrificed on the altar of masculine modernity. And yet, women are by this sacrifice mobilized, like the girls on the coal strings, and become the exemplars of self-abnegation, a model for patriotic bushido. At the same time, of course, Cio-Cio-San is no Western woman, and thus can serve as a symbolic fetish of male patriarchal lineage and imperial desires in an exotic context unconnected to 'real,' that is white, men or women. Cio-Cio-San is the other woman who gives her life to provide the model nuclear family a son and heir, the rented womb and working girl who serves as stark contrast to Pinkerton's leisured and asexual wife. This meaning is, I think, clear as the opera was rewritten for the 1906 Paris production:

BUTTERFLY
   (*She has understood and cries out.*)
Ah! It is his wife!	Ah! è sua moglie!

   (*in a calm voice*)
It is all over for me!	Tutto è morto per me!
All is finished! Ah!	Tutto è finito! ah!

SHARPLESS [the voice of governmental authority]
Have courage.	Coraggio.

BUTTERFLY
They want to take everything from me!	Voglion prendermi tutto!
My son!	Il figlio mio!

SHARPLESS
Make this sacrifice for his welfare ...	Fatelo pel suo bene il sacrifizio.

BUTTERFLY

    (*despairingly*)
Ah! Unhappy mother!	Ah! triste madre!
To abandon my son!	Abbandonar mio figlio!
(*she remains calm and motionless*)	
Enough.	E sia.
To him I owe obedience!	A lui devo obbedir! ([1984] 121)

As Butterfly 'piously kisses the blade' and 'softly reads the words inscribed on it: "Death with honour / Is better than life with dishonour"' we see enacted not just the sacrifice of life for the patriarchal, imperialist nation-state, but the sacrifice of a woman of colour for a white boy-child in a perverted form of social Darwinism and 'scientific' racism.

Ironically, before being banned entirely in a xenophobic sweep, *Madama Butterfly* was thoroughly appropriated by Japanese militarism in the 1930s. The most famous Japanese Cio-Cio-San was undoubtedly Miura Tamaki (1884–1946), whose performance was heard and praised by Puccini himself. In fact, she performed *Madama Butterfly* some 2000 times in Europe. Returning to Japan in the mid-1930s, she continued to perform as Cio-Cio-San, in her own translation, which emphasized, according to the *Asahi Shinbun* (28 June 1936) 'a Japanese woman's pureheartedness' (Groos 'Return,' 183). Today there is a statue to Miura in Nagasaki, showing her in her role as Cio-Cio-San, arm raised and pointing outwards for the small boy with Caucasian features nestled under her arm. The accompanying plaque states that Miura, in singing this role, devoted her life to acquainting the world with the virtues of Japanese womanhood.[5]

We miss a great deal, then, if we see Cio-Cio-San's destruction by Pinkerton as nothing more than the heartless exploitation of a woman of colour by a white male. The woman's self-destructive sacrifice is overdetermined by both the Western imperialist *and* the Japanese imperialist subtexts, despite the fact that those subtexts are at cross-purposes, the one defending Western subjugation of non-European sites, the other an expedient means to avoid such subjugation. Cio-Cio-San is not simply the victim of imperialism, but also its exemplar, providing a displaced model of self-sacrifice for the nation state, and this fetishistic function is inscribed on both her race and her gender. We may feel that it is really Pinkerton who is plunging in the blade, but it is the Meiji Emperor who is holding her arms from behind.

Notes

I would like to thank Professors Thomas Harper, Gaye Rowley, and Sharalyn Orbaugh for their assistance and encouragement in this project. All errors, of course, remain my own.

1 For an examination of the various errors and stereotyping in John Luther Long's original story, David Belasco's play, and Puccini's opera, see Groos, 'Return of the Native.'
2 The translation is adapted from Bernhard Karlgren, *The Book of Odes* (Stockholm: Museum of Far Eastern Antiquities, 1974), 104–5. Cf. Arthur Waley, trans., *The Books of Songs* (1937; New York: Grove Press, 1960), 192. For a popular account of the period, see Barr.
3 For a fine study of Sadayakko, see Kano.
4 The most famous suicides of the Meiji period were those of General Maresuke Nogi and his wife Shizuko, performed on the day of the Meiji emperor's funeral. For the significance of Shizuko's actions, and how they have been interpreted, see Orbaugh, 'General Nogi's Wife.'
5 Dr Thomas Harper, personal communication, 12 March 1999.

Madame Butterfly: Behind Every Great Woman ...

JOY JAMES

Although the most important role may appear to devolve on Madame Chrysanthème, it is very certain that the three principal personages are *myself, Japan*, and the *effect produced on me by that country.*

Pierre Loti, Preface, *Madame Chrysanthème*[1]

[T]he author [Loti] will go on describing cities, in Japan, in Persia, in Morocco, i.e., will go on designating and searchlighting (by emblems of discourse) the space of his desire.

Roland Barthes, 'Pierre Loti: *Aziyadé*' 114

Desiring Production and the Production of Desire

The multiplicity of Pierre Loti – author of *Madame Chrysanthème*, one of the earliest articulations of the Madame Butterfly theme – was navigated with great flexibility by Roland Barthes in his 1971 essay 'Pierre Loti: *Aziyadé*.' Under Barthes's pen the tableaux vivants of Loti by Loti quicken into images of 'desire [as] a force adrift' (119).

Taking Barthes's lead, this chapter will explore the geographies of Loti's desiring production: the contexts, material and imaginary, across which Loti wrote the (multiple) self and its others. For, above all, the sites of transformation of the self, whether they are metaphorical, or occur through the transcriptions of a kind of transvestism, are the spaces of Loti's writings. Identifying the ways in which Loti's *Madame Chrysanthème* relates colonialism and imperialism to gender, 'race,' and class in the construction and representation of the self and its others will show how and where the text intersects with dominant ways of reading colonial sexuality *and* how it works to resist dominant understandings of normative male sexuality. *Madame Chrysanthème* was immensely popular in its own time, and I believe this popularity was due, in part, to the way in which the text articulates sexual ambiguities.[2]

Time/Space/Place Trajectories

[T]here is no binary division to be made between what one says and what one does not say; we must try to determine the different ways of not saying such things, how those who can and those who cannot speak of them are distributed, which type of discourse is authorized, or which form of discretion is required in either case. There is not one but many silences, and they are an integral part of the strategies that underlie and permeate discourses.

Michel Foucault, *The History of Sexuality* 1: 27

Loti's representation of his protagonist, Chrysanthème, is complex and multivalent: Loti evokes and engages contemporary representations of the 'exotic' woman, but, as I will show, his emphasis and attention are elsewhere. In addition to constructing and re-presenting a popular, dominant stereotype of the 'Oriental' woman, Loti's narrative also obliquely addresses what was perhaps a not uncommon experience in the life of the nineteenth-century bourgeois male: same-sex encounters between males are often referred to in contemporaneous literary works, even though their existence was not officially condoned or even acknowledged, except in discourses concerned with policing normative male sexuality.[3] This is a significant point because it directs readers to a problematic terrain that if mapped could provide a picture of previously obscured and, in terms of the dominant culture, silent spaces. More specifically, I am interested in elucidating the ways in which Loti's construction of 'woman' opens onto assertions of other kinds of subjectivities that can be designated as outlawed and outcast in late-nineteenth-century France. I believe that the whispered utterances buried in Loti's texts can be understood in terms of Judith Butler's notions of performativity, as 'that aspect of discourse that has the capacity to produce what it names,' and as 'the discursive mode by which ontological effects are installed' (Butler 4). If Loti's narratives functioned in this way, then his stories, in addition to repeating sexist, racist, and misogynist representations of women that were fundamental to the construction of European bourgeois male identity, also serve to *subvert* normative male sexuality, and to acknowledge and instal space for individuals occupying alternative sexualities. In other words, his stories, by giving shadowy form to male bodies that embraced transgressive sexual practices, contributed to and thickened alternative collective imaginaries, even as they troubled and destabilized hegemonic notions of normative male sexuality.

As **Jonathan Wisenthal** makes clear in his introduction, *Madame Chrysanthème* is fraught with contradictions. Certainly, it is a difficult text with which to work. Loti's disturbing representations of Japan and the young Chrysanthème, coupled with the reality that this poorly written book was not one Loti felt drawn to writing, but rather was a project hastily undertaken primarily for economic gain, makes it a problematic text. However, these difficulties are also the basis of my interpretation: in *Madame Chrysanthème* it is this very fact – the carelessness of Loti's expression – that allows us access to attitudes, values, and beliefs that are paradoxically both more submerged and more obvious than those contained in the crafted storytelling of his other books.

Figuring Loti

Loti was a celebrity in nineteenth-century France. Not only was his work extremely popular and financially successful, he also associated with the rich, famous, and talented people of his day, and was himself a person worthy of note in the popular press. Among the many examples of the formal recognition afforded Loti was his election in 1891 to the Académie Française (he defeated the candidacy of Émile Zola); on the occasion of his death in France in 1923 an enormous state funeral marked his passing, and in 1934 the 'Pierre Loti' museum was inaugurated to celebrate his memory. Loti's influence was pervasive and far-ranging. 'Aziyadé' masquerade balls, where participants dressed as characters from his novel of the same name, were something of a rage in Paris in the early decades of the twentieth century, and when young male 'candidates for entry into the Ecole Navale were asked to state what had inspired their naval vocation, "the great majority said it was through reading Jules Verne and Pierre Loti"' (Hargreaves 82).

Madame Chrysanthème, a formulaic romance about Loti's time in Japan, is presented in its preface as a memoir/travel narrative[4] – 'It is the diary of a summer of my life, in which I have changed nothing, not even the dates' – but in actuality is a story cobbled together from a string of anecdotes and descriptive passages interspersed with stereotypes about the country of Japan and its people. The genre of this narrative is important in that the autobiographical travel narrative constitutes a particularly seductive form of truth telling, because it putatively offers an authoritative vision of a reality accurately rendered. The question of veracity is an unavoidable one in works that purport to be an accurate form of life writing. Factuality in the modern world has been synonymous with authority. In practice, the autobiographical nature of the genre of travel writing both complicates and distorts the representation of non-European cultures, one significant example of which is the Butterfly trope. Loti was in earnest, perhaps more so than he realized, when, as the epigraph of this chapter illustrates, he presented *Madame Chrysanthème* as a tale *primarily* about himself and his relationship to Japan. Furthermore, as I will show, it is in keeping with other nineteenth-century cultural and institutional practices concerned with defining the self in reference to negative identifications of the Other that Loti's representation of the European bourgeois male operates through the staged representation of a Japanese woman. In Loti's work, as in other examples of contemporaneous cultural and institutional production that I cite, people and their customs and habits are presented as static entities in an ahistorical world. Sometimes they are villainized, and sometimes they are romanticized, but always they are diminished and stereotyped; they are constructed as Other, an Other that ultimately serves to construct the identity of those not designated as Other – the white, European, bourgeois male. This notion of defining the self in reference to negative identifications of the Other has in recent years been much theorized and discussed in texts such as Sidonie Smith's *Subjectivity, Identity, and the Body* (10), and as **Sherrill Grace**'s essay demonstrates, formulations such as Smith's continue to provide a useful conceptual framework with which to work. Loti's stories contain many examples of descriptions of an Other negatively identified as all body, animal-like, mindless; identifications that can be understood as operating within Julia Kristeva's notions of the abject. These are but a few of Loti's references to the people of Japan:

> [T]he mousmés come out of their holes like so many mice ... these tiny personages with narrow eyes and no brains. (*Madame Chrysanthème* 1887, 271–2)

> [The] indefinable odour of mousmés, of yellow race, of Japan, which is always and everywhere in the air. (ibid. 278)

> At the moment of my departure, I can only find within myself a smile of careless mockery for the swarming crowd of this Lil[l]iputian curtseying

people, – laborious, industrious, greedy of gain, tainted with a constitutional affectation, hereditary insignificance, and incurable monkeyishness. (ibid. 328)

And it is at those moments that their little slit eyes open, and seem to reveal something like a mind beneath their puppet-like exteriors.

But a mind which, more than ever, seems different in kind from my own; I feel that my thoughts are as distant from theirs as from the fleeting ideas of a bird or the daydreams of a monkey. (ibid. 290–1)[5]

And in *Le Roman d'un spahi* the protagonist refers to a young negress:

[whose hand] had, he could not help feeling, the terrible, chilling look of a monkey's paws.

Yet these hands were small and delicate, and were attached to her stout arms by very slender wrists. But the way in which the palms lacked colour and the half-tinting of the fingers has something *non-human* about it which was terrifying. (trans. Hargreaves, 36–67, italics in the original)

Looking Awry and Seeing Otherwise

As we make our way through *Madame Chrysanthème*, it quickly becomes evident that, in the midst of this crassly racist and misogynist text that is positioned at the genesis of the Butterfly narrative, Loti is also *writing something else*. Even a first reading of *Madame Chrysanthème* reveals that apart from Loti's descriptions of the young Chrysanthème, which are, in fact, often vitriolic, the only passages where the prose is alive and emotionally intense are those that also evoke a homoerotic sensibility. Rather than being structured around the title character, Madame Chrysanthème, the narrative actually threads back and forth through the figure of Yves, a character who, as the object of the narrator's affections and loyalty, holds the storyline together.

When I recognized Yves's place in the structure of the story, I examined the rest of Loti's work and discovered that an emphasis on the expression of an ambiguous sexuality held a prominent place throughout his writings. Moreover, this analysis of the structure of *Madame Chrysanthème* proves to be precisely in keeping with Barthes's reading of Loti's *Aziyadé*. In fact, Barthes's analysis is more applicable to *Madame Chrysanthème* than to *Aziyadé*.[6] Barthes describes the structural function of Loti's young woman protagonist in that story as follows: 'Aziyadé is the neutral term, the zero term of this major paradigm: discursively, she occupies the front rank; structurally, she is absent, she is the place of an absence, she is a fact of discourse, not a fact of desire' (114). As we shall see, this analysis works particularly well in relation to *Madame Chrysanthème.* An interrogation of the quotidian backdrop of *that* text does indeed register particular constructions of subjectivity and identity that mark Chrysanthème as 'the zero term' – 'a fact of discourse.' Once again evoking Butler's work, I suggest that these constructions were a way of writing into the social, or at least implicitly acknowledging, sexual identities that exceeded prescriptions of normative male sexuality. How can these ideas be used to examine the ways in which Loti was, in his work and in his person, actively engaged in what Foucault found to be a common practice in fin-de-siècle France, 'the dissemination and implementation of polymorphous sexualities'?[7]

By the time he arrived in Japan in 1885, Loti was an old hand at turning his various visits to ports-of-call into fictionalized travel narratives. *Madame Chrysanthème* is ostensibly structured around Loti's morganatic marriage arrangements with a young Japanese girl named Okané-San. Indeed, a number of his stories are built around roughly the same plot: Western man travels to 'exotic' land, meets 'Oriental' woman, who immediately recognizes the man as a superior being and falls in love with him; they have a relationship, and the man moves on to the next port, leaving the woman behind. As both **Vera Micznik** and **Melinda Boyd** have shown, *Madame Chrysanthème* is unusual in the larger context of the early Butterfly narratives because the woman does not kill herself or die of a broken heart after the hero departs. Yet, as I have already suggested, in spite of what can be read as the apparent focus on heterosexual relationships, many of Loti's stories also carry a homoerotic charge. Clive Wake addresses this theme of Loti's sexuality and structures his book around the assertion that the novelist was actually a homosexual who perpetrated a heterosexual myth upon his reading public. However, contrary to Wake's interpretation, and in keeping with the historians I referred to above, I argue that the binary of homo/heterosexuality was not so clearly defined. Further, because of the impossibility of maintaining distinct boundaries, it is likely that at least some of the reading public actively engaged, welcomed, and colluded with Loti's representations of diverse sexual identities.

There have been other approaches to the representations of masculinity and sexuality in Loti's writing. Christian Gundermann's 'Orientalism, Homophobia, Masochism' again invokes Barthes in his Freudian-

Lacanian analysis of *Aziyadé*. Gundermann declares that what interests him about the novel 'is precisely the way it wields colonialist stereotypes and simultaneously engenders the potential ... for a "campy" subversion of the stable normative masculinity that purports to lie at the heart of the colonialist project' (151). His analysis of *Aziyadé* figures the central motif of the novel as that of a masked homoerotic relationship, one wherein the Orient, viewed as woman, works to feminize and make into passive (penetrable) objects both its female *and* male subjects. Thus, the male figure that acts as intermediary between the narrator and the woman Aziyadé serves also as an object of desire.

Certainly, if we return to Barthes for a moment, it becomes clear that Loti's *Madame Chrysanthème* is formulaic in more ways than the one referred to earlier:

> A motif appears here – which is visible in other [of Loti's writings] as well: no, *Aziyadé* is not altogether a novel for well-brought-up girls, it is also a minor Sodomite epic, studded with allusions to *something unheard-of and shadowy*.
>
> The paradigm of the two friends is therefore clearly formulated (the friend / the lover), but it has no consequence: it is not *transformed* (into action, into plot, into drama): the meaning remains somehow indifferent. This novel is an almost motionless discourse, which posits meanings but does not resolve them. (111)

Madame Chrysanthème, published eight years after *Aziyadé*, was received by a reading public already well versed in the ambiguities activated in Loti's gendered representations. We know that Loti, who actually spent a total of only thirty-four days in Japan during the visit ostensibly 'chronicled' in *Madame Chrysanthème*, was not much interested in the writing of this story.[8] He did not like the country or the people, but, as he wrote to his sister shortly after his arrival: 'It would be ... a poor piece of investment policy not to profit from my stay by having a bit of a look round the interior and earning my money by spinning a tale out of it' (quoted in Hargreaves, 81). At the same time he wrote to a friend: 'Working hard, writing Japanese novel [*Madame Chrysanthème*], must deliver by August; big money matter. Novel will be daft. Am getting same way myself' (quoted ibid.). Chrysanthème, then, is a kind of lazy version of *Aziyadé*, a version that lacks the defining features that make *Aziyadé* such a good example of the way that the Orient, woman, and normative male sexuality were constituted in relation to one another.

Telling Tales

Not only does the writing, proceeding from desire, constantly touch on the forbidden, alienate the writing subject, and baffle him; but even (this being merely the structural translation of the foregoing) the functional levels are multiple: they tremble within each other.

Barthes, 'Pierre Loti: Aziyadé' 121

In *Madame Chrysanthème*, Yves is a sailor and shipmate of Loti's who accompanies the narrator (Loti) to Japan. The two friends are inseparable. It is Yves who suggests to Loti that he take a wife while he is in Japan, and it is he who later picks out Loti's bride. Thus, it is structurally significant that from the moment of her introduction into the narrative Chrysanthème emerges out of the relationship between the two men. However, very early in the story the narrator begins to worry about the negative effects that his young Japanese wife may be having on his friend Yves. As I have already said, it is significant that this jealous worry and its resolution develop into the main narrative interest in the story. Chrysanthème, rather than being a central character, is figured only as she is perceived, that is, negatively, as a threat and a danger to the relationship between the two men. The productive paradox at play here is figured by Loti's performance of dominant male heterosexuality *and* simultaneous subversion, thereby opening up the spaces of desire recognizable to certain constituencies of his readership.[9] The following passages show how Loti uses displacement strategically. It is displacement that allows Loti to ventriloquize the voice of the bourgeois heterosexual male subject even as he marks out Yves as the primary object of his emotional attachment:

> Yves is now in bed and sleeping under our roof ... Sleep has come to him sooner than to me tonight; for somehow I fancy I had seen long glances exchanged between him and Chrysanthème ... I have left this little creature in his hands like a toy, and I begin to fear lest I should have thrown some perturbation in his mind. I do not trouble my head about this little Japanese girl. But Yves, – it would be decidedly wrong on his part, and would greatly diminish my faith in him. (160)

> [A]s Chrysanthème crouches in front of her smoking-box, I suddenly discover in her an air of low breeding, in the very worst sense of the word ... I should hate her ... if she were to entice Yves into committing a fault, – a fault which I should perhaps never be able to forgive. (162)

> I embarked with Yves on board a sampan; this time it is he who is carrying me off and taking me back to my home ... On land, a delicious perfume of new-mown hay greets us, and the road across the mountains lies bathed in glorious moonlight. (178)

While it can be said that such commentary operates within heterosexual codes of masculine honour and women as property, it is significant that the attention focused on Yves emerges as an obsessive one, and continues throughout the story.

Yves's presence is so keen that on the occasions when he is not present his absence is tangible for the reader. The sublimated erotic tension achieves release when the narrator confronts Yves with his misgivings:

> I risk the remark: 'You will perhaps be more sorry to leave this little Chrysanthème than I am?'
>
> Silence reigns between us.
>
> After which I pursue, and, burning my ships, I add: 'You know, after all, if you have such a fancy for her, I haven't really married her; one can't really consider her my wife.' In great surprise he looks in my face: 'Not your wife, you say? But, by Jove, though, that's just it; she is your wife.'
>
> There is no need of many words at any time between us two; I know exactly now, by his tone, by his great good-humoured smile, how the case stands ... he considers her my wife, and she is sacred. I have the fullest faith in his word, and I experience a positive relief, a real joy, at finding my staunch Yves of bygone days. How could I have so succumbed to the demeaning influence of my surroundings as to suspect him even, and invent for myself such a mean, petty anxiety?
>
> We will never even mention that doll again.
>
> We remain up there very late, talking of other things, gazing the while at the immense depths below our feet, at the valleys and mountains as they become one by one indistinct and lost in the deepening darkness. Placed as we are at an enormous height, in the wide free atmosphere, we seem already to have quitted this miniature country ... (288–9)

The narrator's preoccupation with Yves and the fact that this preoccupation is central to the unfolding of the plot, situates Chrysanthème as Barthes's 'zero term,' in that (again invoking his analysis of *Aziyadé* that I promised earlier to revisit) 'discursively, she occupies the front rank; structurally, she is absent, she is the place of an absence, she is a fact of discourse, not a fact of desire' (114).

Home Truths

Gundermann's attempt, cited above, to establish the possibility of a '*campy* subversion of stable normative masculinity' in Loti's literary production, and its particular positioning in *Madame Chrysanthème*, is consistent with accounts of Loti's personal life. Loti seems always to have been simultaneously constructing and transgressing the prescribed masculine identity of a nineteenth-century bourgeois male. He married a woman, Jeanne Blanche Franc de Ferrière, who was his social equal, and had a child with her, and he also took as a common-law wife Crucita Gainza because of fears about continuance of the family line. He established the young Basque woman in a small house in his hometown and had four children with her. However, he did not spend much time with either of these women. In the course of his career as a naval officer he was, for much of his adult life, away from both homes.

The ambivalent figure that Loti cut was not lost on the French public. A caricature of him (figure 1),[10] one of many published in contemporary magazines, drives home this point. The way that this image details the infamous high-heeled boots Loti teetered around in to give himself more height, the ever-present make-up, the Turkish fez that recalls *Aziyadé*, along with Loti's sexually provocative, precarious balance atop the steeple, and his preoccupation with his own image as he stares into the mirror, suggest a familiar knowledge on the part of the French public with many of the closeted circumstances in his work. The caption, 'Pacha' (pasha in English), refers to a high-ranking Turkish officer. Loti, a high-ranking *French* naval officer, who is identified as such (with the exception of the fez) by the uniform he is wearing, is designated as a 'Turk.' This caption alerts us to the first of many doubles in play here. Loti, as a representative of the French empire, is placed far above the ground in the imperial seat of power: an elevated position from which he is able to survey the entire expanse below. However, he does not occupy this position as intended. Rather, he is lost in the image reflected back from the mirror held in front of him. He is immersed, deeply engaged in this surface. But the reflection in the mirror is ambiguous at best. Finally, we cannot leave this image without further addressing the obvious sexual innuendo. The East, depicted as a place that permits 'transgressive' sexual practices – the penetration of men by other men – is in this image the site of a power reversal: Loti straddling the obviously phallic representation of a mosque can be seen as being penetrated both in terms of (homo)sexual penetration and (contrary to

Figure 1. Caricature of Pierre Loti published in the magazine *Fantasio*, May 1913. *Fantasio* was a student literary magazine founded by Marcel Pagnol and others at the University of Aix-En-Provence in 1913. Pagnol later transformed *Fantasio* into the magazine *Cahiers du sud* (Book – or Notebook – of the South).

the trope of Orientalism that figures, as in Puccini's opera, a feminized East penetrated by the West) as a French subject penetrated by the Turkish 'abject.'

Jonathan Wisenthal's comment, then, that '[i]t is highly appropriate to construct a travesty of the Butterfly narrative, for the story itself is in a way a myth of travesty' (14), is wonderfully illustrated in this image. Furthermore, the caricature itself commits the travesty that is its object because, as Barthes tells us, in the practice of masquerade the costume 'is a problem of identity, and since what is abandoned – or adopted – is a total person, there must be no contagion between the two costumes, the Occidental cast-offs and the new garments; whence those sites of transformation, those transformation chambers ..., those airtight sluices where identities are scrupulously exchanged, one dying (Loti), the other born (Arif) [Loti's masquerade in *Aziyadé*]' (115).

Seen in this light, this caricature is, quite literally, one site of Loti's public undoing.

Still-life on the High Seas

Loti, like a number of his contemporaries, had received training in the visual arts and was an accomplished draftsman. A consideration of some of the many drawings and photographs kept in the Loti archives is instructive in the attempt to acknowledge and confront the silences contained in this work. Photographs of Loti – alone, almost always in costume, and with various of his male friends – when placed beside drawings he made of his fellow shipmates over a period of several decades, provoke distinctly sexualized readings. The four drawings I have included here are compelling. The first (figure 2), made in 1868–9 at the beginning of Loti's naval career, is a composite drawing of Loti's fellow officers and shipmates. The individual images are small in relation to the size of the paper, and each head and shoulders motif is given its own space. The captain of the ship is set in the central space of the composition and further identified with the letter 'C.' In another very similar drawing Joseph Bernard, a close friend of Loti's (they were companions for many years and Loti went to a great deal of trouble to have himself relocated to Bernard's ship when Bernard was promoted to a subsequent position), occupies a place of honour at the drawing's centre. The photograph of Loti and Bernard taken in 1875 (figure 3) is notable for the intensity with which Bernard appears to focus on the young Loti. The above drawing almost certainly uses as its model a simi-

Figure 2. Pierre Loti, Composite drawing of shipmates on *Borda*, 1868–9.

Figure 3. Photograph of Julien Viaud (Pierre Loti) and Joseph Bernard taken aboard the *Borda*.

lar, earlier photograph of Loti and Bernard, taken aboard the vessel *Borda*, on which the pair were stationed for several years. A later drawing made in 1885–6 (figure 4) of sailors on one of Loti's ships, the *Triomphante*, creates a very different impression: the men are no longer represented by pristine head-and-shoulder cameos. These men have bodies, and they are shown in different stages of undress. The scanty undershirts clothe virile, muscular forms that are no longer separated in the pictorial space. The bodies touch, overlap, and intermingle. The harlequin in the centre of the composition is a provocative element alluding to Loti's love of the masquerade. The figures are set against a cloud-

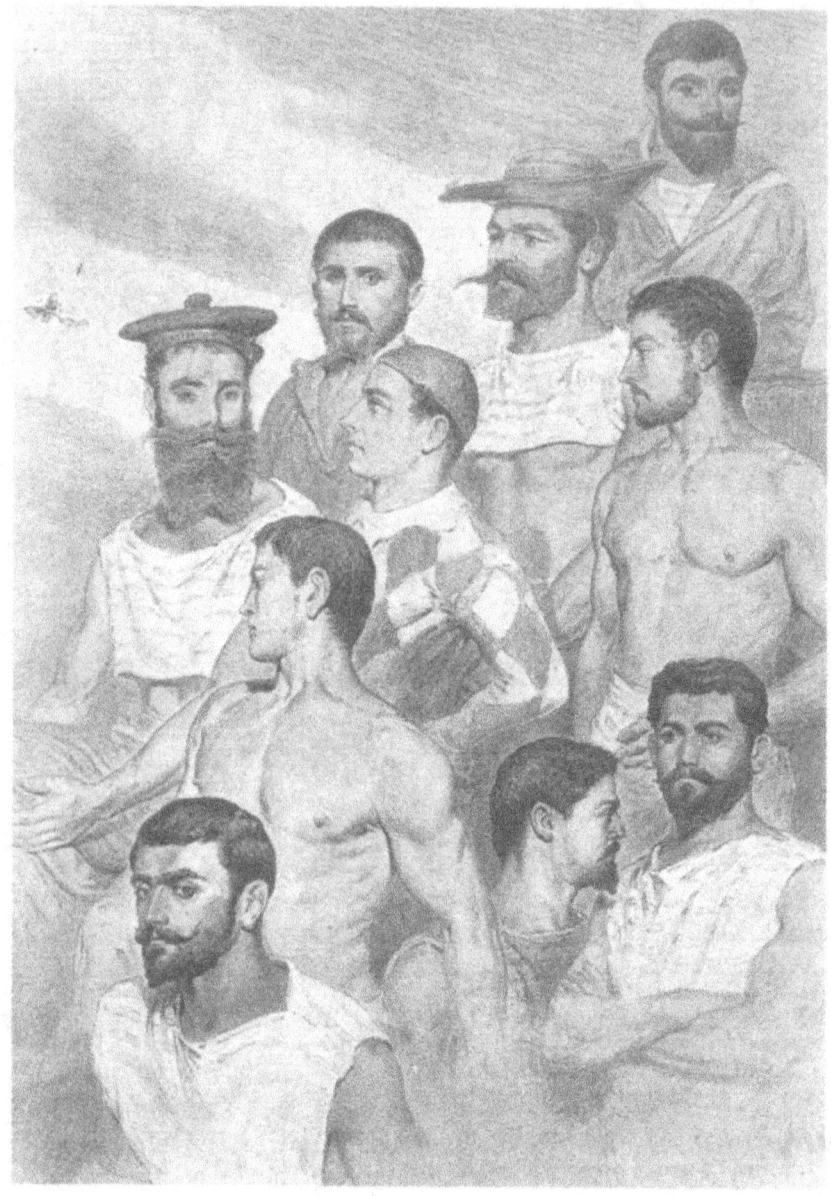

Figure 4. Pierre Loti, Composite drawing of shipmates 1885–6.

swept sky, and a butterfly with a fluid gossamer train (an important and potent symbol for Loti) flies out of the left frame of the drawing.

Figure 5 provides an example of a more extended study executed around the same time, and alludes to a passage in Loti's *An Iceland Fisherman* that details an event aboard ship while crossing the Red Sea: thousands of tiny birds alight on the ship only to die there of exhaustion. In the story the men 'gathered up the little black remains and, with a look of commiseration, spread open the delicate bluish wings. Then they swept them into the deep sea, with long strokes of the broom' (108). *An Iceland Fisherman* has been primarily read as a heterosexual story, but as Richard Berrong shows (*In Love with a Handsome Sailor*) (104–20), Loti's text can also be read as a gay novel. Certainly, the erotic connotations of the above quotation describing the incident, when coupled with this drawing, support such a reading. In the drawing the two men are figured in a formal composition that can be also understood as making ironic references to the moralizing narratives of eighteenth-century genre painting. In addition to the obviously erotic rendering (this drawing would not be out of place in twentieth-century gay visual culture) – muscular limbs and chest, the draped soft lines of the cloth of the men's rolled trousers and the close and familiar proximity of their bodies – the motif of the small, limp birds scattered over the deck and held in the hand have particular associations. In seventeenth- and eighteenth-century genre painting, birds were associated with copulation and the erotic. Not only would Loti's training in visual art have made him aware of the meanings he was calling up in these images, but such readings also circulated in many forms of popular culture. While Berrong's text offers the most extensive and thorough analysis of Loti's appropriation of imagery associated with sexuality in his literary work, other writers have also made similar observations. In her analysis of Loti's *Fleurs d'ennui*, feminist literary theorist Irene Szyliowicz points out that the protagonist (Loti) turns down the invitation of a young and beautiful prostitute 'in favour of a wild horseback ride with his friend,' a character modelled after another of the author's naval companions. Szyliowicz observes: '[T]he horseback ride, a symbol of passion in nineteenth-century literature, usually associated with female characters to identify the unspoken, is here inverted to encompass Loti and his male friend' (86–7).

Tableaux Vivants

In his daily life, Loti's love of dressing-up and disguise was so extensive

Figure 5. Pierre Loti, Extended study, undated.

that Léon Daudet spoke of him 'as putting on a mask to buy a croissant' (cited in Szyliowicz, 23). Indeed, there are numerous references in the secondary literature to Loti's penchant for dressing in exotic attire. Furthermore, Loti's love of costume at times put his career in jeopardy:

> Even when in the navy, he wore makeup, sometimes in excess. One commander recommended that this man never be promoted because he wore too much. But another commander later recommended promotion, in spite of the makeup, insisting that he was an extremely competent officer. (Jay Paul Minn, introduction to Loti, *The Desert*)

> When Loti's ships reached port, he went ashore fully disguised in local dress, and wandered around fixed in the fantasy that he was perceived as a native. If any of his fellow officers or shipmates came across him during his adventures, they knew they were not to acknowledge him in any way and passed by him as if he were a stranger. (Blanch 118)

Loti's preoccupation with masquerade, and his rare ability 'to dress exotically without seeming to be in disguise,' is characterized by Barthes as a 'transvestism' that works to transform (112). This argument is of particular interest to us in reference to a passage from Loti's collection of essays *Japoneries d'automne* (1889), which **Joshua Mostow** has cited in his essay (although to illustrate a different point than the one I will make here). In this quotation Loti describes the annual ball, which he attended, held to celebrate Emperor Meiji's birthday. It would seem that Loti does not disdain *all* Japanese women. He is perfectly able, as on this occasion, to appreciate the distinguished, refined features and devastating self-confidence of the 'countess.' But, is it not the *masquerade of gender* rather than the woman herself that Loti holds up for admiration? Certainly it is nothing to do with class privilege that draws Loti to distinguish this woman, whom he refers to as an 'astonishing parvenue.' After all, what Loti lingers over in his reminiscence of this event are the minutiae of her costume: her white rice-powdered face, impeccably coiffed hair, and her dress, the bodice of which forms 'a slim sheath covered with a stiff embroidery studded with pearls.' I suspect that what Loti – the master of masquerade – recognizes and so admires in this woman is the fact that she is also an accomplished practitioner of the arts of transformation.

Loti's intense love of masquerade also found expression in the 'house of enchantment' that he created for himself in the family home at Rochefort (Genet and Hervé 329). The significance of the nineteenth-century bourgeois interior has been noted by many theorists, and Loti created a particularly hermetic environment, one that prefigured the Paris Exposition of 1900 in its oppressive articulation of the material cultures of many of France's colonial holdings. The interior that he made seems to lurk in some twilight zone between ethnographic fascination and an obsessively articulated dream-world of the Other.[11] In the house's halls and chambers he replicated the environments he had travelled the world to experience. A photo-engraving of Loti standing in what is just a corner of the Turkish room illustrates the excess of the surroundings (figure 6). The rooms were ostentatiously appointed with ethnic decoration and, as well, he owned authentic costumes that complemented each themed setting, which he wore in the elaborate masquerade balls he frequently staged. The archival photograph collection contains dozens of pictures of Loti in these 'exotic' outfits: costumes that run the gamut from the rusticity of Basque peasant clothes to the particularly lavish robes and headpiece borrowed from a member of the Chinese imperial court. The excess exhibited in the printed invitations and menus, as well as that shown in the photographs documenting these balls, is staggering. The photograph of Loti dressed as Osiris (figure 7) shows him ready to take part in a dress-up party at the home of his friend Mme Adam. Nor was he alone in his obsessions: group pictures show that his friends and associates were also ready, willing, and financially able to participate in these extravagant fantasies.

What's in a Name?

Whence comes the name 'Loti?' The nom de plume that Julien Viaud began using in 1872 when he was in Tahiti is the name of an island flower. This was, at the very least, an eccentric choice of name for a naval officer. The origin of this pen name is alternately credited to a Maori girlfriend, who 'pronounced "Loti" over and over again, as proof of her love for him' (Szyliowicz 25), and to Loti's fellow officers, who 'nicknamed him Loti after an Indian flower.'[12] His first name Pierre, was borrowed from a close friend, Pierre Le Cor, who was the model for Yves in *Madame Chrysanthème* and was familiar to Loti's readers through his development as a character in *Fleurs d'ennui* and *Mon frère Yves*. Le Cor and Loti served together for many years, and Loti's journals evince that he harboured an exquisite admiration for his friend: 'When Pierre removes his clothes, one would think he were a Greek statue removing

Madame Butterfly: Behind Every Great Woman ... 215

Figure 6. Photograph of Loti in his home in Rochefort, 1890.

Figure 7. Photograph of Loti dressed as Osiris for a costume party.

his coarse exterior, and one admires him. – In the same bronzed alabaster, hard and polished, are outlined the mobile bulges of his muscles and the powerful lines of an ancient athlete' (Szyliowicz 29).

This statement calls to mind the sensual drawings of Loti's shipmates. What is interesting here is certainly not whether Loti himself could be designated, in today's terminology, as bisexual, straight, or gay. It is more pertinent to our inquiry to ask, What was going on in the performative displays of the masquerade balls and in Loti's extensive use of disguise? And why were his stories – stories that carried a double entendre both sexually and racially, and that constructed such culturally and politically potent stereotypes as 'Butterfly' – so popular?

The After-life of Photographs

A further brief look at some of the material circumstances surrounding the writing of *Madame Chrysanthème* helps to highlight the difficulty, referred to earlier, that is presented by the lack of distinction in the novel between autobiographical account and creative fiction. One of the events Loti describes in *Madame Chrysanthème* is a trip that the narrator (Loti), Yves, and Chrysanthème make to have their photograph taken at the studio of a local photographer. The narrator says: 'To-day, Yves, my mousmé and myself went to the best photographer in Nagasaki, to be taken in a group together ... *We shall send the photograph to France* ... Chrysanthème slowly settles herself in a very affected style, turning in the points of her toes as much as possible, according to the fashion' (Loti 251–2, my emphasis). With these words Loti describes an actual portrait photograph of Loti, Pierre Le Cor, and Okané-San – the young girl who was the model for Chrysanthème – taken while Loti and Le Cor were stationed in Nagasaki in 1885 (figure 8). This image is central to an anecdotal passage in which Loti paints a very unflattering picture as he comments on Japanese society through a description of the busy photographer's crowded shop. In the photograph that is left to us the young girl sits, looking unsure of herself, flanked by the white-suited, standing men. But what place does this photograph hold in the scheme of the larger narrative?

Photographs such as this one were in this period understood as factual evidence. The linking of the photographic event with the veracity of the rest of Loti's narrative demonstrates one of the ways that travel writing functioned, and shows how the genre occupied an ominous position

Figure 8. Photograph of Loti, Pierre Le Cor, and Okané-San in Nagasaki, 12 September 1885.

of power in the construction and representation of peoples, and particularly women, of non-European cultures. In this Japanese cârte-de-visite sent back to his reading public in France, Loti presents just enough detail – the identity of the three people involved and the turned-in feet of the young girl – to communicate a convincing scenario of the event. If the picture and other artefacts are as Loti describes them (and he describes Japanese architecture, household items, and foods, as well as local customs and celebrations in great detail and makes drawings of many of these items), does this confirm that his construction of the young Chrysanthème and of her country, Japan, is an authentic one? Where does fact end and fiction begin?

My point here is not to cite biography to secure the nuances of a written text, but rather to notice the distance that exists between Loti's life and the dominant tropes of exotic female sexuality elicited by his stories. Discovering this distance opens up a reading of *Madame Chrysanthème* as multivalent, and as occupying a place in colonial discourse that was in fact fraught with the needs and desires of competing constituencies. Loti's writings engaged dominant constructions of racialized female sexuality. In works such as *Aziyadé* this construction (in a straight as opposed to 'campy' reading) is fully articulated – the woman is presented as sexually alluring and available, beautiful and mysterious, and devoted to the Western male protagonist. A similar structure recurs in *Madame Chrysanthème*, except that here the construction of an exotic Orient is so fragile that when the young girl removes her clothes for the daily bath, the charade crumbles and – in sharp contrast to the ecstasies evoked in Loti when his friend Le Cor undresses – we are left instead with Loti's unadorned racist and misogynous comments: 'A Japanese woman, deprived of her long dress and her huge sash with its pretentious bows, is nothing but a diminutive yellow being, with crooked legs and flat, unshapely bust; she has no longer a remnant of her artificial little charms, which have completely disappeared in company with her costume' (216).

With this interpretation of feminine identity as masquerade, Loti's text echoes his own extensive use of masks and disguises as ways of playing with, and developing – using both autobiographic fiction and photographic portraiture as prostheses – a multiplicity of complex sexual identities. In this case, there is a resonance between Loti's life and work and Butler's assertions about the performative quality of gender identification and the ways in which sexual binaries can be undone.

Imag(in)ing Culture

In contrast to the use Loti makes of the group portrait above, another photograph of a young girl, found in the Loti archives (which Christian Genet and Daniel Hervé use in *Pierre Loti l'enchanteur* [222] to illustrate, unwittingly it seems, Loti's denigrating representation of Japanese women), presents us, in spite of the way in which Genet and Hervé frame the picture, with a different view: a very beautiful young girl, no more than about thirteen years of age, gazes at the camera with a tentative look that suggests both vulnerability and innocence.

Portrait photographs such as these call up the relationship between photograph and text used by Gauguin in his 1892 painting *Manao Tupapau* (*Spirit of the Dead Watching*). Gauguin travelled to the French colony of Tahiti seeking a new and ostensibly 'primitive' subject matter that would provide an antidote to French bourgeois culture at the end of the nineteenth century. While Gauguin had gathered information on Tahiti at the 1889 World Exposition in Paris (the exposition emphasized France's 'civilizing' mission in relation to its colonial holdings), what is particularly relevant here is that his friend and fellow painter, Émile Bernard, introduced Gauguin to Loti's *Marriage de Loti* (1880). Loti had himself travelled to Tahiti under the auspices of the French navy, married a young girl, and then written a fictionalized account of his experience. Both Bernard and Gauguin were captivated by the author's 'glowing phrases of the Eden-like existence to be enjoyed on the South Sea Island' and his descriptions of 'exotic' Tahitian women:

> A lovely land is Oceania! – Beautiful creatures those Tahitian women; – not classically Greek as to features, but with a beauty of their own which is even more attractive, and antique figures and limbs! Mentally, incomplete creatures whom one loves like the fine fruit or fresh waters and gorgeous flowers ... (214)

> The temper of Tahitians is a good deal like that of children; they are whimsical, perverse, suddenly sulky for no reason at all, always honest and well-meaning, and hospitable in the widest scope of the word ... The contemplative side of man is strangely developed in them; they are alive to every aspect of nature, sad or gay, and open to all the vagaries of imagination. (39–40)

Loti's *Marriage de Loti* is recalled in Gauguin's *Manao Tupapau* painting. Gauguin wrote in *his* autobiographical narrative on Tahiti, *Noa Noa*, which included a reproduction of this painting as well as a photograph of the young woman, Teha'amana, his 'wife' who modelled for the painting: 'I want ... above all (to) render the native mentality and traditional character ... the mood is one of fear. But what sort of fear has possessed her? ... [I]t is, of course, the *tupapau* (spirits of the dead)' (Pollock 12). According to Gauguin, the fear experienced by the young girl in his painting is not rational, not Western fear, but rather springs from a mind less intelligent than that of the man who 'creates' her. Like Loti's Tahitian women, she is mentally 'incomplete ... open to all the vagaries of [the] imagination,' and meant to be 'love[d] like the fine fruit or fresh waters and gorgeous flowers.' While the representation of Chrysanthème in Japan is more derogatory than the romantically enthusiastic evocation of this Tahitian woman, what is evident in both of these examples is the fact that women in Tahiti *and* Japan are constructed as lesser beings compared to their creators: 'incomplete creatures' with 'child-like' or 'animal-like' dispositions.

It is no accident that the circumstances surrounding the painting of *Manao Tupapau* are strikingly similar to those surrounding the writing of *Madame Chrysanthème*. Gauguin and Loti both travelled to foreign lands and 'married' young women. Using their 'wives' as models, both men produced cultural works that re-inscribed and re-presented familiar notions of 'exotic' women. Both men were participating in experiences that engaged them at the level of state, cultural, and personal narratives, and that worked towards securing their fame as artists. Gauguin travelled to the 'exotic' locale of Tahiti with the blessing of the French government: '[He] left France on 1 April 1891 amid considerable publicity equipped with letters from the Ministry of Public Education and the Fine Arts commissioning him to "study and ultimately to paint the customs and landscapes of Tahiti"' (Pollock 12). The impetus behind Gauguin's relocation was an economic as well as a professional move: 'On this French colony he hoped to be able to live cheaply and paint enough to support the intended resumption of his marriage to Mette Gauguin, mother of his five children, with whom he had not lived since 1887' (ibid.). Upon arrival he 'married' a thirteen-year-old, set up house, and went about the business of establishing himself as a force to be reckoned with in the world of nineteenth-century avant-garde painting. But just as Loti was unimpressed by Japan, Gauguin did not like what he found in

Tahiti: 'Almost immediately disappointed by Tahiti, Gauguin nevertheless spent two years there before he managed to persuade the French government to repatriate him' (ibid.). Artists such as Loti and Gauguin were part of a much larger set of forces that regulated the way other cultures were represented. Constructions of 'Oriental' women were supported at many different sites of cultural and institutional power. For example, Loti's *Marriage de Loti* produced images of Tahitian women for public consumption just as his book on Japan worked to circulate and naturalize stereotypical images of Japanese women.

Gauguin's and Loti's images of racialized woman figured as 'exotic,' sexually alluring, and available take us back to the questions provoked by the initial reading of *Madame Chrysanthème*: What was at stake in a society that so enthusiastically embraced these stories? What part did Loti's work – and its significance to the unfolding of the 'Butterfly' narrative – have in the powerful self/other binary that was at play in nineteenth-century Europe? Was he mapping transgression into the spaces of the everyday, and in the process acknowledging and inserting into the social body the possibility of alternative sexual identities – ones that exceeded this binary? The productive paradox at play here is that Loti's work functioned to construct and reinforce images of women that have become a historical trope; yet, as I have maintained, his writing was a subversive voice in the construction of a normative masculine identity in nineteenth-century Europe and its colonies.

Pierre Loti's constructions of the 'Oriental' woman as Other reflects a profound and common ambivalence about sexuality in fin-de-siècle France. His preoccupation with sexuality was at the heart of his stories about non-European cultures. The construction of Madame Chrysanthème was not a construction of the Other at all – in this sense Loti admitted no alterity. His Chrysanthème was primarily a projection of his attempts at and anxieties about self-identity. However, with this assertion, I am not suggesting that his representations did not perform the work of Empire. Not only were they successful in this regard during Loti's lifetime, but the Butterfly narrative continues to have power as a significant cultural and political trope.

Fast Forward

By way of example, David Henry Hwang's play *M. Butterfly* (1986) and

David Cronenberg's film *M. Butterfly* (1993) can, each in its own way, be considered a re-presentation of the underlying tensions that define *Madame Chrysanthème*. If we hold Loti's version of the Madame Butterfly narrative alongside the Hwang/Cronenberg productions, the resonances are clear. A century after *Madame Chrysanthème* was first published *M. Butterfly* gives voice to some of the many silences contained in Loti's work. Not surprisingly, both Hwang's play and Cronenberg's film shift the Butterfly trope in significant, though somewhat differently figured, ways. By framing East–West relations overtly in terms of gender and sexuality, they subvert and complicate, or at the very least open up, the conventional Butterfly narrative, irretrievably altering its power to contain and define the figures it constructs. Through their refusal to fix identities or stave off ambiguities, these productions foreground the political economy of Butterfly's complex narrative tradition, thereby echoing the multiplicity of subject positions produced in *Madame Chrysanthème*. However, as **Richard Cavell**'s essay demonstrates, in terms of projecting the possibility of alternative sexualities, and thereby complexifying the binary of gender, Cronenberg's *M. Butterfly* is the more successful of the two revisionings.

The world of colonial abundance that eighteenth- and nineteenth-century Europe thought lay at its feet quickly became figured as an abyss: an unknown and unknowable foreign space – a zone paradoxically fraught with anxiety and replete with inviting possibility. Loti's narratives participated in Europe's impossible bid to secure a fixed and stable identity for itself in the face of this threat. But they were also fault lines that simultaneously opened up and, if Butler is correct, worked to instal alternative subjective spaces for the paradigmatic bourgeois European male to occupy: ones that resisted the compulsory heterosexuality embedded in the founding identifications of the hegemonic and embodied subjects of modernity. Arguably, Cronenberg's representation of the Butterfly myth occupies the shifting terrain of these developing multiplicities of otherness.

Notes

I am grateful to Richard Berrong for a lively email discussion that took place at the beginning of March 2003, when I sent him this chapter to read. Richard generously made a number of comments, some of which I took up and others that I did not agree with, in an interchange that was most welcome.

1 I am working from translations and that always entails a risk. In relation to this point, however, I would like to stress that I am not attempting to offer either a biographical or a bio-bibliographical reading of Loti.
2 Michel Foucault's *History of Sexuality* series has famously analysed nineteenth-century bourgeois preoccupation with sexuality. See *History of Sexuality,* Introduction: '[Sex] is that aspect of [the bourgeoisie] which troubled and preoccupied it more than any other, begged and obtained its attention, and which it cultivated with a mixture of fear, curiosity, delight, and excitement. The bourgeoisie made this element identical with its body.' Foucault claimed that 'far from being repressed in [nineteenth-century] society [sexuality] was constantly aroused' (148). In her discussion of Foucault's repressive hypothesis, Laura Stoler emphasizes that '[t]his is no dismissal of repression as a "ruse" of the nineteenth-century bourgeois order or a denial that sex was prohibited and masked ... Foucault rejected, not the fact of repression, but the notion that it was the organizing principle of sexual discourse, that repression could account for its silences and prolific emanations' (3). For a further discussion of bourgeois sexuality and colonial representation see Stoler's *Race and the Education of Desire.* Also see Edward Said's *Orientalism* for an analysis of sexuality in terms of East/West relations.
3 There are other contemporaneous examples of literary productions that give weight to Foucault's assertion of a fascination with sexuality in nineteenth-century society and which also echo the homoerotic theme found in Loti's work. I came across one particularly interesting example when I attended a lecture at UBC given by Donna Zapf, 'Tolstoy and the Kreutzer Sonata: Thinking about Music and Its Meaning,' on 3 December 1997. Zapf explored the positioning of music as an irrational Other to the rational self in Tolstoy's novella *The Kreutzer Sonata* (1889). Tolstoy's novella depicts upper-class late-nineteenth-century society in Russia as a society entirely framed by Parisian social life, morals, and manners. Tolstoy parallels the way in which his protagonist Pozdnshev is affected physiologically and involuntarily by music to the effect of women upon men. Male desire is seen as an addiction that inevitably leads to the dissolution of the self, and music, as well as women, are both understood as overwhelmingly powerful in this regard. Tolstoy's novella offers a representation of the upper-class European woman that can be compared to 'woman' as figured in the Orientalist motif and shows that Loti's women are grounded in much broader gendered constructions.
4 In terms of reception, travel narratives were often presented as 'memoir' or 'diary,' and that is part of the problem of their dissemination as 'truth.' The 'armchair traveller' of this era certainly used these narratives to 'learn' about

other cultures. These works functioned on multiple levels and in different ways for different constituencies – the author's intentionality cannot be cited as the defining factor in the ways that this text was able to function – just because Loti *calls* it a diary does not mean that this was its only frame.
5 Quoted in Hargreaves 36–7.
6 See Berrong 18–41.
7 In relation to the threat posed by subjectivities that presented alternatives to those normatively authorized, see Victoria Thompson, 'Creating Boundaries: Homosexuality and the Changing Social Order in France, 1830–1870,' in *Homosexuality in Modern France*, ed. J. Merrick and B.T. Ragan, Jr (New York: Oxford University Press), 102–27. Thompson's essay offers a thorough and insightful analysis of the emergence of homosexuality as a category in nineteenth-century France. She shows that whereas in France in the 1830s and 1840s sexual categories tended to be rather fluid and loosely defined, after the bloody June Days of the 1848 uprising, permeable boundaries came to be associated with disorder and chaos, and that 'cultural categories – in particular those of class, gender, and sexuality – became increasingly fixed' (103). As well, Robert Nye shows, in his essay 'Michel Foucault's Sexuality and the History of Homosexuality in France' (ibid. 225–42), that France was one of the first industrial powers to experience a decline of its population rate, and maps the ways in which concern over this development saw the 'formation of a "natalist" movement whose efforts aimed at solidifying marriage, increasing family size, improving the health of mothers and children, while attempting to stamp out obstacles to reproduction such as alcoholism, pornography, and neo-Malthusian propaganda' (230). This climate made it very easy for 'the homosexual, as someone who threatened the gender balance that was at the basis of all other social distinctions' (Thompson 122), to be viewed with suspicion and fear. During the next few decades the homosexual emerged as a type 'increasingly used to symbolize "a reversal of the regular order"' (ibid. 104). Concomitant with this classification of sexuality into categories presented as 'symmetrical binary opposit[es]' (Eve Kosofsky Sedgwick, *Epistemology of the Closet* [Berkeley: University of California Press, 1990], 9) – hetero- and homosexuality – the homosexual, the 'invert,' became further contained and defined within medical and criminal discourses as aberrant, dangerous to the 'natural' order, and progressively came to function as the dark underside of normative social prescriptions governing identity. All of these changes contributed to what Foucault, in *History of Sexuality*, vol. 1, refers to as a technology of health and pathology that was organized around the positioning of sexuality as 'a medical and medicalizable object' (44).
8 In a section of his book titled 'Literary Imperialism,' Hargreaves quotes the

following conversation, reported in Loti's *Journal intime 1882–1885*, between Loti and his friend Émile Pouvillon: 'I am going to get to work on some Tonkineries, but I find this country so odious that I will do them only with difficulty, and with a very mercenary aim' (81).

9 That the narrative must have been read as a *heterosexual* tale, as well as for its homoerotic content, is indicated by the number of editions published in Viaud's lifetime alone: Richard Berrong cites the number at 222 (121). A circulation of that immensity suggests that the book's readership included both those who were alert to its evocation of diverse sexualities and those who were not.

10 *Fantasio* (a student literary magazine), Genet and Hervé, May 1913, reproduced in *Pierre Loti l'enchanteur* 436.

11 In her presentation of Walter Benjamin's Arcades Project *The Dialectics of Seeing* (1989), Susan Buck-Morss presents analysis of a letter from Adorno to Benjamin in 1935 and says, 'The image of the bourgeois interior is interpreted by both Adorno and Benjamin as an emblem of bourgeois consciousness, which retreats into a subjective, inward realm' (*The Dialectics of Seeing: Walter Benjamin and the Arcades Project* [Cambridge, MA: MIT Press, 1989], 427 n. 97). See also Rosalind H. Williams, *Dream Worlds: Mass Consumption in Late Nineteenth-Century France* (Berkeley: University of California Press, 1982).

12 'Viaud–Pierre Loti,' in *Century Dictionary and Encyclopedia*, ed. Benjamin Smith (New York: Century Company, 1899), 1035. Also both the bibliographical dictionary *Men and Women of the Time* and *Warner's Dictionary of Authors* credit Loti's shipmates with the new name. I am indebted to Daniel O'Leary for alerting me to the translation of Loti's name and for all three of these references.

M. Butterfly: Staging Choices and Their Meanings

RACHEL DITOR AND JAN SELMAN

The following observations began as we prepared for a lab session that explored aspects of David Henry Hwang's *M. Butterfly*. 'The Theatrical Language: Staging Choices and Their Meanings' was part of 'Madame Butterfly in Film, Drama, Opera, and Fiction: An Interdisciplinary Symposium,' held in April 1997. This piece charts our early thoughts as well as our later reflections on the workshop. We wish to acknowledge the participatory nature of the workshop; many of the ideas and perceptions expressed below are the result of generous exchange among symposium participants and guest presenters, some of whom are represented elsewhere in this book.

In response to an invitation to stage scenes from the play for this symposium, we decided to rehearse a number of scenes, with the intention of reworking them during the lab session, in response to the discussions that emerged. We saw the session as a laboratory that could enable conference participants (theorists and practitioners from a variety of disciplines) and presenters to explore how the play text pushed an interpretation, how theatre artists could in turn push around a play through interpretation, and how theories about the story, the play, and the theatre could be embodied on stage. This approach also opened up conversation about the way theatre artists and critics analyse and interpret plays and about ways to build more effective collaborations between playwrights / interpretive theatre artists and theatre academics / cultural critics.

Jan Selman hosted and facilitated the workshop. Rachel Ditor served as the stage director, and Daniel Chen and Steven Cavers, both students in the BA theatre program at UBC, performed the roles of Song and Gallimard, respectively.

The Workshop

JS We began by inviting participants into a 'laboratory' in which we planned to present a selection of very basically staged scenes from the play in order to address the following questions: 'What do you see in this interpretation?' 'What questions does it raise for you?' 'How have the theatre artists interpreted the characters and themes?' 'How else could they be interpreted?' 'How would each interpretive choice alter the play's thesis or impact?' 'What theatre and other theories are useful in considering the play, the characters, the interpretations, the themes?' We wanted to rework scenes in light of the discussion, to illuminate interpretive choices and to test critical theories.

RD If Song and Gallimard can be said to represent the East and the West respectively, and their relationship a microcosm of East–West relations, then character interpretation has implications beyond the straight narrative action of the play. This realization gave me an angle with which to approach the workshop. How do different interpretations of the main characters work to change the meta-message of *M. Butterfly?*

JS The workshop divided itself into two parts. The first focussed upon act 1 and the nature of the relationships and strategies employed by Gallimard and Song, particularly Song.

RD In the early Gallimard-Song scenes in act 1 there is a high level of ambiguity. These scenes are also the audience's first encounters with Song, which make these moments critical to how the audience receives Song's presence, both on her/his own and in relation to Gallimard. What is taken away from or added to our understanding of Gallimard when we first meet the object of his obsession? How do we view Gallimard after this moment? Is he a dupe or are we, too, fascinated and attracted to Song? Where is the audience now – a step removed from Gallimard, or drawn further into the love story? Do we sympathize more or less with Gallimard than we did before we met Song? Has our allegiance switched to Song, or are we still viewing this story strictly from Gallimard's point of view? Later in the play Gallimard's and Song's competition to control the direct address to the audience, and therefore maintain control of the narrative, is much more obvious, but these early scenes present an interesting interpretive challenge.

We presented readings from a variety of scenes in act 1 – including the scene where Song and Gallimard first meet, act 1, scene 6, and their next meeting after the Peking Opera, act 1, scene 8.

JS   The selection of scenes from act 1 omitted all of the most overtly theatrical segments. However, as the lab progressed we discovered the potential in these naturalistic scenes for a high level of theatricality that was not immediately apparent.

RD   Before approaching Song in act 1, scene 6, Gallimard speaks of his attraction to her. He says, 'I wanted to take her in my arms – so delicate, even I could protect her, take her home, pamper her until she smiled' ([1989] 16). Then they meet, talk for a bit – this includes Song's comments on reversing the Butterfly story so that it is a Western woman falling in love with a 'short Japanese business man' (17) – and at the end Song invites Gallimard to hear her sing at the Peking Opera. Gallimard closes this scene, saying to the audience, 'So much for protecting her in my big Western arms' (18). In this scene it seemed clear that Song was in charge, that she had the upper hand, and that Gallimard was taken aback by her beauty and the straightforward manner in which she seemed to present herself and her political views.

In act 1, scene 8 Gallimard meets Song after catching her performance at the Peking Opera. From the beginning of this scene we know that Gallimard is a fish out of water; the sights and sounds there are entirely foreign to him. Song picks him out and calls him to her. Their conversation is both flirtatious and political in nature. This time Gallimard figures he has held his own with her. He closes this scene saying, '[T]onight, I held up my end of the conversation' (22).

JS   And the audience has the choice as to whether to accept or reject, laugh with or at, judge or acquiesce, interpret or take at face value Gallimard's statement. This decision is controlled in part by the author, in part by the creative interpreters, and in part by the audience members.

After we watched the staged readings of excerpts from act 1, the discussion focused upon who the author intended these people to be or, in other words, on character interpretation and motives. We wondered at the play and the apparent shifting sands of Song's levels of knowledge and his/her degree of overt critique of Western assumptions and arrogance. We questioned the make-up of Gallimard: his level of confidence, his experience (or lack of it) in attracting the opposite sex, the nature of his vulnerability. This led us – the actors/director, the reader/

critics, and the playwright / social critics – to a number of possible interpretations of the central characters' early encounters.

We saw that there was a significant interpretive decision to make as to how aggressively and consciously Song pursued Gallimard at their first meeting(s): Was s/he pursuing a political mark or a man? Was s/he sexually engaged or using sex to pursue? Was she actually *pursuing* at their first meeting? How aware was 'she' of her manipulation of him? What mattered more to her, scoring political points or fascinating this man? What mattered more to the playwright – setting up a 'real' story of seduction and political intrigue or posing socio-political insights to the audience? Does Song make the decision to pursue Gallimard during the scene or previous to it? The questions emerged out of participants' private readings of the play as well as observations of the 'performance' of the actors. Which choices might serve the fullest development of the narrative, the socio-political points being made, and the audience's growth of insight? How much is dictated by the play and playwright? How much is imbedded in his writing? How much can be manipulated and selected by the interpreters?

We decided to pose these questions again, but via experimentation with interpretive starting points. In practice. The actors were asked to play the scene of Gallimard and Song's meeting in two divergent ways, one emphasizing the sexual come-on, the other emphasizing an interest in instructing the ignorant Westerner in cultural politics. We wondered which interpretation would better raise the questions that we saw posed by the play/playwright, that is, which theatrical choices would best highlight the intellectual intentions.

RD In restaging these scenes we essentially played with the status between the two characters. Who had the upper hand in the scene? Who was in control of this meeting, and how is that communicated to the audience? This is of interest beyond the surface understanding of the narrative progression involving two lovers; this is also about the East and West negotiating a relationship. As a group we explored two contrasting interpretations.

JS The result was interesting. When act 1, scene 6 was played with overt attention to the sexual come-on, when Song displayed 'herself' carefully and suggestively, the scene was most exciting and engaging, and therefore most effective in 'delivering' the political/intellectual arguments. Is this a matter of sugar-coating a political tract? The separation of the motivation from the dialogue – 'I want to lure him' rather than 'I want to convince him of my political perspective' – allowed for a more complex layering, more spice, and therefore more engagement by the audience. What I wonder is if this simply reveals drama as merely a pleasant way to ingest tough messages, or perhaps something more ...

Inherent in these investigations of alternative interpretations of act 1, scene 6 turned out to be a highlighting of choices of varying levels of audience acknowledgment.

RD   One interpretation involved allowing Gallimard's last line in act 1, scene 8, '[T]onight I held up my end of the conversation' (22), to be true. For the scene to read this way, I asked Daniel Chen, the actor playing Song, to avoid any eye contact with the audience. However, Steven Cavers, playing Gallimard, was free to continue to acknowledge the audience. Playing the scene this way, Gallimard appeared to be more in control of the scene and Song appeared to be a true 'lotus blossom.' All of the edge in Song's political comments was tempered with coyness. There was no shared joke between Song and the audience. This interpretation allowed the audience, like Gallimard, to be fooled and seduced by Song's persona as a delicate, modest, and playful Asian woman. A question arose from this interpretation that we had not dealt with yet: is there a chance that the audience is supposed to be genuinely fooled by Song's real identity? Are we not supposed to know that she is really a man? Does the play work better if the audience experiences the play as Gallimard slowly reveals it to us; or, since Gallimard is telling this story largely through flashbacks, do we know, and should we know, what he knows about Song from the beginning?

Perhaps what is gained by choosing to not reveal too much about Song's real identity has something to do with whom you suspect the audience is. If you assume that the audience is largely white, perhaps there is something to gain by creating a situation where the audience has the potential to fall prey to the same set of stereotypes about Asian women that Gallimard seems to believe.

When we restaged the scene a second time, Song kept direct eye contact with the audience and Gallimard kept his focus on Song, temporarily losing his contact with the audience. Song's direct connection to the audience gave him higher status than Gallimard, and the humour in the scene came to life. For example, Gallimard's last line of the scene was no longer true, more like wishful thinking (he did not appear to have 'held up [his] end of the conversation'). Song read as a much stronger character and the audience had an opportunity to see Gallimard actually in the moment of his infatuation, actually taken with Song as opposed to only talking about it. We saw him lose the perspective that he had at the top of the scene. It was an interesting transformation. In this interpretation it felt as though the audience was sharing a joke with Song from which Gallimard was excluded.

JS We enjoyed being 'in collusion' with Song, and 'knowing more' (feeling superior?) to this gullible lug of a Western male.

RD How does this interpretation play out on a larger scale? The audience is in a position to watch the West being duped by the East, and we are not taken in, as Gallimard is. By sharing jokes with Song s/he is talking to us as equals and by enjoying the humour the members of the audience subtly become Song's co-conspirators. Up until this point, *M. Butterfly* has been Gallimard's story; now, suddenly, when his guard is down, he loses control of the narrative and Song takes over.

JS So, although in selecting only pieces of act 1 to perform and examine we had apparently omitted the 'metatheatrical' moments of the play, we found ourselves, via discussion and practical experiment, right in the middle of an examination of the nature of the theatrical contact with audience that makes the most of this intriguing play. It became clear that this play has an interest in audience that is more deeply embedded than the most obvious 'breakings' of the fourth wall that are suggested in the published text. This play is calling for an ongoing interaction with the audience, from both central characters. The battle that is focal in act 3 can start way back in act 1; a production would want to engage an expression of this competition in the quasi-naturalistic scenes as well as in the play's larger set of staging choices, which play around with who is on stage when, and who is in communication with the audience, verbally and non-verbally. Whereas early reads of the play encourage one to emphasize Gallimard's relation to the audience, with his direct address and all, we discovered that the performance is enhanced when even early in the play Song looks for opportunities to engage the audience intellectually and emotionally; he woos the audience not from the occasion of his first direct address, but, albeit more subtly, from the moment the character arrives on stage.

The second part of the workshop, which focused on act 3, took a somewhat different focus. The workshop participants, which included some who have devoted much thought and scholarship to the play, the film, and other versions of the story, discussed the psychological make-up of Gallimard and his disintegration, the significant differences between the staged and film versions of the last part of *M. Butterfly*, and the playing out of Gallimard's and Song's competition for the audience's sympathies. We also considered the apparent several endings of the play and why it is structured in that way. Some findings that emerged:

1 Gallimard is unravelling; he turns out to have little or no core; the construct he has made of himself throughout the play reveals itself to be false, empty. For the stage actor and director, this idea presents a number of useful tidbits. Perhaps Gallimard, the narrator, should start the play from this moment of crisis; perhaps the entire story is told in order to avoid this terrifying truth?
2 Without the relation to the audience, which is the core drama of the stage play, the film goes rather soft. Noting the film's losses, some of which are due to the film director's and writer's choices to not build a significant, direct-address contact with the viewer, theatre interpreters are encouraged to make very precise choices about the characters' contact with the audience.
3 The substitution of the prisoner audience (in the film) for the live audience (at the play) neglects the film audience as a player. While the scene has an impact in the film, and is held up by some to be a very successful aspect of the film version, the film version loses the active drive that the play derives from its live audience (an audience that has been cultivated, wooed, and cajoled throughout the evening in the theatre). The prison audience is new to us and to Gallimard.
4 The significant shift of power via the shift in control of the narrative continued to engage us. The matter of power via control of access to the audience is clarified in a close look at act 3. These findings should hugely impact theatrical and interpretive choices in earlier parts of the play.
5 An interesting aspect of this discussion arose out of several comments about the rather poor 'double' ('triple'?) ending of the play. Several participants, whether they had read or viewed the play, found the last part of the play problematic. The discussion started with a rather point-blank statement about the weakness of the play. A number of us agreed. But once this statement was on the table there was room to discover much. New territory was revealed by assuming there was

something yet to discover about the play, by assuming there was method in the playwright's madness, by assuming that the choice to apparently end the play three different ways was purposeful rather than merely a failing.

JS Here, in action, was an advantage of getting theorists and artist/practitioners together, of discussing and investigating a play prior to production, prior to any production decisions. *During* a process rather than in an after-the-fact review of a production.

RD If one had this kind of conversation regularly, as part of an exploration before production decisions were made, one might well make much different interpretive choices throughout the three acts; one would progress to one's new knowledge, one's new understanding of the piece.

JS I am reminded that we are in an age where 'discovering a play on your feet' (in rehearsal), while exciting and often effective, can be a huge trap. In that many contemporary playwrights and theatre artists are setting out to use the theatre to expose ideas, themes, and concepts, to set up apparent realities in order to undermine them, theatre in this 'postmodern age' needs different directorial preparation than theatre of a modern age; yet in North America, at any rate, much of our theatre training continues to rely heavily on the methods of the age of realism. Messages from Peter Brooks's *The Empty Space* or from William Ball's *A Sense of Direction* taken to an extreme can miss the boat for much current theatrical work. This exchange among theorists and practitioners highlighted new possibilities.

RD The play is rich and complex enough to allow for any number of interpretations without changing a word of the text. For example, a production could cast a more masculine Song, thereby changing audiences' perception of the dynamic between Song and Gallimard; or a production could give Song more direct play to the audience than Gallimard, thereby undercutting Gallimard's authority as reliable storyteller from the beginning.

JS Such a stance claims much space for the interpretive artists in a theatrical production, and questions the notion of a fixed critical viewpoint or interpretation. It implies that while the play text may well shape the theatrical event and an audience's focus, it cannot and will not fix the meaning. It implies the full possibility for 'revisionist' productions that, at their most extreme, invert the playwright's intended (and unintended) meanings. In my view, without significant rewriting of a text, a fully revisionist production is not possible; the word holds too much power in this society to allow for complete transformation of meaning. However, productions can certainly shift meanings and, at the very least, highlight potential interpretations and skew or bias audiences' potential readings.

RD   I agree. I am not making a pitch for revisionist drama; rather, I am making a point in favour of the artist as critical thinker, social analyst, questioning and investigating a script in an effort to ensure the most relevant, challenging, and engaging presentation of a play.
    As we discovered, in a play that deals so much with the breaking of boundaries, the breaking of the fourth wall is no accidental thing and deserves close examination. In the end, what interests me most as a director are the questions regarding which character breaks that boundary, and when, and to what end.
    Perhaps it is Hwang's choice to keep breaking the fourth wall that accounts for much of what attracts me to this play. The constant breaking of the fourth wall, the characters' drive to connect with the audience, to woo them, to compete for their support, to have them present as witness, makes the audience an equal and necessary player in the event.

JS   As in debate, or sports events. This is a level of audience energy and engagement we strive for in the theatre. The closest I have seen us get to this goal is in highly participatory theatre performances.

RD   However, after a later conversation with actors Daniel and Steven I was forced to question my appreciation of *M. Butterfly*'s attempt as a script to keep existing in the here and now. I thought that the very form of the play meant that *M. Butterfly* could always, on some level, remain relevant to an audience because of the fact that it seeks to involve its audience in a live event.

JS   To debate the issues, in essence, in the here and now, even as the story dates itself.

RD But what about the content? The following comment of Daniel Chen's forced me to question whether or not the issues in this play are still as relevant now as when they were written, in 1986.

> In the end I feel like Gallimard is still seated on this, not a pedestal, but he's the one who has been victimized by the seducer who is 'female' and is 'Asian.' And so that is the perception the audience is left with ... Once the play is over and Song storms off and Gallimard has his monologue at the end, it just makes him such a martyr ... I don't see how many people will sympathize with Song. You walk away and think, 'Gee, that's so sad he killed himself.' And Song just walks away.

Certainly Hwang has attempted to rewrite the Madame Butterfly story in such a way as to empower the character of Song. Song survives, and it is Gallimard who is unable to accept the reality of his/their situation. Yet Daniel Chen feels our sympathies may lie more with Gallimard – that his pain occludes the triumph of Song's empowerment. Is this a sign of the times in which the play was written? Is this last movement of the play indicative of the fact that many say we are currently living in a *culture of confession*, a time when we have equated testifying with survival?

JS So what of this play that has attracted so much critical attention? For me, the question of the power relationships between text/playwright and production / interpretive artists is central to the critics'/theorists', as well as the director/interpreters', work. The play text charts territory; a production works with that territory, emphasizing and de-emphasizing elements of theme and action. So in the case of this play, I read, listen, analyse, and ponder with a high degree of interest as its meanings and implications are unpacked. In the case of *M. Butterfly*, the playwright and the critics' and theorists' comments that followed close on the heels of its successful early productions, point us to questions of race and gender construction. (In many ways, this play does the critics' work for them vis-à-vis the earlier artworks that use the Butterfly story.) Soon we are into musings on the play's misogyny. As a woman with social equality as an aim, I am forced to question Hwang's questioning. Can, indeed, two male characters effectively question female constructs? Can a male author? Critics with more insights than I tell me 'no.'

As an activist and a theatre director and a woman, I pause. On one hand, one can, at this point, refuse to play. But the interpreter in me wants to ask a number of further questions before putting this play script away on the shelf. The play script is a chart, meant to provide a score for a production rather than sit as a piece of literature. Is the rigid construction of 'the female' established in order to provoke the debate, or indeed to, however unconsciously, reinforce it? Ultimately, I think Hwang, and other overtly politicized playwrights who have waded into this murky and controversial zone of gender construction (such as Wertenbaker, Churchill, Brennan, and Brecht) do us a service. This play allows audience, critic, and artist to confront the questions; this act of confrontation, this deep inquiry, rather than the conclusions individuals may reach and the judgments they may make, is surely the point. Thanks are due to those artists who stick their necks out, and to those critics who continue to demand that we wrestle, rather than settle, with these themes.

Bibliography

Abbate, Carolyn. 'Opera; or, the Envoicing of Women.' In *Musicology and Difference: Gender and Sexuality in Music Scholarship*, ed. Ruth A. Solie. Berkeley: University of California Press, 1993.

Absalom, Roger. *Italy Since 1800: A Nation in the Balance?* New York: Longman, 1995.

Adas, Michael. *Machines as the Measure of Men*. Ithaca: Cornell University Press, 1989.

Adorno, Theodor W. 'Bourgeois Opera.' In Levin, 25–43.

Akiyama, Aisaburo. *Geisha Girl*. 3rd edition. Yokohama: Yoshikawa Book Store, 1937.

Altman, Rick. 'Dickens, Griffith and Film Theory Today.' In *Classical Hollywood Narrative*, ed. Jane Gaines, 9–48. Durham and London: Duke University Press, 1992.

Appiah, Anthony Kwame, and Henry Louis Gates, Jr, eds. *Identities*. Chicago: University of Chicago Press, 1995.

Arblaster, Anthony. *Viva la Libertà! Politics in Opera*. New York: Verso, 1992.

Ardoin, J. 'Puccini and the Phonograph.' *Opera Quarterly* 2 (1984): 114–20.

Ashbrook, William. *The Operas of Puccini*. Ithaca: Cornell University Press, 1985.

Ashbrook, William, and Harold Powers. *Puccini's Turandot*. Princeton: Princeton University Press, 1991.

Ashcroft, Bill, Gareth Griffiths, and Helen Tiffin. *The Empire Writes Back: Theory and Practice in Post-Colonial Literatures*. London: Routledge, 1989.

Association for Asian Studies. *Abstracts of the 1997 Annual Meeting*. Ann Arbor, MI: Association for Asian Studies.

Aston, W.G. *A History of Japanese Literature* (1899). Repr. Tokyo: Charles E. Tuttle, 1972.

Atlas, Allan W. 'Crossed Stars and Crossed Tonal Areas in Puccini's *Madama Butterfly.*' *19th Century Music* 14.2 (Fall 1990): 186–96.
Barr, Pat. *The Coming of the Barbarians: A Story of Western Settlement in Japan 1853–1870.* London: Macmillan, 1967.
– *The Deer Cry Pavilion: A Story of Westerners in Japan 1868–1905.* Harmondsworth: Penguin, 1968.
Barthes, Roland. 'Pierre Loti: *Aziyadé.*' Trans. Richard Howard. In *New Critical Essays*, 105–21. New York: Hill and Wang, 1980.
Beard, William. *The Artist as Monster: The Cinema of David Cronenberg.* Toronto: University of Toronto Press, 2001.
Beasley, W.G. *Japan Encounters the Barbarians: Japanese Travellers in America and Europe.* New Haven: Yale University Press, 1995.
Beaulieu, Janick. Review of *Madame Butterfly*, directed by Frédéric Mitterrand. *Séquences* 183 (March–April 1996): 45–6.
Belasco, David. *The Heart of Maryland and Other Plays.* Ed. and intro. Glenn Hughes and George Savage. Princeton: Princeton University Press, 1941.
– 'Madame Butterfly: A Tragedy of Japan.' In *Representative American Plays: From 1767 to the Present Day*, ed. Arthur Hobson Quinn, 621–36. 7th edition. New York: Appleton-Century-Crofts Inc., 1957.
– *Six Plays.* Boston: Little, Brown, 1928.
– *The Theatre through Its Stage Door.* Ed. Louis V. Defoe. New York: Harper, 1919.
Belton, John. *Widescreen Cinema.* Cambridge, MA: Harvard University Press, 1992.
Berg, Karl Georg. 'Das Liebesduett aus Madama Butterfly: Überlegungen zur Szenendramaturgie bei Giacomo Puccini.' *Die Musikforschung* 38 (March 1985): 183–94.
Bernardi, David. 'The Voice of Whiteness: D. W. Griffith's Biograph Films (1908).' In *The Birth of Whiteness: Race and the Emergence of U.S. Cinema*, ed. Daniel Bernardi, 103–28. New Brunswick, NJ: Rutgers University Press, 1996.
Berrong, Richard. *In Love with a Handsome Sailor: The Emergence of Gay Identity and the Novels of Pierri Loti.* Toronto: University of Toronto Press, 2003.
Bhabha, Homi K. 'Dissemination: Time, Narrative, and the Margins of the Modern Nation.' In *Nation and Narration*, 291–322. London and New York: Routledge, 1990.
Billington, M. 'Miss Saigon and Madama Butterfly: The Orient Expressed.' *Opera Canada* 34.2 (1993): 16–17.
Bird, Isabella. *Unbeaten Tracks in Japan* (1880). London: Virago, 1984.
Biss, R. 'Nagasaki mon amour: Auckland Opera's *Madama Butterfly.*' *Music New Zealand* 26 (Spring 1994): 30–1.
Blanch, Lesley. *Pierre Loti: Portrait of an Escapist.* London: Collins, 1983.

Bongie, Chris. *Exotic Memories: Literature, Colonialism, and the Fin de Siècle*. Stanford: Stanford University Press, 1991.
Bordwell, David, Janet Steiger, and Kristin Thompson. *The Classical Hollywood Cinema: Film Style and Mode of Production to 1960*. New York: Columbia University Press, 1985.
Borges, Jorge Luis. 'Pierre Menard, Author of the *Quixote*.' In *Labyrinths*, ed. Donald A. Yates and James E. Irby. New York: Modern Library, 1983.
Brauton, R. Henry. *Building Japan, 1868–1876*. Sandgate, VT: Japan Library, 1991.
– *Schoolmaster to an Empire: Richard Henry Brauton in Meiji Japan 1868–1876*. New York: Greenwood Press, 1991.
Breakwell, Ian. *An Actor's Revenge*. London: BFI Publishing, 1995.
Bronfen, Elizabeth. *Over Her Dead Body: Death, Femininity and the Aesthetic*. New York: Routledge, 1992.
Brooks, Peter. *The Melodramatic Imagination: Balzac, Henry James, Melodrama and the Mode of Excess*. New Haven: Yale University Press, 1976.
Browne, Nick. 'The Undoing of the *Other* Woman: Madame Butterfly in the Discourse of American Orientalism.' In *The Birth of Whiteness: Race and the Emergence of U.S. Cinema*, ed. Daniel Bernardi, 227–56. New Brunswick, NJ: Rutgers University Press, 1996.
Brug, M. 'Leb' wohl, mein Blutenreich: Robert Wilson und Myung-Whun Chung entkitschen in Paris Madama Butterfly.' *Opernwelt* 1 (January 1994): 12–15.
Bryson, Norman. 'Westernizing Bodies: Women, Art, and Power in Meiji Yōga.' In *Gender and Power in the Japanese Visual Field*, ed. Joshua S. Mostow, Norman Bryson, and Maribeth Graybill. Honolulu: University of Hawai'i Press, 2003.
Budden, Julian. *Puccini: His Life and Works*. Oxford: University Press, 2002.
Burch, Noel. 'Porter, or Ambivalence.' *Screen* 19. 4 (Winter 1978–9): 91–104.
Buscombe, Ed. 'Sound and Color.' In *Movies and Methods Volume II: An Anthology*, ed. Bill Nichols, 83–92. Berkeley: University of California Press, 1985.
Butler, Judith. 'Extracts from Gender as Performance: An Interview with Judith Butler.' *Radical Philosophy* 67 (Summer 1994). Available at http://www.leeds.ac.uk/ics/but-int1.htm.
Capote, Truman. 'The Duke in His Domain' (1956). In *A Capote Reader*, 517–44. New York: Random House, 1987.
Carner, Mosco. *Madama Butterfly: A Guide to the Opera*. Foreword by Victoria de los Angeles. London: Barrie & Jenkins, 1979.
– 'In Defence of Puccini.' In *Puccini's* Madame Butterfly, ed. Eric Crozier. London: Sadler's Well's Opera Book, John Lane, 1946.

- 'Mrs. F. B. Pinkerton 1 & 2 (Four Versions of Butterfly).' *Opera* 35 (December 1984): 1325–9.
- *Puccini.* London: Duckworth, 1992.
- *Puccini: A Critical Biography.* 2nd edition, London: 1974. 3rd edition, New York: Holmes and Meier, 1992.

Carney, Raymond. *American Vision: The Films of Frank Capra.* Cambridge: Cambridge University Press, 1986.

Cavell, Richard. 'Transvestic Sites: Postcolonialism, Pedagogy, and Politics.' In *Dangerous Territories: Struggles for Difference and Equality in Education,* ed. Leslie Roman and Linda Eyre, 99–112. New York: Routledge, 1997.

Chang, Hsaio H. 'Cultural/Sexual/Theatrical Ambivalence in *M. Butterfly.*' *Tamkang Review* 23.1–4 (1993): 735–55.

Charest, Rémy. *Robert Lepage: Quelques zones de liberté.* Quebec: Les éditions de l'instant même, 1995.

Chin, Frank. 'Come All Ye Asian American Writers of the Real and the Fake.' In *The Big Aiiieeeee! An Anthology of Chinese American and Japanese American Literature,* ed. Jeffrey Paul Chan et al., 1–92. New York: Meridian, 1991.

Chion, Michael. *Audio-Vision: Sound on Screen.* Trans. Claudia Gorbman. New York: Columbia University Press, 1990.
- *La voix au cinéma.* Paris: Cahiers du cinéma, 1982.

Chow, Rey. 'The Dream of a Butterfly.' In *Human All Too Human,* ed. Diana Fuss, 61–92. New York: Routledge, 1996.
- *Ethics after Idealism: Theory-Culture-Ethnicity-Reading.* Bloomington: Indiana University Press, 1998.

Christiansen, Rupert. *Prima Donna: A History.* London: Bodley Head, 1984.

Cleary, Thomas. *The Japanese Art of War: Understanding the Culture of Strategy.* Boston and London: Shambhala, 1991.

Clément, Catherine. *Opera, or the Undoing of Women.* Trans. Betsy Wing, foreword by Susan McClary. Minneapolis: University of Minnesota Press, 1988.

Clunas, Craig. *Superfluous Things: Material Culture and Social Status in Early Modern China.* Urbana: University of Illinois Press, 1991.

Conrad, Peter. *A Song of Love and Death.* New York: Poseidon Press, 1987.

Conroy, Francis, Sandra Davis, and Wayne Patterson. *Japan in Transition: Thought and Action in the Meiji Era, 1868–1912.* London: Associated University Presses, 1984.

Cook, David. *A History of Narrative Film.* 3rd edition. New York: Norton, 1996.

Corazzol, Adriana Guarieri. 'Opera and Verismo: Regressive Points of View and the Artifice of Alienation.' *Cambridge Opera Journal* 5 (1993): 39–53.

Corse, S. '"Mi chiamo Mimi": The Role of Women in Puccini's Operas.' *Opera Quarterly* 1 (1983): 93–106.

Cronenberg, David, dir. *M. Butterfly*. With Jeremy Irons, John Lone, Barbara Sukowa, and Ian Richardson. Geffen Pictures. Videocassette, Warner, 1993.

Crook, Barbara. 'M. Butterfly's Wings Clipped by Lack of Passion.' Review of *M. Butterfly* by David Henry Hwang. Arts Club Theatre, Vancouver. *Vancouver Sun*, 21 January 1993: D2.

– 'Shades of Gray: Allan Gray Delves Deep into His Troubled Life to Portray a Deluded Man.' *Vancouver Sun*, 18 January 1993: C1.

Cusick, Susanne. 'Gender and the Cultural Work of a Classical Music Performance.' *repercussions* 3 (Spring 1994): 77–110.

Dalby, Liza. *Geisha*. Berkeley, Los Angeles, London: University of California Press, 1983.

Dauthendey, Max. *Die Acht Gesichter am Biwasee*. Munich: Langen Müller, 1958.

– *Gesammelte Werke*. Munich: Albert Langen, 1925.

de Gruchy, John. 'The Institutionalization of *Japonisme* in Britain: From Aesthetics to Modernism.' Centre for Japanese Research, Research Paper no. 10, Institute of Asian Research, University of British Columbia, 1996.

– *Orienting Arthur Waley: Japonisme, Orientalism, and the Creation of Japanese Literature in English*. Honolulu: University of Hawai'i Press, 2003.

Deleuze, Gilles. *Masochism: An Interpretation of Coldness and Cruelty*. New York: George Braziller, 1971.

De Quincey, Thomas. *The Confessions of an English Opium Eater* (1821). Harmondsworth: Penguin, 1987.

Dewey, John, and Alice Dewey. *Letters from Japan and China*. New York: Dutton, 1920.

Dickins, Frederick Victor. *Primitive and Mediaeval Japanese Texts*. Oxford: Clarendon Press, 1906.

DiGaetani, John. 'David Henry Hwang.' In *A Search for Postmodern Theatre: Interviews with Contemporary Playwrights*, 161–74. New York: Greenwood Press, 1991.

– *Puccini the Thinker: The Composer's Intellectual and Dramatic Development*. 2nd edition. New York: Peter Lang, 2001.

Dizikes, John. *Opera in America: A Cultural History*. New Haven: Yale University Press, 1993.

Doane, Mary Anne. 'Film and the Masquerade: Theorizing the Female Spectator.' In *Issues in Feminist Film Criticism*, ed. Patricia Erens. Bloomington: Indiana University Press, 1990.

Du, W. 'From M. Butterfly to Madama Butterfly: A Retrospective View of the Chinese Presence on Broadway.' *Dissertation Abstracts* 53.3201a (March 1993).

Dufwa, Jacques. *Winds from The East*. Stockholm: Almqvist & Wiksell, 1981.

Dunn, Leslie C., and Nancy A. Jones, eds. *Embodied Voices: Representing Female Vocality in Western Culture*. Cambridge: Cambridge University Press, 1994.

Duus, Peter. *The Abacus and the Sword: The Japanese Penetration of Korea 1895–1910.* Berkeley: University of California Press, 1995.
Earle, Joe. *Splendors of Imperial Japan: Arts of the Meiji Period from the Khalili Collection.* London: Khalili Family Trust, 2002.
Edwards, Osman. *Japanese Plays and Playfellows.* London: William Heinemann, 1901.
Eisler, Paul E. *The Metropolitan Opera: The First 25 Years.* New York: North River Press, 1984.
Fabian, I. 'Eindrucke einer Opernreise durch Amerika.' *Opernwelt* 2 (February 1994): 11–16.
Fält, Olavi K. *The Clash of Interest: The Transformation of Japan in 1861–1881 in the Eyes of the Local Anglo-Saxon Press.* Trans. Malcom Hicks. Rovaniemi: Pohjois-Suomen historiallinen yhdistys, 1990.
– 'The Image of Japan in Finland Prior to the Russo-Japanese War.' In *Europe Interprets Japan*, ed. Gordon Daniels, 95–102, 259–61. Kent: Paul Norbury, 1984.
Findley, Timothy. *The Butterfly Plague.* New York: Viking, 1969.
Foucault, Michel. *The History of Sexuality: An Introduction,* vol. 1. Trans. Robert Hurley. London: Penguin, 1981.
Frieze, James. 'Channelling Rubble: *Seven Streams of the River Ota* and *After Sorrow.*' *Journal of Dramatic Theory and Criticism* 12.1 (1997): 133–42.
Fukuyama, Francis. 'The End of History.' *The National Interest* 16 (Summer 1989): 3–18.
Furman, Nellie. 'Opera, or the Staging of the Voice.' *Cambridge Opera Journal* 3.3 (1991): 303–6.
Garber, Marjorie. 'The Occidental Tourist: *M. Butterfly* and the Scandal of Transvestism.' In *Nationalisms and Sexualities*, ed. Andrew Parker et al., 121–46. New York: Routledge, 1992.
– *Vested Interests: Cross-Dressing and Cultural Anxiety.* New York: Routledge, 1991.
– *Vice Versa: Bisexuality and the Eroticism of Everyday Life.* New York: Simon and Schuster, 1995.
García Márquez, Gabriel. *Chronicle of a Death Foretold.* Trans. Gregory Rabassa. New York: Alfred A. Knopf, 1983.
Gavazzeni, Gianandrea. 'Il valore della "pause" nella Madama Butterfly di Puccini.' In *Music senza aggettivi: Studi per Fedele D'Amico.* Florence: Olschki, 1991.
Genet, Christian, and Daniel Hervé. *Pierre Loti: L'enchanteur.* Liguge, Poitiers: Aubin Imprimeur, 1988.
Ghérardi, Evariste. *Le théâtre italien.* 6 vols. Paris: Pierre Witte, 1718.
Giradi, M. 'Madama Butterfly, una tragedia esotica.' In *Madama Butterfly, di Giacomo Puccini*, 1529–51. Venice: Teatro la Fenice, 1989.

Gledhill, Christine, ed. *Home Is Where the Heart Is: Studies in Melodrama and the Woman's Film*. London: British Film Institute, 1987.
Gossman, Lionel. *The Empire Unpossess'd: An Essay on Gibbon's Decline and Fall*. Cambridge: Cambridge University Press, 1981.
Grace, Sherrill. 'Incorporating "Butterfly" in Plays by Henry David Huang and Robert Lepage.' *The Hannan Ronshu* 10.2 (2001): 11–25.
Graf, Herbert. *Opera for the People*. New York: Da Capo, 1973.
Greenhalgh, Paul. *Ephemeral Vistas: The Expositions Universelles, Great Exhibitions and World's Fairs, 1851–1939*. Manchester: Manchester University Press, 1988.
Greenwald, H.M. 'Comment and Chronicle.' *19th-Century Music* 15 (1991): 166–7.
– 'Recent Puccini Research.' *Acta Musicologica* 65 (1993): 23–50.
Griffen, John. 'Broadway Gender-bender Comes to the Big Screen.' *Montreal Gazette*, 8 October 1993: C1.
– 'Cronenberg's *M. Butterfly* Has Canadian Quality of Reserve.' *Montreal Gazette*, 12 September 1993: F2.
Grilli, Peter, ed. *Japan in Film: A Comprehensive Annotated Catalogue of Documentary and Theatrical Films on Japan Available in the United States*. New York: Japan Society, 1984.
Groen, Rick. 'When Illusions Collide with Deceptions.' *Globe and Mail*, 9 September 1993: C1.
Groos, Arthur. 'Cio-Cio-San and Sadayakko: Japanese Music-Theatre in *Madama Butterfly*.' *Monumenta Nipponica* 54.1 (Spring 1999): 41–73.
– 'Illica's Butterfly: The First Version of Act I.' In *I libretti di Puccini e la letteratura de suo tempo: Perspektiven der Opernforschung* 3. Frankfurt: Bern, 1993.
– 'The Lady Vanishes: The Lost Act of Madama Butterfly.' *Opera News* 59 (January 1995): 16–19.
– 'Lieutenant B.F. Pinkerton: Problems in the Genesis of an Operatic Hero.' *Italica* 64 (1987): 654–75.
– 'Madame Butterfly: The Story.' *Cambridge Opera Journal* 3.2 (1991–2): 125–58.
– 'Return of the Native: Japan in *Madama Butterfly* / *Madama Butterfly* in Japan.' *Cambridge Opera Journal* 1.2 (July 1989): 167–94.
Groth, K.U. 'Liege: Puccini, Madama Butterfly.' *Opernwelt* 33 (1992): 38+.
Gundermann, Christian. 'Orientalism, Homophobia, Masochism: Transfers between Pierre Loti's *Aziyadé* and Gilles Deleuze's "Coldness and Cruelty."' *Diacritics* 24 (Summer–Fall, 1994): 151–67.
Gunning, Tom. *D.W. Griffith and the Origins of American Narrative Film*. Urbana and Chicago: University of Illinois Press, 1994.
Gurney, A.R. 'Far East.' In *Collected Plays 1992–1999*. Lyme, NH: Smith and Kraus, 2000.

Hadden, J. Cuthbert. *Favorite Operas*. London: T.C. and E.C. Jack, 1910.
Halberstam, David. *The Fifties*. New York: Villard Books, 1993.
Hansen, Miriam. *Babel and Babylon: Spectatorship in American Silent Film*. Cambridge: Harvard University Press, 1991.
– 'Early Cinema – Whose Public Sphere?' In *Early Cinema: Space, Frame, Narrative*, ed. Thomas Elsaesser with Adam Barker, 228–46. London: BFI Publishing, 1990.
Hargreaves, Alec G. *The Colonial Experience in French Fiction: A Study of Pierre Loti, Ernest Psichari and Pierre Mille*. London: Macmillan, 1981.
Harvie, Jennifer. 'Transnationalism, Orientalism, and Cultural Tourism: *La Trilogie des Dragons* and *The Seven Streams of the River Ota*.' In *Theatre sans frontières: Essays on the Dramatic Universe of Robert Lepage*, ed. Joseph I. Donahue, Jr and Jane M. Koustas, 109–25. East Lansing: Michigan State University Press, 2000.
Hayes, John P. *James A. Michener: A Biography*. New York: Bobbs-Merrill, 1984.
Hearn, Lafcadio. *Japan: An Interpretation*. New York: Grosset and Dunlap, 1904.
Heath, Mary Renner. 'Exoticism in Puccini: The Japanese Melodies in *Madama Butterfly*.' *Opera Journal* 13.4 (1980): 21–8.
Hegel, G.W.F. *The Philosophy of History*. Trans. J. Sibree. New York: Dover, 1956.
Hein, Laura, and Mark Selden, eds. *Living with the Bomb: American and Japanese Cultural Conflicts in the Nuclear Age*. London and New York: M.E. Sharpe, 1997.
Henderson, Brian. '*The Searchers*: An American Dilemma.' In *Movies and Methods Volume II: An Anthology*, 429–49. Berkeley: University of California Press, 1985.
Heung, Marina. 'The Family Romance and Orientalism: From Madame Butterfly to Indochine.' In *Visions of the East: Orientalism in Film*, ed. Matthew Bernstein and Gaylyn Studlar, 158–83. New Brunswick, NJ: Rutgers University Press, 1997.
Hinsch, Bret. *Passions of the Cut Sleeve*. Berkeley: University of California Press, 1990.
Hishida, Seiji. *Japan as a Great Power*. New York: Columbia University Press, 1905.
Hoare, J.E. *Japan's Treaty Ports and Foreign Settlements: The Uninvited Guests 1858–1899*. Folkstone: Japan Library, 1994.
Holland, A.K. 'Puccini as Craftsman.' In *Puccini's* Madame Butterfly, ed. Eric Crozier. London: Sadler's Wells Opera Book, John Lane, 1946.
Holmes, Colin, and A.H. Ion. 'Bushidù and the Samurai: Images in British Public Opinion, 1894–1914.' *Modern Asian Studies*, 14.2 (1980): 309–29.
Holmund, Christine. 'Displacing Limits of Difference: Gender, Race, and Colonialism in Edward Said and Homi Bhabha's Theoretical Models and Marguerite Duras's Experimental Films.' *Quarterly Review of Film and Video* 13 (1991): 1–22.

Hopkinson, Cecil. *Bibliography of the Works of Giaccomo Puccini 1858–1924.* New York: Broude, 1968.

Huang, Martin. *Literati and Self-Re/Presentation: Autobiographical Sensibility in the Eighteenth Century Chinese Novel.* Stanford: Stanford University Press, 1995.

Hunt, Nigel. 'The Global Voyage of Robert Lepage,' *Drama Review* 122 (1989): 104–18.

Huston, John, dir. *Barbarian and the Geisha, The.* Produced by Eugene Frenke. 104 minutes. Twentieth Century Fox, 1958. Videocassette, 1988.

Hutcheon, Linda, and Michael Hutcheon. *Bodily Charm: Living Opera.* Lincoln: University of Nebraska Press, 2000.

– *Opera: Desire, Disease, Death.* Lincoln: University of Nebraska Press, 1996.

Hwang, David Henry. *M. Butterfly.* New York: Dramatists Play Service, 1988; Plume-Penguin, 1989.

Ikegami, Eiko. *The Taming of the Samurai: Honorific Individualism and the Making of Modern Japan.* Cambridge, MA: Harvard University Press, 1995.

Irwin, Robert. 'The Theorists of Baghdad; Footnotes to Fairbanks: Lessons in "Reading the History of Orientalist Cinema."' Review of *Visions of the East: Orientalism in Film,* ed. Matthew Bernstein and Gaylyn Studlar (New Brunswick, NJ: Rutgers University Press, 1997). *TLS*, 30 May 1997: 18–19.

Jackson, Stanley. *Monsieur Butterfly: The Story of Giacomo Puccini.* New York: Stein, 1974.

John, Nicholas, ed. *Madama Butterfly.* English National Opera Guide Series no. 26. London: John Calder, 1984; repr. 1990.

Johnson, L.B. 'At Lyric Opera, a Kabuki-style Butterfly.' *High Fidelity / Musical America* 33 (June 1983).

Kano, Ayako. *Acting Like a Woman in Modern Japan: Theater, Gender, and Nationalism.* New York: Palgrave, 2001.

Kaplan, E. Ann. *Looking for the Other: Feminism, Film, and the Imperial Gaze.* New York and London: Routledge, 1997.

Karlgren, Bernhard. *The Book of Odes.* Stockholm: Museum of Far Eastern Antiquities, 1974.

Keene, Daniel. *Cho Cho San.* Sydney: Currency Press, 1987.

Keene, Donald. 'The Sino-Japanese War of 1894–95 and Its Cultural Effects in Japan.' In *Tradition and Modernization in Japanese Culture,* ed. Donald H. Shively. Princeton: Princeton University Press, 1971.

Kelsky, Karen. 'Flirting with the Foreign: Interacial Sex in Japan's "International Age."' The *Global / Local: Cultural Production and the Transnational Imaginary,* ed. Rob Wilson and Wimal Dissanayake, 173–92. Durham: Duke University Press, 1996.

Kerman, Joseph. *Opera as Drama.* New York: Vintage, 1952.

Kestner, Daniel. 'Bridge of Dreams: How Western Perceptions of a Distant Land Led to the Flowering of *Japonisme.*' *Opera News* 59 (January 1995): 8

Kinsey, Alfred. *Sexual Behaviour in the Human Female.* Philadelphia: Saunders, 1953.

Koestenbaum, Wayne. *The Queen's Throat: Opera, Homosexuality, and the Mystery of Desire.* New York: Poseidon, 1993.

Kondo, Dorinne K. '*M. Butterfly*: Orientalism, Gender, and a Critique of Essentialist Identity.' *Cultural Critique* (Fall 1990): 5–29.

Kong, Foong Ling. 'Pulling the Wings Off Butterfly.' *Southern Review* 27.4 (1994): 418–31.

Kristeva, Julia. *Black Sun: Depression and Melancholia.* Trans. Leon S. Roudiez. New York: Columbia University Press, 1989.

– *Powers of Horror: An Essay on Abjection.* Trans. Leon S. Roudiez. New York: Columbia University Press, 1982.

Lacoue-Labarthe, Philippe. 'The Caesura of Religion.' In Levin, 45–77.

Lampert-Greaux, Ellen. 'Cinematic Realism at the Met.' *Theatre Crafts International* 29 (April 1995).

Landy, Marcia. *The Cinematic Uses of the Past.* Minneapolis: University of Minnesota Press, 1996.

Lane, Christopher. *The Ruling Passion: British Colonial Allegory and the Paradox of Homosexual Desire.* Durham: Duke University Press, 1995.

Le Fanu, Mark. 'On Some Lesser-Known Films by Mizoguchi.' In *Mizoguchi: The Master,* ed. Gerald O'Grady. Toronto: Cinématèque Ontario, 1997.

Lehmann, Jean-Pierre. 'Images of the Orient,' In John, 7–14.

Leiter, Samuel L. *Kabuki Encyclopedia.* Westport, CT.: Greenwood Press, 1979.

Leonardi, Susan J., and Rebecca A. Pope. *The Diva's Mouth: Body, Voice, Prima Donna Politics.* New Brunswick, NJ: Rutgers University Press, 1996.

Lepage, Robert, and Ex Machina. *The Seven Streams of the River Ota.* London: Methuen, 1996.

Levin, David, ed. *Opera through Other Eyes.* Stanford: Stanford University Press, 1994.

Liao, Ping-hui. '"Of Writing Words for Music Which Is Already Made": *Madama Butterfly, Turandot* and Orientalism.' *Cultural Critique* 16 (1990): 31–51.

Lindenberger, Herbert. *Opera: The Extravagant Art.* Ithaca and London: Cornell University Press, 1984.

Littlejohn, David. *The Ultimate Art: Essays Around and About Opera.* Berkeley: University of California Press, 1992.

Locke, Ralph P. 'Constructing the Oriental "Other": Saint-Saëns's *Sampson et Dalila.*' *Cambridge Opera Journal* 3 (November 1991): 261–302.

– 'What Are These Women Doing in Opera?' In *En Travesti: Women, Gender Sub-*

version, Opera, ed. Corinne E. Blackmer and Patricia Julianna Smith. New York: Columbia University Press, 1995.
Long, John Luther. *Madame Butterfly*. New York: Century, 1903.
– 'Madame Butterfly.' In John, 25–59.
– *Miss Cherry Blossom of Tokyo*. Philadelphia: Lippincott, 1895; repr. 1903, 1905.
Loti, Pierre. *The Desert*. 1895. Trans. Jay Paul Minn. Salt Lake City: University of Utah Press, 1993.
– *L'exilée; par Pierre Loti*. Paris: Calmann-Levy, 1896.
– *Fantôme d'Orient*. 42nd edition. Paris: Calmann-Lévy, 1899.
– *Un jeune officier pauvre, fragments de journal intime rassemblés par son fils, Samuel Viaud*. Paris: Calmann-Lévy, 1924.
– *Madame Chrysanthème*. Paris: Kailash, 1993.
– *Madame Chrysanthemum*. 1887. Trans. Laura Ensor. London: KPI, 1985.
– *The Marriage of Loti*. 1880. Trans. Clara Bell. London: KPI, 1986.
Lye, Colleen. '*M. Butterfly* and the Rhetoric of Antiessentialism: Minority Discourse in an International Frame,' In *The Ethnic Canon: Histories, Institutions and Interventions*, ed. David Palumbo-Liu, 260–89. Minneapolis: University of Minnesota Press, 1995.
Ma, Karen. *The Modern Madame Butterfly: Fantasy and Reality in Japanese Cross-cultural Relationships*. Rutland: Charles T. Tuttle, 1996.
Ma, Ruiqi. 'The Ideology of Cultural and Gender Misunderstandings in D.H. Hwang's *M. Butterfly*.' *Canadian Review of Comparative Literature* 23 (December 1996): 1053–63.
Macdonald, Ray S. *Puccini: King of Verismo*. New York: Vantage, 1970.
MacKerras, Colin, *The Rise of the Peking Opera, 1770–1870: Social Aspects of the Theatre in Manchu China*. Oxford: Clarendon Press, 1972.
'Madama Butterfly.' *Opera News* 58 (January 1994): 26–9.
Mahling, Christoph-Hellmut. *The Japanese Image in Opera, Operetta and Instrumental Music at the End of the Nineteenth and during the Twentieth Century: Tradition and Its Future in Music*. Osaka: Mita, 1991.
Manalanson, Martin F., IV. 'Your Cio-Cio-San.' In *Premonitions: The Kaya Anthology of New Asian North American Poetry*, ed. Walter K. Lew, 344–5. New York: Kaya, 1995.
Marchetti, Gina. *Romance and the 'Yellow Peril': Race, Sex and Discursive Strategies in Hollywood Fiction*. Berkeley: University of California Press, 1993.
Marcus, Greil. *Lipstick Traces: A Secret History of the Twentieth Century*. Cambridge: Harvard University Press, 1989.
Mark, Lindy Li. 'Kunju and Theatre in the *Pinhua Baojian*.' *Chinoperl Papers* 14 (1986): 37–59.

Martin, Robert K. 'Gender, Race, and the Colonial Body: Carson McCullers's Filipino Boy, and David Henry Hwang's Chinese Woman.' *Canadian Review of American Studies* 23.1 (1992): 95–106.
Marx, Joseph. *Nagasaki: The Necessary Bomb?* New York: Macmillan, 1971.
May, Lary. *Screening Out the Past: The Birth of Mass Culture and the Motion Picture Industry.* Chicago: University of Chicago Press, 1980.
McCartney, Maxwell, and Paul Cremona. *Italy's Foreign and Colonial Policy 1914–1937.* London: Oxford University Press, 1938.
McClary, Susan. *Feminine Endings: Music, Gender, and Sexuality.* Minnesota: University of Minnesota Press, 1991.
McClintock, Anne. *Imperial Leather: Race, Gender and Sexuality in the Colonial Contest.* London: Routledge, 1995.
McLaren, Malcolm. *Fans.* Columbia. 1984
Meech-Pekarik, Julia. *The World of the Meiji Print: Impressions of a New Civilization.* New York: Weatherhill, 1986.
Metalious, Grace. *Peyton Place.* Cutchogue, NY: Buccaneer Books, 1994.
Metastasio, Pietro. *Opere.* 11 vols. Venice: Zatta, 1800–2.
Michener, James. *Sayonara.* New York: Random House, 1954.
– *Tales of the South Pacific.* New York: Macmillan, 1947.
Mitterrand, Frédéric, dir. *Madame Butterfly.* 129 min. Videocassette, Erato Films, 1995.
Mordden, Ethan. *Demented: The World of the Opera Diva.* New York: Franklin Watts, 1984.
Moy, James S. 'David Henry Hwang's *M. Butterfly* and Philip Kan Gotanda's *Yankee Dawg You Die*: Repositioning Chinese American Marginality on the American Stage.' *Theatre Journal* (March 1990): 48–56.
Mulvey, Laura. *Visual and Other Pleasures.* London: Macmillan, 1989.
Murray, Janet H. *'Hamlet' on the Holodeck: The Future of Narrative in Cyberspace.* New York: Free Press, 1997.
Ng, Maria Noëlle. *Three Exotic Views of Southeast Asia: The Travel Narratives of Isabella Bird, Max Dauthendey, and Ai Wu, 1850–1930.* New York: EastBridge, 2002.
Norton-Welsh, C. 'Coburg.' *Opera* 45 (February 1994): 212–13.
Nygren, Scott. 'Boundary Crossings: Japanese and Western Representations of the Other.' *Quarterly Review of Film and Video* 14.3 (1993): 85–93.
– 'Doubleness and Idiosyncracy in Cross-Cultural Analysis.' *Quarterly Review of Film and Video* 13 (1991): 173–87.
Onoto, Watanna. *A Japanese Nightingale.* London: Archibald Constable, 1904.
Oppens, K. 'Ewig die Zweite: 50 Jahre New York City Opera: Drei Urauffuehrungen, Tippets Midsummer Marriage und die originale Butterfly.' *Opernwelt* 34 (December 1993): 40–3.

Orbaugh, Sharalyn. 'General Nogi's Wife: Representations of Women in Narratives of Japanese Modernization.' In *In Pursuit of Contemporary East Asian Culture*, ed. Xiaobing Tang and Stephen Snyder. Boulder, CO: Westview Press, 1996.

Osborne, Charles. *The Complete Operas of Puccini: A Critical Guide*. London: Gollancz, 1981.

Parakilas, J. 'The Soldier and the Exotic: Operatic Variations on a Theme of Racial Encounter, Part I.' *Opera Quarterly* 10 (1993–4): 31–56.

Parker, R. 'Counterpoint: A Key for Chi? Tonal Areas in Puccini.' *19th-Century Music* 15 (March 1992): 229–34.

Parouty, M. 'Opera Bastille: Madama Butterfly face à son destin.' *Diapason-Harmonie* 400.20 (January 1994).

Pedlar, Neil. *The Imported Pioneers: Westerners Who Helped Build Modern Japan*. Folkstone: Japan Library, 1990.

Pevere, Geoff. 'Believing Is Seeing.' Review of *M. Butterfly*, directed by David Cronenberg. *Globe and Mail*. 1 October 1993: C1+.

Phillips-Matz, Mary Jane. *Puccini: A Biography*. Boston: Northeastern University Press, 2002.

Plaut, Eric A. *Grand Opera: Mirror of the Western Mind*. Chicago: Ivan R. Dee, 1993.

Poizat, Michel. *The Angel's Cry: Beyond the Pleasure Principle in Opera*. Trans. Arthur Denner. Ithaca: Cornell University Press, 1992.

Pola Bunka Kenkyūjo, ed. *Bakumatsu/Meiji Bijin-chū* [Notebook of Beautiful Women from the Late Edo and Meiji Periods]. Bessatu Rekishi Tokuhon, no. 563. Tokyo: Shinjinbutsu Ôrai-sha, 2001.

Pollock, Griselda. *Avant-Garde Gambits, 1888–1893: Gender and the Colour of Art History*. London: Thames and Hudson, 1992.

Ponnelle, Jean-Pierre, dir. *Madama Butterfly*. By Giacomo Puccini. With Mirella Freni and Plácido Domingo. Wiener Philharmoniker, cond. Herbert von Karajan. Videocassette, London, 1974.

Porter, Andrew. 'Musical Events (Clipped Wings).' *The New Yorker*, 23 July 1984: 96+.

Potyra, M. 'Musikdrama intensiv dargeboten: Eindringliche Inszenierung von Puccinis Madama Butterfly im Landestheater.' *Orchester* 42 (January 1994): 52.

Powers, Harold. 'One Halfstep at a Time: Tonal Transposition and "Split Association" in Italian Opera.' *Cambridge Opera Journal* 7 (1995): 135–64.

Powils-Okano, Kimiyo. *Puccinis 'Madama Butterfly.'* Bonn: Verlag für systematische Musikwissenschaft GmbH, 1986.

Preston, Stuart. *Farewell to the Old Opera House*. New York: Doubleday, 1966.

Puccini, Giacomo. *La Fanciulla del West: Opera in tre atti*. Milan: Ricordi, 1911.

– *Madama Butterfly* (score). Milan: Ricordi, 1907. Repr. New York: Dover, 1990.

- *Madama Butterfly.* Piano vocal score. Milan: Ricordi, 1944.
- *Madama Butterfly.* Libretto by Luigi Illica and Giuseppe Giacosa. English ed. based on R.H. Elkin. In John, 67–125.
- 'Madama Butterfly.' In *Seven Puccini Librettos,* 177–257. Trans. William Weaver. New York: Norton, 1981.
- *Madama Butterfly.* With Renata Tebaldi and Carlo Bergonzi. Orchestra e cor dell' Accademia de Santa Cecilia. Decca 411 634-2. 1985.

Raffaelli, Laure. Ed. *Rome.* New York: Knopf, 1994.

Remen, Kathryn. 'The Theatre of Punishment.' *Modern Drama* 37.3 (1994): 391–400.

Rewa, Natalie. 'Clichés of Ethnicity Subverted: Robert Lepage's *La Trilogie des Dragons.*' *Theatre History in Canada* 11.2: 148–61.

Rich, Frank. '"M. Butterfly," a Story of a Strange Love, Conflict and Betrayal.' Review of *M. Butterfly* by David Henry Hwang. *New York Times,* 21 March 1988: C13.

Robinson, Paul. 'The Opera Queen: A Voice from the Closet.' *Cambridge Opera Journal* 6 (1994): 283–91.

Rosselli, John. *Italy: The Decline of a Tradition, the Late Romantic Era: from the Mid Nineteenth Century to World War I.* Englewood Cliffs, NJ: Prentice-Hall, 1991.

Rushmore, Robert. *The Singing Voice.* New York: Dodd, Mead, 1971.

Russo, J.P. 'Puccini, the Immigrants, and the Golden West.' *Opera Quarterly* 7 (1990): 4–27.

Said, Edward W. *Culture and Imperialism.* New York: Knopf, 1992.
- *Orientalism.* New York: Vintage, 1978.
- 'Orientalism Revisited.' *Cultural Critique* 1 (Fall 1988).

Sansom, G.B. *The Western World and Japan.* London: Cresset Press, 1950.

Schatz, Thomas. *Hollywood Genres.* New York: Random House, 1981.

Schiller, Friedrich. *Turandot, Prinzessin von China. Schillers Werke,* 2: 1–146. Weimar: Hermann Böhlaus, 1949.

Schwab, Raymond. *The Oriental Renaissance.* Trans. Gene Patterson-Black and Victor Reinking. New York: Columbia University Press, 1984.

Searson, C. 'First Night Fiascos.' *Classic CD* 45 (February 1994): 204–6.

Seigle, Cecilia Segawa. 'A Samurai's Daughter.' *Opera News* 58 (January 1994): 8+.
- 1993. *Yoshiwara: The Glittering World of the Japanese Courtesan.* Honolulu: University of Hawai'i Press, 1993.

Shevstova, Maria. 'Of "Butterfly" and Men: Robert Wilson Directs Diana Soviero at the Paris Opéra.' *New Theatre Quarterly* 11.41 (February 1995): 3–11.
- 'On Playing Madame Butterfly.' Interview with Diana Soviero. *New Theatre Quarterly* 11.41 (February 1995): 12–16.

Shimakawa, Karen. '"Who's to Say?" Or, Making Space for Gender and Ethnicity in *M. Butterfly.*' *Theatre Journal* 45 (1993): 349–61.
Shionoya, Kei. *Cyrano et les samurai: Le théâtre japonais en France et l'effet de retour.* Paris: Publications orientalistes de France, 1986.
Shohat, Ella. 'Gender and Culture of Empire: Toward a Feminist Ethnography of the Cinema.' *Quarterly Review of Film and Video* 13 (1991): 45–84.
Skloot, Robert. 'Breaking the Butterfly: The Politics of David Henry Hwang.' *Modern Drama* 23.1 (March 1990): 59–66.
Smith, Sidonie. *Subjectivity, Identity, and the Body: Women's Autobiographical Practice in the Twentieth Century.* Bloomington: Indiana University Press, 1993.
Spence, Jonathan D. *The Search for Modern China.* New York: Norton, 1990.
Stead, Alfred. *Great Japan: A Study in National Efficiency.* London: John Lane, Bodley Head; New York: John Lane, 1906.
Stoler, Ann Laura. *Race and the Education of Desire: Foucault's History of Sexuality and the Colonial Order of Things.* Chapel Hill: Duke University Press, 1995.
Street, Douglas. *David Henry Hwang.* Boise, ID: Boise State University, 1989.
Studlar, Gaylyn. *In the Realm of Pleasure: Von Sternberg, Deitrich, and the Masochistic Aesthetic.* Urbana and Chicago: University of Illinois Press, 1988.
Suner, Asuman. 'Postmodern Double Cross: Reading David Cronenberg's *M. Butterfly* as a Horror Story.' *Cinema Journal* 37.2 (Winter 1998): 49–64.
Szyliowicz, Irene L. *Pierre Loti and the Oriental Woman.* London: Macmillan, 1988.
Tambling, Jeremy. *Opera and the Culture of Fascism.* Oxford: Clarendon Press, 1996.
– *Opera, Ideology and Film.* Manchester: Manchester University Press, 1987.
Tambling, Jeremy, ed. *A Night in at the Opera: Media Representations of Opera.* London: John Libby, 1994.
Tennyson, Alfred. 'Locksley Hall.' In *The Norton Anthology of English Literature*, 1867–73. New York: Norton, 1968.
Testa, Bart. 'Technology's Body: Cronenberg, Genre, and the Canadian Ethos.' *Post Script* 15.1 (Fall 1995): 39–56.
Tindall, Gillian. *Countries of the Mind: The Meaning of Place to Writers.* London: Hogarth Press, 1991.
Treitler, Leo. 'Gender and Other Dualities of Music History.' In *Musicology and Difference: Gender and Sexuality in Music Scholarship*, ed. Ruth A. Solie, 23–45. Berkeley: University of California Press, 1993.
Ueno, Chizuko. 'Genesis of the Urban Housewife.' *Japan Quarterly* 34.2 (April–June 1987): 130–42.
– 'The Position of Japanese Women Reconsidered.' *Current Anthropology* 28.4 (August–October 1987): S75–84.
Vance-Watkins, Lequita, and Aratani Mariko, eds. and trans. *White Flash / Black*

Rain: Women of Japan Relive the Bomb. Minneapolis, MN: Milkweed Editions, 1995.
van Rij, Jan. *Madame Butterfly: Japonisme, Puccini, and the Search for the Real Cho-Cho-San.* Berkeley, CA: Stone Bridge Press, 2001.
Wake, Clive. *The Novels of Pierre Loti.* The Hague: Mouton, 1974.
Waley, Arthur, trans. *The Book of Songs* (1937). New York: Grove, 1960.
Walser, Robert. 'Deep Jazz: Notes on Interiority, Race, and Criticism.' In *Inventing the Psychological*, ed. Joel Pfister and Nancy Schnog. New Haven: Yale University Press, 1997.
Wedekind, Frank. *The Lulu Plays and Other Sex Tragedies.* Trans. Stephen Spender. London: John Calder, 1977.
White-Parks, Annette. *Sui Sin Far / Edith Maude Eaton.* Chicago: University of Illinois Press, 1995.
Wilde, Oscar. 'The Ballad of Reading Gaol.' In *The Collected Works of Oscar Wilde*, 822–39. Leicester: Blitz, 1990.
– 'The Decay of Lying.' In *The Artist as Critic: Critical Writings of Oscar Wilde*, ed. Richard Ellmann. New York: Vintage, 1969.
Wilkinson, Endymion. *Misunderstanding: Europe vs. Japan.* Rev. edition. Tokyo: Chuokoron-Sha, 1982.
Williams, Linda. 'Film Bodies: Gender, Genre, and Excess.' *Film Quarterly* 44.4 (1991): 2–13.
Wilson, Colin. *The Outsider.* Boston: Houghton Mifflin, 1956.
Wong, Jan. *Red China Blues: My Long March from Mao to Now.* Toronto: Doubleday, 1996.
Yamakawa, Kikue. *Women of the Mito Domain: Recollections of Samurai Family Life.* Trans. Kate Wildman Nakai. Tokyo: University of Tokyo Press, 1992.
Yokoyama, Toshio. *Japan in the Victorian Mind.* London: Macmillan, 1987.
Young, Robert. *Colonial Desire.* London: Routledge, 1995.
Youngblood, J. 'Views and Viewpoints: Why Music Critics Disagree.' *College Music Symposium* 23 (1983): 193+.
Zelechow, Bernard. 'The Opera: The Meeting of Popular and Elite Culture in the Nineteenth Century.' *History of European Ideas* 16.1–3 (1993): 261–6.
Zhang Cixi, comp. *Qingdai Yandu liyuan shiliao, xubian* [Historical Materials on Peking Theatre in the Qing Dynasty, Continuation]. Peiping, 1937; repr., 4 vols. Taipei: Xuesheng shuju, 1965.
Žižek, Slavoj. '"The Wound Is Healed Only by the Spear That Smote You": The Operatic Subject and Its Vicissitudes.' In Levin, 25–44.

Contributors

Melinda Boyd recently completed her PhD in Musicology in the School of Music at the University of British Columbia.

Richard Cavell is a professor of English in the Department of English at the University of British Columbia.

Rachel Ditor is a theatre director and dramaturg based in Vancouver.

Sherrill Grace is a professor of English in the Department of English at the University of British Columbia.

Joy James is a sessional lecturer in the Women's and Gender Studies program at the University of British Columbia, and in the School of Critical and Cultural Studies at Emily Carr Institute of Art and Design.

Susan McClary is a professor of musicology in the Department of Musicology at the University of California, Los Angeles.

Brian McIlroy is a professor of film studies in the Department of Theatre, Film and Creative Writing at the University of British Columbia.

Kate McInturff is a sessional lecturer in the Department of English and the Institute of Women's Studies at the University of Ottawa.

Vera Micznik is an associate professor of musicology in the School of Music at the University of British Columbia.

Joshua S. Mostow is a professor of Japanese literature and culture in the Department of Asian Studies at the University of British Columbia.

Maria Ng is an associate professor of English in the Department of English at the University of Lethbridge.

Jan Selman is a professor of theatre in the Department of Drama at the University of Alberta.

Bart Testa is a senior lecturer of cinema studies in Innis College at the University of Toronto.

Jonathan Wisenthal is a professor emeritus of English in the Department of English at the University of British Columbia.

Index

Actor's Revenge, An, 121n2
Adas, Michael, 170–1, 173
Adorno, Theodor Wiesengrund, 164, 169n4, 226n11
Akiyama, Aisaburo, 41
Appiah, Anthony Kwame, 170
Arblaster, Anthony, 81
Ashbrook, William, 27, 34nn11, 19
Aston, W.G., 190
Atlas, Allan, 35n22, 47, 56

Ball, Lucille, 127
Ball, William, 234
Barthes, Roland, 196, 200–1, 201–2, 203, 204, 207, 213
Beard, William, 91, 121n3
Beasley, W.G., 172
Beaulieu, Janick, 70
Belasco, David: historical context, 4; Westerner, 5. See also *Madame Butterfly* (play)
Belton, John, 129
Benjamin, Walter, 226n11
Bernard, Émile, 220
Bernard, Joseph, 207–9
Berrong, Richard, 211, 226n9

Berry, Chuck, 127
Bertolucci, Bernardo, 106
Bhabha, Homi K., 137, 138, 148, 151n6
Bird, Isabella, 175
Birth of a Nation, The, 107, 108
Bizet, Georges, 17n10
Blanch, Lesley, 213
Blue Angel, The, 103
Borges, Jorge Luis, 23
Boublil, Alain, 4, 11, 136
Bouriscot, Bernard, 9, 120n1, 137, 138
Brando, Marlon, 127, 129, 130–1, 132, 135
Brecht, Bertolt, 31, 237
Brennan, Kit, 237
Bridge on the River Kwai, The, 134–5
Brooks, Peter, 133, 234
Browne, Nick, 24, 35n25, 69–70, 83, 93, 95, 106–7, 111, 115
Bryson, Norman, 184
Buck-Morss, Susan, 226n11
Burch, Noel, 110
Burroughs, William, 127
Buscombe, Ed, 129
Busoni, Ferrucio, 23, 27, 163

Butler, Judith, 197, 201, 219, 223

Callas, Maria, 83, 84
Capote, Truman, 130
Carner, Mosco, 27, 28, 35n20, 180n5
Carney, Raymond, 133
Cavers, Steven, 227, 231, 235
Cézanne, Paul, 106
Chang, Hsaio H., 77
Charest, Rémy, 138, 139, 146
Chen, Daniel, 227, 231, 235-6
Chion, Michel, 99
Chow, Rey, 93, 96, 103, 118, 120, 122n7, 161, 168
Christiansen, Rupert, 83-4, 85
Churchill, Caryl, 237
Cixi, 178
Clément, Catherine, 12, 21, 25
Close, Glenn, 76
Conder, Josiah, 182
Conrad, Peter, 73-4, 83, 84, 85
Cronenberg, David: Westerner, 5. See also *Dead Ringers*; *Fly, The*; *M. Butterfly* (film); *Naked Lunch*; *Scanners*; *Videodrome*

Dalby, Liza, 37, 39-40, 41, 43, 57nn3, 6-7
Daudet, Léon, 213
Dauthendey, Max, 172-3, 179n3
Dean, James, 127
de Gruchy, John, 191-2
Deleuze, Gilles, 121n6
Delibes, Léo, 17n10
De Quincey, Thomas, 171
Destinn, Emmy, 34n11
Dewey, Alice, 176, 177
Dewey, John, 176, 177
Dickins, Frederick Victor, 182
Dizikes, John, 73, 75

Dufwa, Jacques, 172

Eaton, Winifred, 175
Edwards, Osman, 58n9, 186-7, 190

Fält, Olavi K., 174
Farewell My Concubine, 121n2
Farrar, Geraldine, 70, 83
Fassbinder, Rainer Werner, 106
Findley, Timothy, 157-8
Flaubert, Gustave, 116
Fly, The, 96
Fortin, Simon, 150n2
Foucault, Michel, 73, 74, 197, 201, 224nn2, 3, 225n7
Fox, Samuel Middleton, 191
Franc de Ferrière, Jeanne Blanche, 205
Freni, Mirella, 63
Freud, Sigmund, 106, 108, 129
Frieze, James, 151n7
Fukuyama, Francis, 158-9

Gainza, Crucita, 205
Garber, Marjorie, 65, 66, 160
Garbo, Greta, 117
Garcia Márquez, Gabriel, 22
Gates, Henry Louis, Jr, 170
Gauguin, Paul, 220-2
Genet, Christian, 213, 220
Gentlemen Prefer Blondes, 133
Ghérardi, Evariste, 163
Giacosa, Giuseppe, xiii n2, 4, 5, 17n13
Gilbert, W.S., 17n10
Ginsberg, Allen, 127
Gish, Lillian, 113-14, 117
Glass, Philip, 151n3
Gledhill, Christine, 129
Gossman, Lionel, 162
Graf, Herbert, 72-3

Gray, John, 88n6
Great Train Robbery, The, 110
Greenhalgh, Paul, 174, 176
Griffith, D.W., 111. See also *Birth of a Nation, The*; *Musketeers of Pig Alley*
Groos, Arthur, 16n6, 18n13, 38, 41, 62–3, 69, 70, 185, 186, 192–3, 194, 195n1
Guess Who's Coming to Dinner, 134
Guinness, Alec, 134
Gundermann, Christian, 201–2, 205
Gunning, Tom, 107
Gurney, A.R., xii–xiii

Hadden, J. Cuthbert, 76
Halberstam, David, 127
Haley, Bill, 127
Hammerstein, Oscar, II, 4
Hansen, Miriam, 113–14, 116, 117
Hardy, Thomas, 12
Hargreaves, Alec G., 198
Harper, Thomas, 195n5
Harrison, Wallace, 74
Harvie, Jennifer, 151n7
Hayes, John P., 127
Hearn, Lafcadio, 190–1
Hegel, Georg Wilhelm Friedrich, 171, 178
Hein, Laura, 124
Henderson, Brian, 126
Herrmann, Bernard, 104–5
Hervé, Daniel, 213, 220
Heung, Marina, 91, 102, 115
Hisama, Ellie, 29
Hishida, Seiji, 173–4
Hoare, J.E., 124
Holland, A.K., 23, 27, 33n7
Holmes, Colin, 192
Hoshi, Shizuko, 67, 71n5
Huang, Ying, 64, 70

Hwang, David Henry: historical context, 4; on *Madama Butterfly*, 9–10, 32; Westerner, 5. See also *M. Butterfly* (play)

Ibsen, Henrik, 18n16
Ikegami, Eiko, 189
Illica, Luigi, xiii n2, 4, 5, 17n13, 164
Ion, A.H., 192
Irons, Jeremy, 92, 95, 120
Irwin, Robert, 125

Jam, Jimmy, 33n5
Jit, Krischen, 69

Kano, Ayako, 195n3
Kawakami, Otojirō, 185–6
Kawakami, Sadayakko, 185–6, 192, 193
Kaye, Stanley F., 70
Keene, Donald, 185–6
Kelsky, Karen, 155–6
Kerman, Joseph, 25, 33n4, 34n13
Kerouac, Jack, 127
King, Martin Luther, Jr, 126
Kinsey, Alfred, 127
Kiyoko, Horiba, 123
Kluge, Alexander, 106
Kobbé, Gustav, 33n8
Koestenbaum, Wayne, 83, 85
Kondo, Dorinne, 28, 39
Kristeva, Julia, 42, 43, 46, 199
Krusceniski, Salomea, 34n11

Lacoue-Labarthe, Philippe, 169n3
Landy, Marcia, 106
Lane, Christopher, 161
Lang, Fritz, 93
Le Cor, Pierre, 214–18, 219
LeFanu, Mark, 186

Lehmann, Jean-Pierre, 181, 182
Leoncavallo, Ruggero, 150n2, 163
Lepage, Robert: *Dragons Trilogy, The*, 138, 139, 151n7; *the far side of the moon*, 138. See also *Seven Streams of the River Ota, The*
Lewis, Terry, 33n5
Liang, Ning, 64, 70
Liao, Ping-hui, 56–7, 57n2
Lindenberger, Herbert, 74
Logan, Joshua. See *Sayonara*
Lone, John, 92, 119
Long, John Luther: historical context, 4; Westerner, 5. See also *Madame Butterfly* (short story)
Loti, Pierre, 183–4, 196–226; *Aziyadé*, 200–1, 202, 219; *Fleurs d'ennui*, 214; historical context, 4; *An Iceland Fisherman*, 211; *Le Marriage de Loti*, 220–2; 'marriage' in Nagasaki, 4–5; *Mon frère Yves*, 214; *Le Roman d'un spahi*, 200; Westerner, 5. See also *Madame Chrysanthème*
Louie, Alexina, 151n3
Ludwig, Christa, 63
Lye, Colleen, 69, 72, 77

Ma, Karen, 28
Ma, Ruiqi, 68
MacArthur, Douglas, 126
Macaulay, Thomas Babington, 179n1
Madama Butterfly (opera, Puccini): Cio-Cio-San as geisha, 21, 36–58, 102; Cio-Cio-San's suicide, 12–13, 54–6, 145, 149–50, 193–4; Japan aestheticized in, 7; love duet, 21–3, 52–4, 58n11, 141–2, 149; Orient infantilized in, 7; Suzuki, 59–60, 61–4; as tragedy, 17n11, 115–17; and *Turandot*, 170, 178–9; 'Un bel dì,' 24–5, 56, 167–8

Madame Butterfly (film, Olcott), 91, 106–8, 112–13
Madame Butterfly (play, Belasco): and *The Birth of a Nation*, 107, 108; Cho-Cho-San as geisha, 45; Japan aestheticized in, 8; Orient infantilized in, 5–6
Madame Butterfly (short story, Long): Japan aestheticized in, 8; Orient infantilized in, 6
Madame Chrysanthème (Loti), 196–205, 217, 222; Chrysanthème as rashamen, 44–5; ending, 15–16; Japan aestheticized in, 7–8; Orient infantilized in, 6; representation as subject in, 9
Manalansan, Martin F., 156–7, 158
Marchetti, Gina, 36, 93, 107, 109, 110, 112–13, 115, 116–17, 125
Marcus, Greil, 155
Márquez, Gabriel Garcia. See Garcia Márquez, Gabriel
Martin, Robert K., 160
Marx, Joseph, 124
Mascagni, Pietro, 17n10, 164
Massenet, Jules, 17n10
M. Butterfly (film, Cronenberg), 68, 69, 71, 91–104, 117–20, 160–1; Chin, 65, 67; and *Madame Chrysanthème*, 222–3; non-Asian elements, 4
M. Butterfly (play, Hwang): Chin, 59–60, 64–71; and *Madame Chrysanthème*, 222–3; in performance, 227–37; Song Liling, 77–87, 119–20, 228–32; and *The Seven Streams of the River Ota*, 136–42, 146–50; 'Woman' in, 6
McCarthy, Joseph, 126
McClintock, Anne, 18n14, 42–3, 46, 158–9, 162, 168, 174–5
McLaren, Malcolm, 31, 155, 158
McNally, Terence, 150n2

Meech-Pekarik, Julia, 183–4
Meeting Venus, 76
Men, The, 130
Messager, André, 17n10
Metalious, Grace, 127
Metastasio, Pietro, 163
Metropolitan Opera House, 73–5
Meyerbeer, Giacomo, 17n10, 164
Michener, James, 127–8
Minn, Jay Paul, 213
Mitterand, Frédéric, 31, 64, 70, 71n6
Miura, Tamaki, 69, 70, 83, 194
Monroe, Marilyn, 127, 133
Montalban, Ricardo, 131
Monteverdi, Claudio, 163, 167
Morris, William, 191
Moy, James, 68
Mulvey, Laura, 105
Murray, Janet, 158
Musketeers of Pig Alley, 114–15

Nagasaki, 4–5, 16n5, 40–1, 123–4, 194
Naipaul, V.S., 18n14
Naked Lunch (film), 96
New York City Opera, 74–5
Nietzsche, Friedrich, 162
Nowra, Louis, 150n2
Nye, Robert, 225n7

Offenbach, Jacques, 150n2
Olcott, Sidney. See *Madame Butterfly* (film)
O'Leary, Daniel, 226n12
Onassis, Aristotle, 84
On the Waterfront, 130
Orbaugh, Sharalyn, 195n4
Osborne, Charles, 33n8

Pagnol, Marcel, 206
Parks, Rosa, 126
Perry, Matthew, 16n5

Picasso, Pablo, 106, 163
Pickford, Mary, xii, 91, 106–8, 114–15, 117
Plaut, Eric A., 82, 86
Plowright, Rosalind, 83
Pollock, Griselda, 221, 222
Ponnelle, Jean-Pierre, 14, 63, 169n6
Porgy and Bess, 87n4
Powils-Okano, Kimiyo, 48, 58n10
Presley, Elvis, 127
Pretty Woman, 76
Psycho, 104–5, 108
Puccini, Giacomo: historical context, 4; *Bohème, La*, 104; *La Fanciulla del West*, 165; *Tosca*, 20; *Turandot*, 170, 178–9; Westerner, 5. See also *Madama Butterfly* (opera)

Quinn, Arthur, 61

Remen, Kathryn, 72, 73
Rewa, Natalie, 138, 151n7
Roberts, Julia, 76
Rodgers, Richard, 4
Root, Derek, 157
Rushmore, Robert, 83
Ruskin, John, 191
Russell, Ken, 84, 136

Said, Edward, 138, 169n7, 178, 224n2
Saint-Saëns, Camille, 17
Sansom, G.B., 163
Sayonara (film), 123, 127–35
Scanners, 96
Schatz, Thomas, 123
Schoenberg, Arnold, 106, 162, 163, 169n3
Schönberg, Claude-Michel, 4, 11, 136
Sedgwick, Eve Kosofsky, 225n7
Seigle, Cecilia Segawa, 38, 39, 40, 41–2, 57n3

Selden, Mark, 124
seppuku, 187–91
Seven Streams of the River Ota, The, 142–50
Severini, Gino, 163
Shakespeare, William, 13, 18n16
Shanghai Express, 103
Shaw, Bernard, 17n12, 18n16, 191
Shionoya, Kei, 186
Smith, Sidonie, 137, 138, 148, 149, 151n8, 199
Sondheim, Stephen, 4
Spence, Jonathan D., 171, 177, 178
'Star-Spangled Banner, The,' 11, 23, 47, 56, 166
Stead, Alfred, 192
Stein, Gertrude, 162
Stoler, Ann Laura, 74, 224n2
Stoppard, Tom, 18n16
Stradella, Alessandro, 34n15
Strauss, Richard, 17, 28, 34n14, 150n2, 163
Streetcar Named Desire, A (film), 130
Studlar, Gaylyn, 121n6
Subusawa, Mari Yoriko, 127
Sullivan, Arthur, 17n10
Sumie, Terai, 123
Sweeney, Charles W., 16n5
Syberberg, Hans-Jürgen, 106
Szyliowicz, Irene, 211, 214

Tambling, Jeremy, 16n2, 30, 158, 163–5, 166–7
Tara, Miiko, 131–2
Te Kanawa, Kiri, 83
Teahouse of the August Moon, The, 130
Tennyson, Alfred, 171, 179n1
Thompson, Victoria, 225n7
Thomson, Virgil, 162
Thriller, 104–5

Toll of the Sea, 129
Tolstoy, Leo, 224n3
Treitler, Leo, 35n26
Tremblay, Michel, 150n2
Truman, Harry, 126

Ueno, Chizuko, 187
Uncle Tom's Cabin (film), 110

van Rij, Jan, 16n6
Verdi, Giuseppe, 11, 12, 17n10, 28, 164, 165
Viaud, Julien. *See* Loti, Pierre
Victoria, Queen, 178
Vietnam War, 4, 14, 29, 82, 94–5, 118, 126
Visconti, Luchino, 106
Viva Zapata, 130

Wagner, Richard, 28, 47
Wake, Clive, 201
Walser, Robert, 33n5, 34n9
Wertenbaker, Timberlake, 237
Wild One, The, 130
Wilde, Oscar, 3, 8, 17n10, 18n16, 161
Wilkinson, Endymion, 60
Wilson, Colin, 130
Wong, Anna May, 129
Wong, Jan, 66, 71n4

Yamakawa, Kikue, 188
Yeats, William Butler, 13
Young, Robert, 83

Zapf, Donna, 224n3
Zelechow, Bernard, 72–3
Žižek, Slavoj, 162–3
Zola, Émile, 198
Zorn, John, 29

www.ingramcontent.com/pod-product-compliance
Lightning Source LLC
Chambersburg PA
CBHW052016070526
44584CB00016B/1777